JOURNEY
Pacific Coast Highway

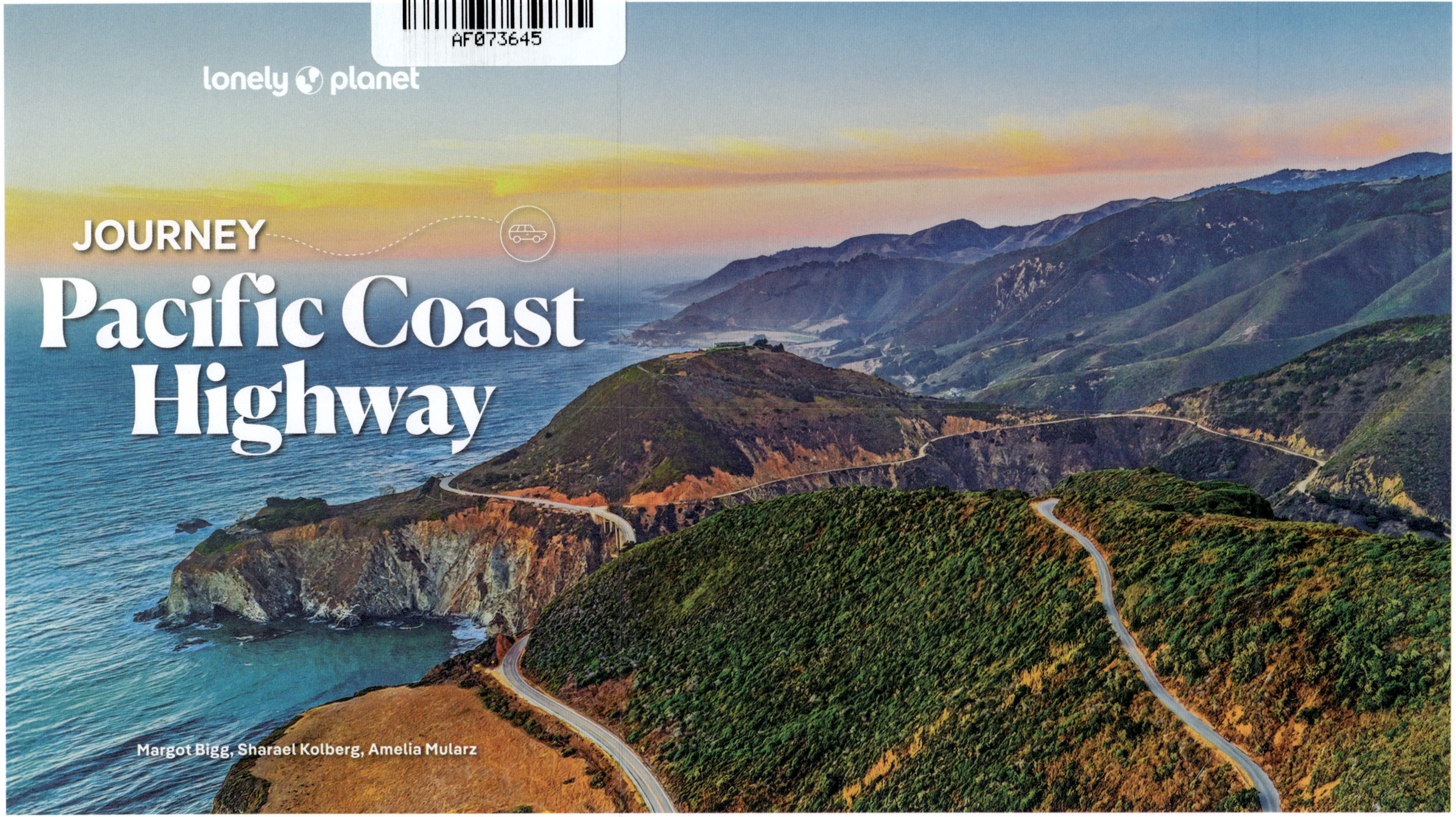

Margot Bigg, Sharael Kolberg, Amelia Mularz

Stretching from the palm-fringed shores of San Diego to the redwood forests of the far north, the Pacific Coast Highway offers the ultimate introduction to California. In just one road trip, you can see the city lights of Los Angeles and San Francisco, cruise along the coastal bluffs of Big Sur and find yourself face-to-trunk with the world's most colossal trees. Whether you drive just a segment or cover the entire coast, you can expect spectacular scenery, delightful towns and ocean sunsets for as far as the eye can see.

Contents

Plan Your Trip

- My Pacific Coast Highway 4
- Life's a Beach 8
- Hiking Heaven 12
- Culinary California 16
- On a Mission 20
- Weird & Wonderful 24
- 6 Ways to Do the Pacific Coast Highway 28

Go to p30 for the full route map

The Drive

SOUTH COAST
- City Guide: San Diego 34
- San Diego to Los Angeles 42
- City Guide: Los Angeles 62
- Los Angeles to Santa Barbara 72

CENTRAL CALIFORNIA
- City Guide: Santa Barbara 94
- Santa Barbara to San Luis Obispo 100
- San Luis Obispo to Carmel-by-the-Sea 118
- Carmel-by-the-Sea to San Francisco 140
- City Guide: Santa Cruz 156

Golden Gate Bridge (p172), San Francisco

NORTHERN CALIFORNIA
- City Guide: San Francisco 168
- San Francisco to Mendocino 176
- Mendocino to Eureka 198
- Eureka to Crescent City 218

Toolkit

- First Time 238
- Money 239
- On the Road 240
- Cycling 244
- Where to Stay 245
- Access, Attitudes & Safety 246
- Responsible Travel 248
- The Spotter's Guide 250

INSIGHT ESSAYS

- The Happiest Place on Earth 60
- Surf Culture 88
- A Cultural History of the Coast 116
- Big Sur: A Creative's Muse 136
- Surviving Climate Change 162
- The Napa Valley 194
- Legends of the Coast 216
- The Return of the Condor 234

Previous page: Pacific Coast Highway at Big Sur (p126)

My Pacific Coast Highway

Margot Bigg @margotbigg

I still remember my first trip down the Pacific Coast Highway. I was maybe seven years old, and my parents thought it'd be fun to take a road trip from Portland to San Francisco via the redwood forest. This was my first proper trip to the forest, and while my memories are hazy, I still remember the excitement of taking our car through a tree and visiting a gift shop inside a hollowed-out redwood trunk. Although I've driven that stretch of the PCH countless times since, I still get a little giddy when I know that redwood groves are around the next bend.

Margot Bigg writes about experiential travel for publications around the world. She's a huge fan of road tripping and loves taking the scenic route whenever possible. Margot wrote the front and back sections and the Northern California (p167) chapters, plus an essay on the Yurok Condor Restoration Program (p234).

Margot in the redwoods

MY FAVORITE VIEWS

The Marin Headlands
The Golden Gate Bridge and San Francisco look larger than life when viewed from the north. p180

Elk
Spectacular sea stack views add to the appeal of this upscale getaway near Mendocino. p192

The Tall Trees Grove
Redwoods stretching into the sky, as far as the eye can see. p226

MY FAVORITE STOPS

Stearns Wharf, Santa Barbara
Historic wharf with souvenir shops, dining and fishing. p98

Big Sur River Inn
Hotel and restaurant with Adirondack chairs in the river. p133

Garrapata State Park
Two miles of scenic hiking trails along the coast. p134

Sharael Kolberg
@SharaelTravels

Having lived in various places along the Pacific Coast Highway, I've driven it from top to bottom numerous times. I am continually drawn to the rhythm of the coast – the smooth, swervy road, shrill cry of seagulls, melodic waves and tang of salty air. Although the highway does pass through cities, it's the small, charming towns, where surfboards are strapped to car rooftops and everyone waves hello, that make the journey memorable. I always visit the neighborhood coffee shop to support the community, chat with the locals and browse the bulletin board. The people can be just as pleasant as the scenery.

Apart from writing about adventure and wellness travel for Lonely Planet, she hosts the Sharael Travels podcast. Sharael wrote the Santa Barbara City Guide (p94), the Central California chapters (p93) and an essay about how Big Sur inspires creativity (p136).

Sharael at Stearns Wharf (p98), Santa Barbara

MY FAVORITE ROADSIDE EATERIES

Crystal Cove Shake Shack, Newport Beach
Burgers and shakes are even more indulgent with ocean views. p54

Neptune's Net, Malibu
This PCH pitstop has been serving seafood since the 1950s. p78

Nepenthe, Big Sur
Come for the history (Kerouac was here!), stay for the apple pie and sunset views. p131

Amelia Mularz @ameliamularz

As an Angeleno, Laguna Beach might be my favorite weekend escape along the Pacific Coast Highway. It's beach, but with a side of adventure. It's not just plopping down on a patch of sand; it's scrambling around tide pools and rocky outcrops to find the perfect little cove for your towel and a beach read. It's watching the surfers and even hopping on a board yourself, then wandering into town – salty hair and all – to find something organic and fresh to eat.

Amelia Mularz is a Midwest-born, LA-based writer who loves to tell stories about travel and design. Amelia wrote the South Coast chapters (p33).

Anita Isalska @lunarsynthesis

Hwy 1 is the thread that connects my years on the West Coast: from weekend escapes out of the Bay Area, to following my heart – and Oregon's otherworldly shores – up to Seattle. My golden rule: stop at roadside fruit stalls. Sensory memories are incredibly powerful and your trip will come flooding back the next time you bite a juicy-to-bursting peach.

Anita writes about travel, technology and wellness. She wrote the Santa Cruz (p156) and San Francisco city guide chapters (p168), and an essay on climate change along the PCH (p162).

David Gibb @HappyWanderlusters

As a former beach-loving resident of Encinitas, California, I love taking early morning strolls along the town's Moonlight Beach. It's also a great spot to jump into a lively afternoon pickup game of beach volleyball – meeting new friends under the blazing sun. Sipping a Classic Old Fashioned at the historic Hotel del Coronado and catching sunsets at Sunset Cliffs round out my list of favorite local pastimes.

David is an adventurous, globe-trotting travel writer – whose heart still resides in Encinitas, CA. He wrote the San Diego city guide (p34).

Andrew Bender @wheresandynow

No place represents LA quite like Griffith Park, 4300 acres of mountains, hiking trails, the zoo and museums. Here, my must-do is the Griffith Observatory, perched on a promontory allowing all seekers to look upward through telescopes at the infinity of stars above, or just to contemplate how, in the city below, a star of tomorrow may be about to get that big break.

Andrew's dozens of Lonely Planet titles include California, Japan and Amsterdam. Andrew wrote the Los Angeles city guide (p62) and the essay on Disneyland (p60).

James Gulliver Hancock @gulliverhancock

I lived in LA for three years and we used to drive up the PCH all the time. It was always funny to see Hollywood movies that ended with them driving up this stretch of road and wondering how they got from one side of LA to the other so quickly! We used to go camping up the coast among the sequoias and the PCH was always a stunning way to get there – the seals, the windswept trees that looked like giant bonsai.

James drew the illustrated map at the start of this book.

Christabel Lobo @whereschristabel

Carmel-by-the-Sea truly feels like a storybook town – quaint cottages with shingled roofs and art galleries tucked into hidden courtyards. Its beauty is effortless, but Carmel is also fiercely protective of its character. There are no street numbers, no neon signs, and strict building codes that leave it frozen in time – and, more importantly, charm. It's a place to let the sea sweep you to your rightful slow coastal pace.

Christabel is a writer and illustrator. She wrote essays on the legends (p216) and the cultural history of the Pacific Coast Highway (p116).

Carmel-by-the-Sea (p144)
DAVID A LITMAN/SHUTTERSTOCK

Life's a Beach

From SoCal's sunny sands to the windswept coastlines of the chilly north, California's beaches are as diverse as they are beautiful.

CLOSE YOUR EYES and imagine a California beach scene. The chances are high that you'll picture long stretches of sand punctuated by beach towels and swimsuit-clad bodies, plus a sprinkling of surfers or palm trees. What you're less likely to envision, unless you've spent a lot of time in Northern California, is a fog-engulfed shoreline flanked by ancient woodlands with nary a human in sight. And yet both images are equally representative of California's massive coastline.

A Cool Journey

While most of California's coast technically has a Mediterranean climate, Southern California is where you'll find the beachiest of vibes. Head to the beaches of San Diego (p34) or Orange County (p51) and you're sure to see plenty of people swimming, sunbathing and building sandcastles, especially between late spring and fall. Visit Pismo Beach (p114), Malibu (p76), Rincon Point (p82) or Huntington Beach (p56) and you may even see surfers gliding along massive waves, but they may be in wetsuits. Because of a current that brings frosty weather down from Alaska, the waters in this part of the Pacific are noticeably chilly, and even Southern California waters can hover in the 65–70°F range in the height of summer.

Water temperatures begin to drop as you make your way north, and while the Central Coast is a great place for a nippy dip in the height of summer, by the time you get up to the Monterey Bay area, you might find it a tad too cold to swim. Temperatures really begin to drop in the San Francisco Bay area, where you should always have a sweater on hand, even in the middle of

Pismo Beach (p114)
FROM LEFT: XPIXEL/SHUTTERSTOCK, HANNATOR/SHUTTERSTOCK

the summer. The farther north you get, the more the beaches (and weather) will start to feel like the Pacific Northwest, which translates to cool temperatures and plenty of rainfall.

Coastal Creatures

Sea life abounds all along the coast of California, but you'll see a lot more marine creatures in areas that don't get a lot of human traffic. Tide pools have the most obvious abundance of sea creatures, and starfish, anemones, barnacles and crabs make frequent appearances in pools up and down the coast. You're likely to see plenty of birds, too, from squawking seagulls – who aren't afraid to steal a snack from unguarded picnics – to black oystercatchers, small shorebirds with extra-long vermilion beaks that make them look like little avian Pinocchios. Depending on when you visit, you may even see a Western snowy plover (p193), a threatened species known to nest in Pacific Coast sands.

Humans (and their dogs) aren't the only mammals that frequent the California coast, and, along with migrating whales, you may spot sea lions, seals and otters during your journey. These creatures are commonly found in areas with large underwater kelp forests, including around San Miguel in the Channel Islands (p81), home to one of the world's largest seal colonies, as well as in the waters of the massive Monterey Bay National Marine Sanctuary (p134), which protects waters from the Bay Area clear down to Cambria (p126).

SURFING USA

Although surfing (and the surfer-dude trope) has long been associated with the California coast, the sport wasn't actually introduced to the state until the early 20th century. While archaeological evidence of wave-riding has been found in coastal communities across the planet, modern surfing traces its roots to Polynesian cultures and was introduced to the rest of the world via Hawaii.

BOOKS SET ON THE CALIFORNIA COAST

Malibu Rising (Taylor Jenkins Reid)
A story of one night in socialite Malibu in the early 1980s, and how quickly things can go up in flames.

Big Sur and the Oranges of Hieronymus Bosch (Henry Miller)
A memoir detailing the years Miller spent on the Big Sur coast and the many interesting characters he met during his stay.

Cannery Row (John Steinbeck)
A fictionalized portrait of life in Monterey during the Great Depression.

HIGHLIGHTS

1 La Jolla Cove, San Diego, p29
San Diego–area beach popular with snorkelers, divers and swimmers thanks to its crystal-clear waters. You can often spot sea lions and seals at nearby Children's Pool Beach.

2 Huntington State Beach, Huntington Beach, p56
This 121-acre beach has enough room for surfing, swimming, sunbathing and playing beach volleyball, with amenities ranging from restrooms to restaurants, plus several surf schools.

3 Rincon Point, Carpinteria, p82
This famous surf spot offers some seriously spectacular breakers and not much else (beyond sand). It's great for experienced surfers or anyone who wants to watch them in action.

4 Pfeiffer Beach, Big Sur, p132
One of the best places in California to watch the sunset is at Pfeiffer Beach, where you can watch the sun descend behind a tiny hole in an offshore sea stack named Keyhole Arch.

5 Glass Beach, Fort Bragg, p205
See colorful fragments of ocean-polished glass on this beach, which was once used as a dumpsite (that's where the glass came from).

6 Trinidad Head, Trinidad, p225
Trade sand for hiking trails and make your way to this towering bluff to take in views of offshore sea stacks that provide homes for large colonies of seabirds. Bring binoculars.

Hiking Heaven

Don't expect to spend all of your time behind the wheel: the Pacific Coast Highway offers ample opportunities to get out and stretch your legs.

THE CALIFORNIA COAST has some seriously great hikes, from short strolls along beachfront bluffs to longer forays that take you deep into groves of old-growth redwoods. Although some journeys – such as the remote Lost Coast Trail (p208) – are best approached on overnight backpacking trips, there are loads of easier options along the coast, many of which are less than a mile long. A growing number of trails across the state are wheelchair-friendly, too; the Rails-To-Trails Conservancy *(railstotrails.org)* publishes a comprehensive map of accessible options at *traillink.com/stateactivity/ca-wheelchair-accessible-trails*. If you're new to hiking, it's best to start with an easier hike and read descriptions before you set out. Trails are generally rated as either easy, moderate or strenuous based on a combination of length, elevation gain and obstacles found along the way.

Gearing Up

While you'll probably see a few hikers garbed in hiking clothes from head to toe, hiking isn't an activity that requires a lot of specific equipment, or even special shoes. If you're attempting a hike that's listed as easy to moderate, you'll usually be fine with regular tennis shoes (provided they have some traction). For rockier terrain, hiking boots with ankle support can be helpful, though many people opt to wear trail-running shoes, which combine the flexibility and comfort of a running shoe with the traction of a hiking boot.

Wearing long pants that cover your legs and ankles is generally a wise choice, especially if you're hiking in forests where thorny blackberry bushes, stinging nettles and itch-inducing poison oak can ruin your hike. Trousers are also

The Lost Coast (p208)

FROM LEFT: WABENO/SHUTTERSTOCK, ROBERT STOLTING/SHUTTERSTOCK

a smart choice in grasslands (including those on coastal bluffs), which are a prime habitat for Pacific Coast and western black-legged ticks; the latter are known to carry Lyme disease. A sun hat is also a good idea. Even people who don't typically sunburn sometimes find themselves more prone to burns when hiking at the beach.

The California Coastal Trail

While the Pacific Crest Trail (PCT), a 2650-mile trail that stretches from Mexico to Canada, is a bucket-list item for many hikers, trekking the entirety of the Pacific Coast isn't as doable, largely because there's not a single trail that runs along the length of the coast – at least not for now. The California Coastal Trail Association is out to change that, and has been working with stakeholders across the state to help create a 1200-mile California Coastal Trail (CCT; *californiacoastaltrail.org*). Once the trail is complete, it will be possible to walk from the border with Mexico to the border with Oregon without having to get in a car or try your luck walking along the edge of a busy highway.

They've started by supporting projects that connect smaller segments of the coast together, such as the Humboldt Bay Trail (p222) between Eureka and Arcata. The Humboldt Bay Trail is also part of a similar, if slightly less ambitious, project known as the Redwood Trail, which seeks to connect San Francisco Bay with Humboldt Bay over the course of 307 miles.

DOUGLAS FIR CONES

The easiest way to recognize the cone of a Douglas fir during a hike is by looking for 'bracts' (scales) that resemble the bottom half of a mouse as viewed from above, with two legs and a tail sticking out. According to legend, there was once a great forest fire and mice had nowhere to go. A mighty Douglas fir allowed the little rodents to hide in its cones, saving them from the fire.

OTHER WAYS TO GET OUT & PLAY

Moutain biking
Rent a mountain bike and hit the trails or get a fat-tire bike and take a ride on the beach.

Paddleboarding
Explore Pacific Coast rivers on a stand-up paddleboard or aboard a kayak.

Surfing
Catch a wave on a surfboard or a beginner-friendly boogie board.

HIGHLIGHTS

① **Broken Hill Trail, Torrey Pines State Natural Reserve, Del Mar, p46**
This popular 2.5-mile trail offers beautiful views of the Pacific Ocean from atop sandstone cliffs. Come in the winter and you may end up spotting a whale.

② **Griffith Park, Los Angeles, p67**
Choose your own adventure at this urban hiking hot spot where you can trudge all the way up to the iconic Hollywood sign or take a trail to the Griffith Observatory.

③ **West Cliff Drive, Santa Cruz, p161**
Stroll 3 miles from Natural Bridges State Beach to the boardwalk, stopping en route to dip your toes in the surf at Cowell's Beach or have a glass of wine at Vino by the Sea.

④ **Devil's Slide Trail, Pacifica, p153**
Enjoy incredible views of the Pacific Ocean with a walk or bike ride along this 1.3-mile multi-use trail on a repurposed stretch that was formerly part of the PCH.

⑤ **Pygmy Forest Trail, Van Damme State Park, Mendocino, p193**
A quarter-mile boardwalk trail that leads through a grove of 'pygmy' trees that are over a century old but still only measure between 6 inches and 8 feet tall.

⑥ **Tall Trees Grove Trail, Redwood State and National Parks, p226**
A 4.5-mile hike into a grove of old-growth redwoods that includes the Libby Tree, which was once the tallest known tree on Earth.

Culinary California

Global influences and local ingredients, not to mention great wine, mean visitors to California are in for a real treat.

A MAJOR CHARACTERISTIC of California cuisine is an emphasis on organic, locally sourced ingredients. Farm-to-table dining, which emphasizes sourcing ingredients directly, traces its modern origins to Californians such as Pasadena cookbook author Helen Evans Brown and Berkeley restaurateur Alice Waters. While the concept of serving fresh, locally sourced food is hardly novel in the grand scheme of things, the environmental and nutritional impact of large-scale agricultural practices inspired chefs to look locally – and sometimes in their own backyards – for ingredients. This translates to menus that focus heavily on seasonal ingredients that are available in abundance, from creamy avocados in Southern California to earthy forest-foraged mushrooms on the North Coast.

Global Flavors

Spend much time in California, especially in larger cities, and you'll notice that some of the most popular places to eat serve flavors from around the globe. Go to any major city and you'll find everything from Burmese cuisine to Iranian fare, and even small cities usually have Chinese, Indian, Thai and Vietnamese restaurants.

Mexican food is ubiquitous in most of the state, although well-known dishes such as tacos and burritos are often pretty Americanized (or, more specifically, California-ized), and include fillings that you'd unlikely find south of the border, such as rice. Some of the best street food in California is Mexican, from tamales sold by roadside vendors to tacos served hot from taco trucks. You can buy single tacos for a quick snack, or get a selection for a full meal. Or, if you

Must-Try Californian Dishes

Cioppino
An Italian-American style of seafood stew originating in San Francisco and featuring a mix of Dungeness crab, shrimp, scallops and more cooked with tomatoes and wine.

Cobb Salad
A hearty mix of greens, tomatoes, bacon, hard-boiled eggs, avocado and cheese; invented at Hollywood's Brown Derby restaurant in the 1930s.

Mission Burrito
A massive burrito filled with meat, cheese, beans and rice; named for San Francisco's Mission District where it originated.

Left: Cobb salad; Above: Burrito; Right: *Cioppino* (seafood stew)

visit Oxnard, just north of Los Angeles, you can try a few different spots by going taco-hopping on the **Oxnard Taco Trail** (p79).

Of course, many ingredients that are popular in California today did not come to the state by way of migration. Indigenous foods that are popular in Californian cuisine include Chinook salmon, huckleberries and all sorts of mushrooms, from California golden chanterelles to king boletes (usually called porcinis by the time they make it to the plate).

Wine Counties of California

While California has made a name for itself on America's culinary map, the state is even more famous for its wine. In fact, around 81% of wine produced in the United States comes from California and most is produced either on or within a short distance of the Pacific Coast.

The **Napa Valley** (p184) is the most famous wine region in the state, if not the country, drawing in wine lovers from across the globe who come to try globally acclaimed Cabernet Sauvignon. Just next door, the **Sonoma Valley** (p184) region is better known for Pinot Noir, and offers a more laid-back (and budget-friendly) alternative to Napa.

The Central Coast is another major wine-producing region, particularly around Paso Robles in San Luis Obispo County and farther south in the Santa Barbara area. Cooler weather means areas closest to the Pacific are great for growing pinot noir and chardonnay, while Rhône varietals do well as you move slightly inland.

ACORNS

Although acorns don't typically feature on most menus in California these days, they were a major staple for a number of Native American tribes for thousands of years. One of the most common ways to process them involved roasting, shelling and grinding the nuts before sifting them into a flour. Members of some tribes continue to eat acorns to this day, often in the form of a nutritious mush known as *wiiwish*.

BEST WINE-TASTING EXPERIENCES

Chateau Montelena, Napa Valley, p184
Historic Napa Valley winery whose Chardonnay earned the top score at the 1976 'Judgement of Paris' wine competition, helping put Napa on the global wine map.

Wine Train, Napa, p184
A vintage wine train that chugs from downtown Napa to nearby tasting rooms.

Lompoc Wine Ghetto, Lompoc, p109
An industrial park complex housing a group of wineries and tasting rooms.

Chateau Montelena (p184)

FROM LEFT: XPIXEL/SHUTTERSTOCK, NATURE'S CHARM/SHUTTERSTOCK

On a Mission

Learn about Spanish cultural and architectural influence by visiting California's missions.

IF YOU SPEND much time traveling by road between San Diego and Sonoma County, you'll probably pass by a Spanish mission or two. These historic buildings were constructed in the late 18th and early 19th centuries by Franciscan priests, and most remain active to this day, serving as tourist attractions and active parishes (and providing inspiration for the Mission Revival stye of architecture). While visiting these structures can be a real treat for architecture lovers, irrespective of faith, the backstory of California's 21 missions is far from beautiful.

History

Starting in 1769, Spanish priests and civilian supporters were sent from Baja California (or 'lower California,' which is now part of Mexico) to Alta ('upper') California to create a series of missions, each within a day's horseback ride of the last. There were two driving ideas behind the missions. The priests were mainly concerned, or so it appeared, with converting Native Americans to Catholicism. However, the biggest backing came from the Spanish crown, which was set on expanding its territory during a time when large swathes of the Pacific Coast were yet to be 'claimed' by other European forces, despite a large presence of Russian, English and French traders and trappers in the region.

And so they began, and for more than half a century, Spanish Empire–backed priests would build a total of 21 missions, usually near Native American villages. Along with Catholicism, the settlers introduced diseases such as tuberculosis and measles that ended up killing large numbers of people who, having never been exposed to such sicknesses, had zero immunity. Some

Mission San Juan Capistrano (p53)
FROM LEFT: TONY_PAPAGEORGE/SHUTTERSTOCK, ALIZADA STUDIOS/SHUTTERSTOCK

Indigenous people converted to Catholicism and became religious leaders themselves, while others resisted or rebelled.

In 1821, Mexico gained independence from Spain and gained territorial control over Alta California. In 1833, the Mexican government passed a secularization act that ultimately transferred ownership of the missions from the Franciscans. Instead of the land being returned to Indigenous people, much of it ended up in the hands of *Californios* (descendants of Spanish settlers) through land grants. The Alta California territory became part of the US in 1850 at the end of the Mexican–American War, and many of the missions were progressively given back to the Catholic Church in the decades that followed.

The California Missions Trail

Today, the 21 missions are promoted together as part of the California Missions Trail, part of which coincides with the Pacific Coast Highway. The route is also known as El Camino Real (The Royal Road). The term originally referred to a network of roads between the missions, but now refers to an established modern route that includes parts of Hwy 101 along with I-5 and California State Rte 82. It starts in San Diego (p34) at San Diego de Alcala, which was the first of the missions, and ends at the final mission to be constructed, San Francisco Solano, in the city of Sonoma (p183).

ADOBE

Also known as mud bricks, adobe bricks were one of the main components that went into constructing the missions of California. Adobe bricks are typically made of a mix of mud and other organic material, such as straw, and while this type of material is associated with the Spanish (at least in the US), it's been used all over the world for millennia.

CALIFORNIA MISSIONS IN FILM

Vertigo (1958)
A character by the name of Madeline falls from the bell tower of the Mission of San Juan Bautista in this Hitchcock classic.

Incubus (1966)
Mission San Antonio de Padua was one of the key filming locations of this Esperanto-language film starring William Shatner of *Star Trek* fame.

Pee-wee's Big Adventure (1985)
Parts of the interior of Mission San Fernando Rey de España were used to depict the Alamo, where Pee-wee famously searched for the basement.

HIGHLIGHTS

① Mission San Juan Capistrano, San Juan Capistrano, p53
Considered the birthplace of Orange County, this mission combines a historic landmark with a botanical garden and a museum featuring a wide array of artifacts, from coins and documents to an antique saddle.

② Mission Basilica San Buenaventura, Ventura, p80
Beautiful blue-and-white tile work and whitewashed walls are just the beginning of what this beautiful mission, elevated to minor basilica status in 2020 under Pope Francis, has to offer.

③ Old Mission Santa Barbara, Santa Barbara, p97
On a 15-acre hill overlooking Santa Barbara and the Pacific Ocean, this beautiful spot features a cemetery, an old church and a nine-room museum full of art and artifacts.

④ La Purísima Mission, Lompoc, p109
Dating to 1787, this sprawling mission park features beautifully restored whitewashed buildings and easy access to around 25 miles of hiking trails.

⑤ Mission San Luis Obispo De Tolosa, San Luis Obispo, p124
This L-shaped mission, built in stages, features a museum and a bell tower that still uses the services of bell ringers rather than a more modern automatic system.

⑥ Carmel Mission, Carmel-by-the-Sea, p144
Within easy walking distance of downtown Carmel-by-the-Sea, this active mission is notable for housing California's first library.

Weird & Wonderful

From optical illusions to unusual petting zoos, the Pacific Coast has plenty of oddities worth pulling over for.

ROADSIDE ATTRACTIONS HAVE been an integral part of the American road-trip experience since the get-go. In the early days of long-distance motor travel, enterprising folks with a talent for art and construction began building giant statues of everything from fruit to ducks with hopes of beckoning road-weary tourists to pull over and take a look – and spend some money. While colorful structures are common in flatter parts of the interior US, many such spots found along the Pacific Coast – such as the drive-through redwood trees found in **Leggett** (p205), **Klamath** (p228) and on the **Avenue of the Giants** (p210) – are somewhat integrated into the natural environment. Others, such as the **Mystery Spot** (p160) in Santa Cruz and **Confusion Hill** (p207) in Mendocino County, rely on the use of optical illusions to draw in the crowds.

Modern Stops

While roadside attractions aren't being built at the same rate that they used to be, they still pop up from time to time, sometimes by accident. In fact, one of the newest roadside attractions on the Pacific Coast Highway – the **Cardiff Kook Statue** (p47) in Encinitas – wasn't initially intended to draw gawks and groans. This 6-foot-tall sculpture, which depicts a man on a surfboard, was initially intended to be a simple nod to the city's surf community. However, when the statue was unveiled in 2007, local surfers were less than impressed, critical of everything from the statue's surfing form to his proportions. As a response, pranksters began dressing the statue up in costumes inspired by everyone from Elvis Presley to former US Supreme Court justice and feminist icon Ruth

THE PACIFIC COAST HIGHWAY IN MUSIC

Pacific Coast Highway by the Beach Boys
Leave it to the most California-centric band ever to pen a song about Hwy 1.

Pacific Coast Highway by the Hip Abduction
This PCH-themed song, featuring songwriter Trevor Hall, covers the road from Los Angeles up to the redwoods in Humboldt County.

Bixby Canyon Bridge by Death Cab for Cutie
The narrator of this melancholy tune travels from San Francisco to Big Sur's most famous bridge.

Left: Drive-Thru Tree Park (p205); Right: Mystery Spot (p160)

Bader Ginsburg, and now you'll never be sure just how the famous surfer will be garbed when you visit.

Architectural Oddities

Some of the weirdly wonderful spots along the route weren't necessarily meant to make people stop and take a look, but they're still worth a pit stop to see. In La Jolla, **Sunny Jim's Sea Cave** (p39) beckons, daring visitors to descend 145 steps into a sandstone cave tunnel that served as the former residence of engineer and artist Gustav Schultz.

At the California Polytechnic State University in San Luis Obispo, the **Architecture Graveyard** (p122) is another worthwhile stop. Here, over two dozen student-built structures sit in various states of disrepair; the oldest date back to the mid-1960s. Roughly 40 miles up the road in San Simeon, **Hearst Castle** (p126) merits at least a few hours. This opulent landmark mansion, now managed by California State Parks, was built over a period of nearly two decades and features grand halls (some look like they were plucked from medieval Europe) and sprawling courtyards filled with fountains and statuary.

On the North Coast, the **Sea Ranch Chapel** (p191) is considerably less grand, measuring roughly the size of a small American garage. Still, its colorful stained-glass windows, sweeping roof and carved wooden interiors make it worth a stop, particularly if you're interested in seeing an example of the Sea Ranch community's signature architecture style.

BIOLUMINESCENT WAVES

Go for an evening walk along a Southern California beach in the summer and you may notice a mystical glow on the ocean waves. What you're witnessing is bioluminescence, a natural phenomenon that occurs when there's a large population of plankton known as dinoflagellates present. When waters are disturbed (such as by the force of the ocean or the swish of a kayak paddle), these emit a star-like shimmer that illuminates the waters around them.

ODD ANIMAL ENCOUNTERS

Canzelle Alpacas, Toro Canyon, p86
This family-run farm experience has everything from peacocks to llamas plus, of course, alpacas.

Bison Paddock, San Francisco, p174
Visit Golden Gate Park to see buffalo (aka bison) hanging out in a meadow, just as they have since the late 19th century.

Ostrichland, Buellton, p110
Feed snacks to unsettlingly massive birds at this 32-acre property that's home to over 150 ostriches and emus.

Sea Ranch Chapel (p191)

6 Ways to Do the Pacific Coast Highway

The Pacific Coast Highway takes you from one end of California to the other, but there are plenty of ways to approach the journey. These are some ways you can build the trip of a lifetime.

1 South to North
Time *At least a week*

Many people start in San Diego and drive all the way up the coast, wrapping up in Crescent City or continuing north to Oregon and Washington. It's easy to do in a week as long as you don't run into any road closures, but you can extend your journey quite significantly if you make long stops in major cities or do a lot of detours.
Possible overnights Los Angeles, Santa Barbara, San Luis Obispo, Carmel, San Francisco, Mendocino, Eureka

Bixby Bridge (p134)

See p30 for the full route map

2 In Reverse
Time *At least a week*

While this book outlines the journey from south to north, you can just as easily start in the north. This takes you through redwood forests and along the rugged Mendocino, Sonoma and Marin coastlines, over the Golden Gate Bridge into San Francisco and down past the Monterey Bay. From here, you'll continue along the Big Sur and Central coasts, weaving your way down to Southern California and wrapping up in San Diego.
Possible overnights Eureka, Mendocino, San Francisco, Carmel, San Luis Obispo, Santa Barbara, Los Angeles

3 Los Angeles to San Francisco
Time *4 days*
Best for *Time-pressed travelers who want a taste of the coast*

While plenty of people zip between San Francisco and Los Angeles on I-5, it's much more fun to take the Pacific Coast Highway instead. Just head north past Santa Barbara and along California's Central Coast before crossing into scenic Big Sur (road repairs permitting). From here, continue north along the Monterey Bay and through Santa Cruz, following Hwy 1 past Half Moon Bay and into San Francisco.
Possible overnights Santa Barbara, San Luis Obispo, Monterey, Santa Cruz

Carmel-by-the-Sea (p144)

For essential trip tips, see p237

4 Winter Warriors
Time *At least a week*
Best for *Crowd avoiders and budget travelers*

Bundle up and take a winter journey along the Pacific Coast Highway. While snow isn't usually an issue, you may run into some ice at higher elevations, so be extremely careful. Expect big waves (especially during the annual king tides in winter) and lots of rain. Hiking trails are empty during this time of year, and tend to get muddy.
Possible overnights Los Angeles, Santa Barbara, San Luis Obispo, Carmel, San Francisco, Mendocino, Eureka

5 Weekends Away
Time *2 nights*
Best for *Time-pressed urbanites*

You can see little segments of the Pacific Coast on weekend trips from major cities across the state. Santa Barbara and the surrounding wine regions are ideal for a weekend from Los Angeles. Travelers based in San Francisco should consider a weekend up north in Mendocino, but could just as easily head south for a weekend in Carmel-by-the-Sea or on the Big Sur coast.
Possible overnights Mendocino, Carmel, Santa Barbara

6 On a Bike
Time *3–4 weeks*
Best for *Serious cyclists*

Cycling the Pacific Coast promises to be both challenging and rewarding. Many people can pull it off in three weeks, but giving yourself four weeks is ideal if you want to pace yourself and take city breaks along the way. Consider starting in the north if you do this journey in late summer or fall to avoid NorCal rain and SoCal heat.
Possible overnights Los Angeles, San Luis Obispo, Big Sur, Santa Cruz, Eureka

WHEN TO GO

Jun–Aug
Summer is peak season all along the route, and campsites and hotels book up well in advance. The weather is usually great, with crowds to match.

Sep–Nov
Crowds dwindle in September after the Labor Day Weekend at the beginning of the month, but temperatures stay warm into early October.

Dec–Feb
The low season brings with it cool temperatures and minimal crowds, but it's not ideal for camping and hiking in the northern sections.

Mar–May
Temperatures start to warm up, especially in Southern California, but crowds remain smaller, except during spring-break school holidays and the Memorial Day Weekend at the end of May.

The Drive

A stage-by-stage, mile-by-mile account of the route. Your journey begins here.

NORTHERN CALIFORNIA
San Francisco to **Mendocino**, p176
Mendocino to **Eureka**, p198
Eureka to **Crescent City**, p218

END — Crescent City
Eureka
Mendocino

PCH near Torrey Pines State Natural Reserve (p46)
GLOWING EARTH PHOTOGRAPHY/SHUTTERSTOCK

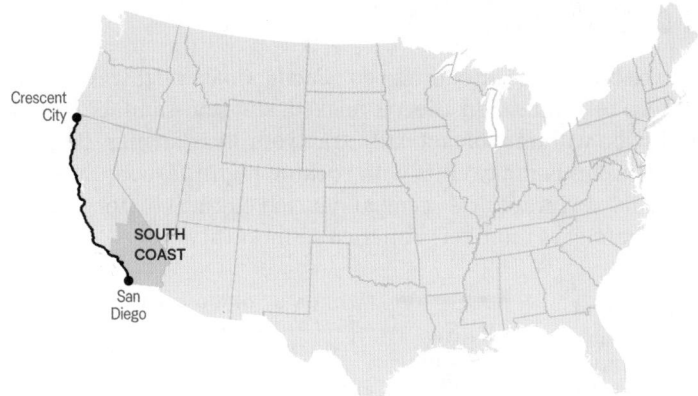

SOUTH COAST

A road by any other name would look as sweet... As you wind your way along Southern California's shoreline, the Pacific Coast Highway takes on many monikers. Torrey Pines Road, Camino del Mar, Carlsbad Boulevard, US-1 – these are all other names for the Pacific Coast Highway, or PCH (psst: SoCal locals never say 'the' in front of 'PCH.') But one thing remains consistent: you're in for endless ocean views, legendary beach towns and nonstop culinary temptations. One other thing that's consistent: your GPS will continually try to lure you to the I-5, which runs parallel to PCH for a good portion of the southern coast. Try to resist. PCH hugs the coast as tight as a surfer's wetsuit and offers the best views.

CITY GUIDE:
San Diego

La Jolla (p39)

Whether you're beginning or ending your Pacific Coast Highway journey at this southern terminus, San Diego's relaxed, suit-and-sandals, live-and-let-live beach vibe will unapologetically grab your heartstrings. Blending stunning beaches and craggy cliffs with rocking nightlife, countless culinary delights, a vibrant arts scene and a rich cultural history, San Diego embodies its shameless moniker: 'America's Finest City.'

Getting Around

Driving For the ultimate in freedom and flexibility, driving is your best option for exploring all that Greater San Diego offers. It'll save a lot of transit time and scheduling headaches in the long run.

Parking Parking can be a nightmare, and is expensive around downtown and other touristy areas. City parking garages typically charge $20 to $35 per day, and lots fill up fast, especially during special events. With patience, along with the ability and desire to walk a bit further, you can score cheaper options.

Public transportation San Diego's Metropolitan Transit System (MTS) operates a network of buses and trolleys ($2.50/6 per ride/day pass) throughout the region. Service can sometimes be a bit spotty, with limited hours and routes in some areas, so be sure to plan trips in advance. For public transportation schedules and trip planning, go to *sdmts.com*.

HOW MUCH FOR A

Fish taco $3-6

Carne asada fries $8-12

Balboa cocktail $15

Ticket to San Diego Zoo $83 adult, $73 child (3-11 years)

WORDS BY **DAVID GIBB**

David is an adventurous, globetrotting travel writer – whose heart still resides in Encinitas, CA

Arriving

By air A few miles northwest of downtown, refreshingly modest San Diego International Airport (SAN; *san.org*), America's busiest single-runway airport, serves as primary hub for commercial air travel. Airport car rentals abound; however, cheaper rates can often be scored downtown, just a short jaunt away (you'd have to board a shuttle to the Consolidated Rental Car Center anyway). Hop aboard the Rte 992 bus ($2.50, 30 minutes) to Santa Fe Depot, the downtown Amtrak station. Use a pre-loaded PRONTO card, the Metropolitan Transit System (MTS) app, or pay with credit/debit cards. Taxis are readily available but rideshares like Uber and Lyft typically offer better rates ($15 to $25, 10 to 15 minutes).

By rail Many opt for Los Angeles' larger LAX airport, hopping aboard Amtrak's Pacific Surfliner train (running south from San Luis Obispo) for a short but scenic ride into San Diego's charming downtown station, Santa Fe Depot. Built in 1915, its stunning Spanish Colonial Revival architecture serves as a fitting welcome.

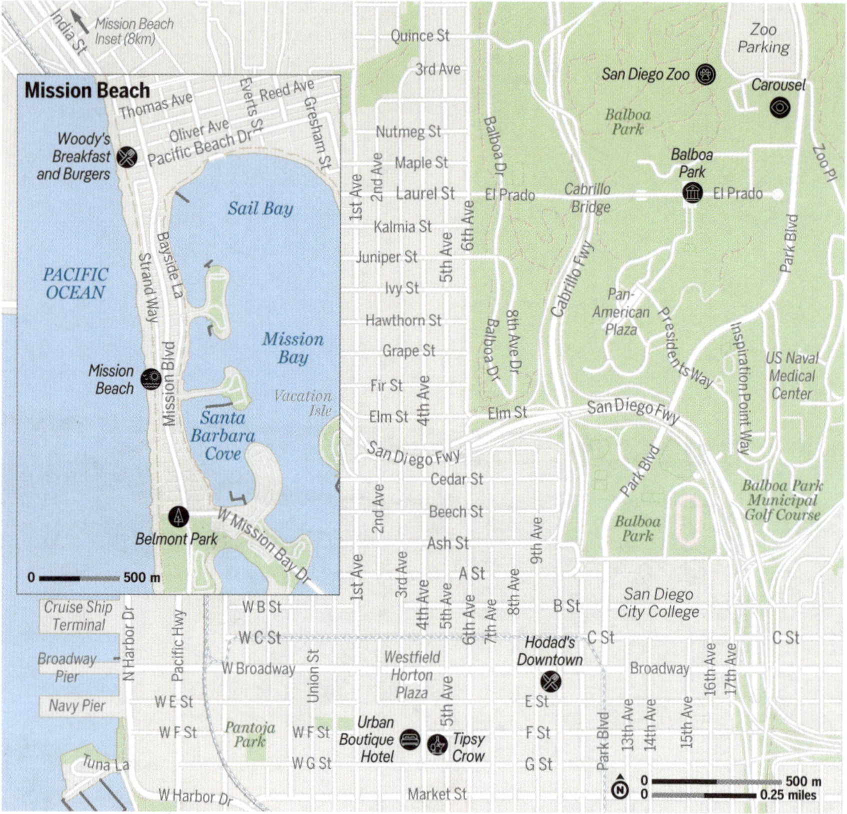

A DAY IN SAN DIEGO

Stroll **Mission Beach**'s 2-mile boardwalk, watching the sunrise. Stop and enjoy breakfast at beloved **Woody's Breakfast and Burgers** (woodyssd.com). Then enjoy nostalgic fun at **Belmont Park** (belmontpark.com; free; 11am-10pm), packed with rides, games and treats. Tip: ride the Giant Dipper rollercoaster on Tuesdays for just $1.

Explore the lush gardens at 1200-acre **Balboa Park** (p38), take in a couple of museums, then reach for the coveted brass ring atop a colorfully painted horse on the popular Victorian-era **Carousel**. Time permitting, visit some of your favorite (furry) relatives over at the **San Diego Zoo**.

Devour a jaw-breaking burger at **Hodad's Downtown** before enjoying a 10-block leisurely stroll to the **Gaslamp Quarter** (p38), then relax with a nightcap at an intimate lounge. Find late-night fun at one of the rowdier spots, like **Tipsy Crow** (thetipsycrow.com; noon-2am) – ask about their secret underground tunnels.

Where to Stay

San Diego boasts an eclectic mix of accommodation options, ranging from large chain hotels to historical boutique hotels, trendy bed-and-breakfasts and exquisite vacation rentals. If the food scene, nightlife and proximity to attractions like Balboa Park and museums are important, grab a spot downtown (pricey parking surcharges, though). Hit Pacific Beach if you prefer a youthful, edgy college vibe, or head to Mission Beach for a smorgasbord of private vacation rentals, including beachfront villas with golden sand and white-capped waves beckoning you.

BEST PLACES TO STAY

Urban Boutique Hotel $$
Fifty-five charming, clean (but small) rooms in the heart of Little Italy. *urbanboutiquehotel.com*

Manchester Grand Hyatt $$
Convenient downtown four-star hotel near Seaport Village. *hyatt.com*

Pendry San Diego $$$
Chic, five-star boutique hotel, with a rooftop pool, in the Gaslamp Quarter. *pendry.com*

Hotel del Coronado $$$
Iconic Victorian seaside gem entertains with stories and amenities. *hoteldel.com*

Where to Eat

San Diego offers a cornucopia of dining options, ranging from food trucks and taquerias to upscale bistros and Michelin-starred restaurants. Little Italy, once defined by its incredible pasta and pizza, has become a destination for a diverse range of culinary hot spots. Hit Old Town for traditional Mexican food, or Pacific Beach for some of SoCal's finest Cali-Baja dishes.

FROM MEXICO & THE SEA, WITH LOVE

With San Diego's large Chicano population and proximity to the border, Mexican food is a cornerstone of its culinary landscape. Tacos and burritos are everywhere – food trucks, taquerias, upscale restaurants – with fish tacos (beer-battered fish and shredded cabbage smothered in creamy avocado and chipotle sauces) considered the region's signature dish.

Another San Diego staple is carne asada fries, a meat-lover's dream. Marinated skirt steak is piled high on a bed of fries, crowned with melted cheese, fresh guacamole (taken as seriously here as pizza is in Chicago) and a dollop of sour cream. California burritos, another foodie favorite, feature marinated carne asada, fries, pico de gallo, guacamole, sour cream and cheese (notice a trend?). Blending regional palates with Mexican flair, some of SoCal's finest Cali-Baja creations are found at eateries in Old Town and Pacific Beach.

Seafood dishes run a tight second-place finish. Sample a tasty bowl of *cioppino* (seafood stew) or try a sweet-and-spicy ceviche dish.

VALENTYN VOLKOV/SHUTTERSTOCK

BEST PLACES TO EAT & DRINK

Hodad's Downtown $$
Savory, jaw-breaking, mammoth-sized burgers. *hodadsdowntown.com;* hours vary

Sportsmen's Seafood $$
Secret-recipe Italian fish and chips. Delish tuna and salmon jerky, too. *sportsmensseafood.com;* 11am-8pm

Assenti's Pasta $$
Handmade artisan GMO-free pasta, cut fresh to order. Chef's kiss good! *assentispasta.com;* 9am-5pm Mon-Sat

Raised by Wolves $$
Tantalizing cocktails aplenty at this throwback to speakeasies. Reservations needed. *raisedxwolves.com;* hours vary

Gaslamp Quarter

 Explore Downtown: Gaslamp Quarter & Seaport Village

Blending contemporary and Victorian-era architecture, the Gaslamp Quarter evokes the spirit of a bygone era – a horse-drawn carriage would seem at home along Fifth Ave's cobblestone streets. Covering more than 16 blocks, this was once ground zero for gambling dens, seedy saloons and cathouses. Now it's the heart of modern, downtown San Diego, with pulsating nightlife, museums, theaters, art galleries and over 100 eateries. Enjoy live jazz at Horton Plaza Park or imbibe at an intimate cocktail lounge.

Looking for retail therapy? **Seaport Village** *(seaportvillage.com)*, a downtown shopping destination covering 14 acres, boasts dozens of shops and restaurants. Tip: fans of Bugs Bunny and the Looney Tunes won't want to miss the Chuck Jones Gallery.

Left: Balboa Park

BARRIO LOGAN'S CHICANO HERITAGE

Nowhere is San Diego's Chicano heritage more evident than in the neighborhood of Barrio Logan, formerly known as Logan Heights. An influx of Mexican refugees settled here in the early 1900s, forming the world's largest Chicano community. Despite challenges, it has evolved into a vibrant epicenter of Chicano culture. Now showcasing the largest collection of Chicano murals in the world, Barrio Logan first embraced art as a means of telling stories of its history and struggles in the 1960s.

When the city announced plans to build the Coronado Bridge in the 1970s, locals peacefully protested, leading to the creation of Chicano Park. This 7-acre park, situated under the concrete pillars of the freeway overpass, showcases over 100 murals. Many blend art with activism, featuring powerful themes deeply rooted in the community's social and political history.

Since 2015, Border X Brewing has hosted Chicano-Con, an annual event spotlighting Chicano artists, that runs concurrently with San Diego Comic-Con each July. Worth a stop, the **Chicano Park Museum & Cultural Center** *(chicanoparkmuseum.org; 11am-5pm Thu-Sun)* honors the park's history and art.

 Go Wild at Balboa Park's San Diego Zoo

Balboa Park *(balboapark.org/explorer/museums)* is packed with fun. Museums and gardens beckon as talented buskers entertain, carillon bell chimes fill the air, and outdoor theatre shows pack summer crowds. And whatever you do, don't miss the park's world-renowned **San Diego Zoo** *(zoo.sandiegozoo.org)*.

Spanning 100 acres and home to 680 species, the zoo is celebrated for its conservation efforts – and for providing its 12,000 animals with domains mimicking their natural habitats. That includes pandas Xin Bao and Yun Chuan, a pair of new arrivals from China.

Explore the grounds by hopping aboard a guided double-decker tour bus or Skyfari Aerial Tram. Parking's free – but get there early.

Fun in La Jolla

Perfect for adventurous families and shopoholics, La Jolla blends stuffy business suits with beach sandals. Cliffside sunsets, stunning beaches and frolicking sea lions round out the fun.

HOW TO

Parking: There are many free parking spaces at the La Jolla Shores lot...but aim to get there early.

La Jolla Cove offers free parking along Coast Blvd (near Scripps Park and Children's Pool), but the limited spots disappear quickly.

Free parking is permitted along La Jolla's residential streets – but stay mindful of posted time limits, as enforcement is aggressive.

While those seeking retail therapy should hit the many boutique shops lining Prospect St, San Diego's equivalent of Rodeo Drive, others looking for a more natural and relaxing vibe should head straight for the stunning beaches and towering cliffs at La Jolla Shores and La Jolla Cove.

With an easily accessible, wide sandy beach with a scenic boardwalk, calm waters and year-round lifeguards, La Jolla Shores embraces a laid-back, beach-bum attitude.

Resting below majestic seaside cliffs less than 2 miles away, La Jolla Cove preaches a truly authentic SoCal beach experience. Beachgoers descend stairs (various access points) to share the sand and calm, clear waters with snorkelers and scuba divers. Adventurous types may opt to descend 145 creaky and often slippery wooden steps at **Sunny Jim's Sea Cave** *(cavestore.com; adult/child $13/7)*, meandering their way through spooky sandstone cliff tunnels (once used by smugglers), ending their sea cave journey with a spectacular ocean view.

A few blocks south of the cove, Children's Pool offers a small seawall-protected beach, a common gathering spot for California seals and sea lions.

Above: California sea lion; Left: La Jolla Cove

Across to Coronado

Coronado is a picturesque retreat offering luxury beach resorts, historic hotels, fabulous dining options and a family-friendly beach.

HOW TO

Getting here: While you'll probably crave the experience of driving across Coronado Bridge, you can also hop aboard the **Flagship Ferry** *(coronadoferrylanding.com; return $18, under child 3 free)*, departing downtown from Broadway Pier and the San Diego Convention Center (bikes free, service animals only, schedules online). Tip: ride free 5:40am to 8:50am and receive a free return ticket for the afternoon.

Parking: Free street parking is abundant in Coronado, although you may need to walk a couple of blocks from Orange Ave (the main drag, where metered spots are 25¢ per hour). Pay-by-license-plate parking is also available at the Coronado Ferry Landing.

The Famous Bridge

Opened in 1969, the 2.12-mile Coronado Bridge seduces with its sultry blue sea and sky-colored curves. Towering 200ft high above San Diego Bay, it's supported by 27 concrete girders as powerful as...well... California gym rats.

Often seen in movies and TV shows, this landmark bridge was immortalized during the eight-season run of the detective show *Simon & Simon* (1981–89), where it featured prominently in the show's opening credits.

The Even-More-Famous Hotel

The world's largest resort hotel when it opened in 1888, Hotel del Coronado (known as 'The Dell' to locals), with elegant Victorian grandeur, remains the Mona Lisa of the Coronado landscape. Boasting a storied past, the hotel has featured in many iconic movies, including *Some Like It Hot* (1959) starring Marilyn Monroe. Offering opulent amenities, including tennis, golf and expansive pools, it remains a classic San Diego destination experience. If you're going to splurge once during your visit, do it here. Nonguests can stroll the opulent lobby, restaurants and hotel gardens. Tip: ask for one of the original 400 rooms, or you may find yourself in one of the newer, boring sections. Thrillseekers and ghosthunters should request room 3502 or 3327, both considered hotbeds of paranormal activity.

Fun in the Sand & Water

Known for its soft white sand and gentle waves, family-favorite Coronado Beach stretches along the Pacific Coast for more than

AS THE SUN SYMBOLICALLY SETS

If you're ending your fantastic PCH adventure here, it's rather serendipitous that the perfect place to watch the sunset awaits you. Sunset Cliffs, along the western bank of the Point Loma peninsula, provides a breathtaking vista – the cliffs seemingly ablaze during the nightly spectacle. Descend the stairs (known as the Stairway to Heaven) adjacent to Sunset Cliffs Natural Park, at the extreme south end of Sunset Cliffs Blvd (at Ladera St). The sandy beach below marks the ideal spot to end your trip.

Left: Hotel del Coronado; Below: Coronado Beach

1.5 miles, affording stunning views of the San Diego skyline. Popular with sun worshippers, beachcombers and sandcastle architects, it's also a haven for avid water-sports enthusiasts. Paddleboarders, kayakers and jet-skiers converge to share the waters, with the Coronado Bridge providing a captivating backdrop. Kayaks and paddleboards are available for rent at both the **Boathouse** *(619-522-2655)* and **SUP & Saddle** *(supandsaddle.com)*, which also offers bike rentals. Fully accessible, the beach has changing rooms, bathrooms and showers available.

San Diego

Winding away from San Diego, this stretch of PCH, heading through the heart of California's quintessential beach towns, is the kind of drive that inspires a lifestyle change. Every time I cruise it, I think: *I need to work on my surfing. Is middle age too late to learn to skateboard? Should I join a beach volleyball league?* This is the coastline of the Beach Boys' 'Surfin' USA' and the Mamas & the Papas' 'California Dreamin'.' Even the most staunch city sightseers will want to hop out of the car and feel sand between their toes.

Amelia Mularz

Los Angeles

133 MILES · 4.5 HOURS' DRIVE

THIS LEG:

- San Diego
- Torrey Pines State Natural Reserve
- Del Mar
- Cardiff
- Downtown Encinitas
- Leucadia
- Oceanside
- San Onofre State Beach
- Capistrano Beach
- Laguna Beach
- Newport Beach
- Huntington Beach
- Long Beach
- Los Angeles

PCH at Newport Beach (p55)
TOMTOMDOTCOM_TBIRDAERIAL/SHUTTERSTOCK

Driving Notes

Passing through a string of iconic beach towns means you'll get a good look at the bakeries, breweries and board shops that fuel the area. But you'll also run into lights and pedestrian crossings galore, so bring your patience. If you're ever in a hurry, you can always hop over to I-5 for the fastest route.

Breaking Your Journey

Each beach town on the route has lodging, shopping and top-notch dining, so it's a matter of finding room in your belly for yet another award-worthy taco joint. If you've got budgeting on the brain, you may want to avoid spending the night in Orange County's major beach destinations, such as Laguna Beach and Newport Beach for Encinitas and Oceanside.

Amelia's Tips

BEST MEAL Burgers, malts and ocean views make Crystal Cove Shake Shack (p54) a must.

FAVORITE VIEW Heisler Park, Laguna Beach, has walking trails, gardens and clifftop cove views.

ESSENTIAL STOP Charming San Juan Capistrano (p52) is worth the detour.

ROAD-TRIP TIP Pack a beach go-bag that's separate from your suitcase. That way you can pull over for a swim.

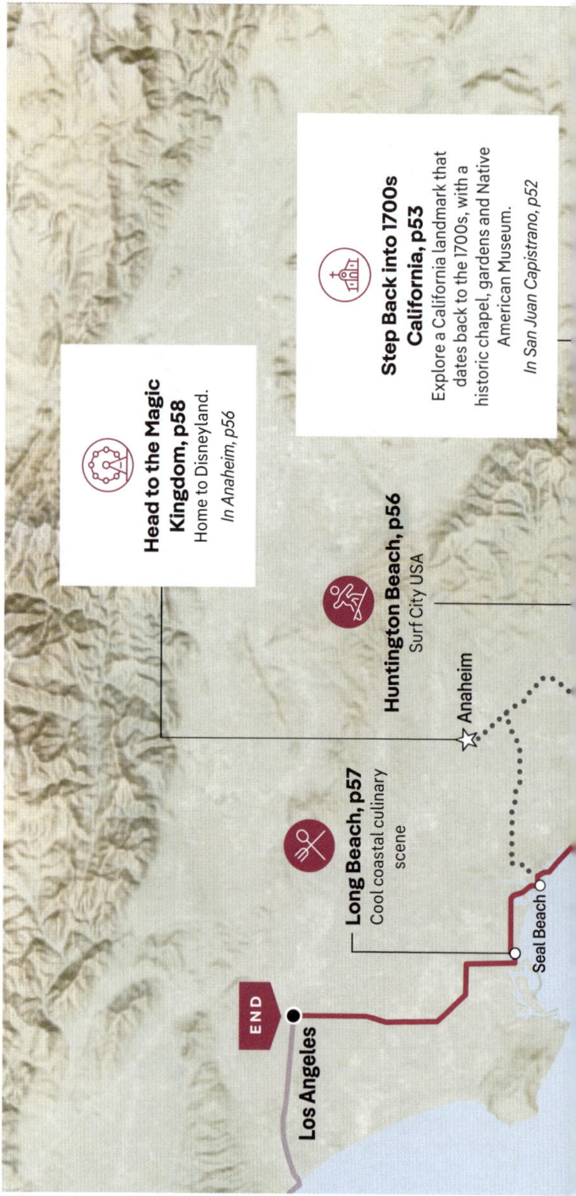

Step Back into 1700s California, p53
Explore a California landmark that dates back to the 1700s, with a historic chapel, gardens and Native American Museum.
In San Juan Capistrano, p52

Head to the Magic Kingdom, p58
Home to Disneyland.
In Anaheim, p56

Huntington Beach, p56
Surf City USA

Long Beach, p57
Cool coastal culinary scene

Anaheim

Seal Beach

END — Los Angeles

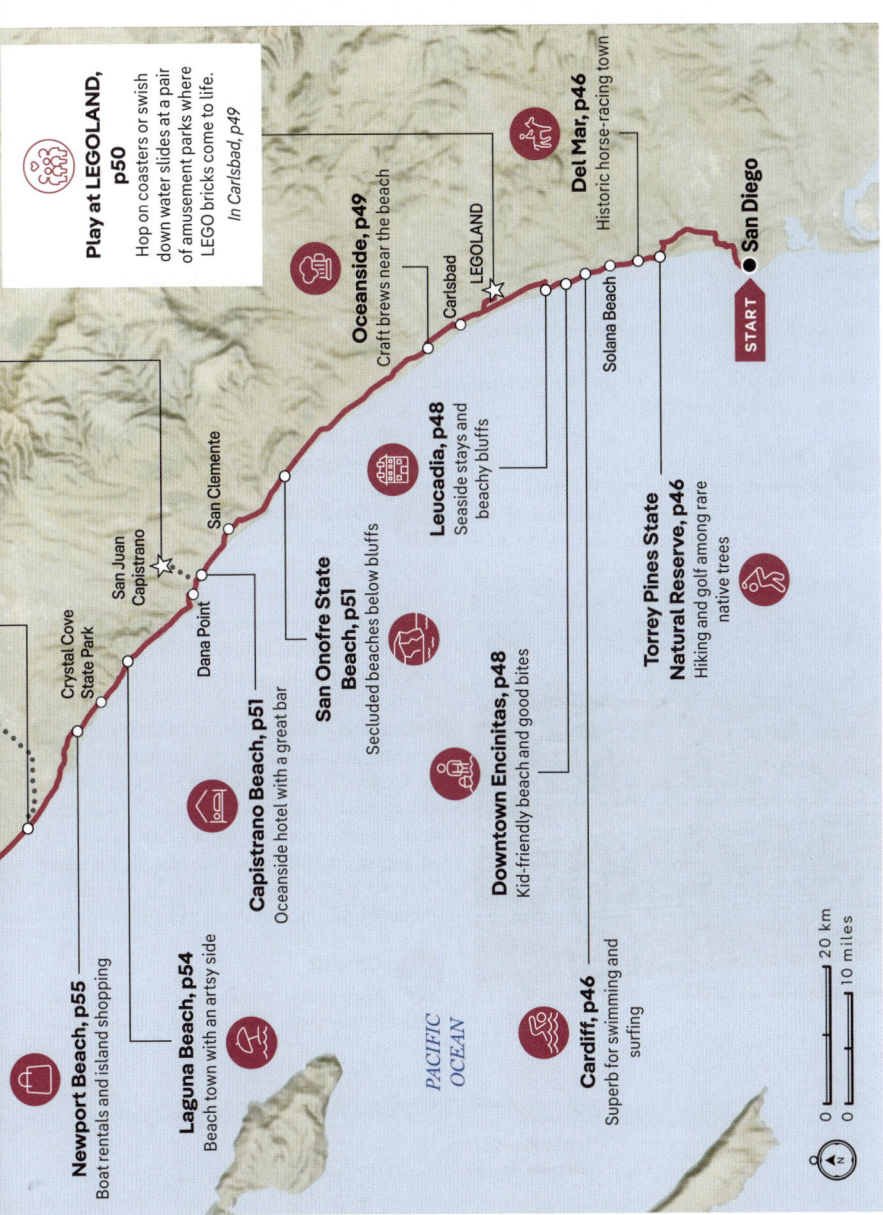

Torrey Pines State Natural Reserve

Leaving San Diego, hop on Torrey Pines Rd – the name for PCH in these parts – to the **Torrey Pines State Natural Reserve** *(parks.ca.gov)*. Named after the rarest native pine in the US, this 2000-acre reserve is a paradise for outdoor lovers of all kinds. Some might take a more luxe approach and hit the links at **Torrey Pines Golf Course** *(torreypines.com; 18 holes for nonresidents from $92)*, while others may prefer a hike. The 2.5-mile Broken Hill Trail meanders along sandstone cliffs and past wildflowers and the reserve's namesake trees. In the winter, keep your eyes peeled for whales.

Del Mar

Continuing north, you'll pass Torrey Pines State Beach (part of the reserve and not a bad place to stop for a dip) and soon you'll notice the road name changes to Camino del Mar. That's your first sign you've entered the historic horse-racing town: Del Mar. If you're driving through during summer (July through early September) or fall (November), you may be able to catch a race at the **Del Mar Thoroughbred Club** *(dmtc.com)*, where they like to say 'the turf meets the surf.' Even when it's not a race day, the track, which doubles as the Del Mar Fairgrounds, also regularly hosts concerts.

For shopping, beeline to **Del Mar Plaza** *(delmarplaza.com)*, where you'll find vacation-perfect looks at **Urban Beach House**, and beach reads at **Camino Books**. The plaza also has dining with ocean views, including the easy-breezy java spot **Kini Koffee** *($)* and flatbread-and-beer-slinging **Monarch Ocean Pub** *($$)*.

Solana Beach

The water views keep coming as you cross the San Dieguito River and soon cross into Solana Beach, where our favorite coastal road becomes Hwy 101. You'll pass shops and restaurants along Hwy 101 – **Achilles Coffee** *(achillescoffeeroasters.com; $)* is especially great for a caffeine fix and selection of sandwiches named after San Diego destinations – but swing over to Cedros Ave for more unique shops. Running parallel to Hwy 101, the **Cedros Avenue Design District** *(cedrosavenue.com)* has dozens of independent boutiques and galleries packed into just a few blocks. Within walking distance of the design district, **Fletcher Cove** is a beloved beach in the area, especially if you have little ones, as it has a playground.

Cardiff

Keep your swimsuit on, because just north of Solana Beach you'll cruise past a series of state

Del Mar

Hike or golf in an outdoor paradise named for rare pines

Fletcher Cove

beaches and reefs that are supreme for surfing, swimming, tide pooling and diving. Technically, Cardiff (or its full name Cardiff-by-the-Sea) is part of Encinitas, but its natural attractions are so alluring, it deserves a stop all its own. **Cardiff State Beach** *(parks.ca.gov; vehicle day-use fee from $15)* is equipped with road-tripper–friendly amenities, including bathrooms, showers and ample parking. Just north, you'll find another state beach, **San Elijo**, which is worth a visit to see the infamous **Cardiff Kook Statue** (right on Hwy 101 at Chesterfield Dr). A 6ft bronze ode to beginner surfers, the statue is often dressed in silly (some might say humiliating) clothes, a tradition among local pranksters.

BEST PLACES TO EAT

Salt + Lime, Del Mar $$
A SoCal success story, Salt + Lime won over San Diego taste buds as a food truck before becoming a bricks-and-mortar joint serving up Baja-style tostadas and tacos. *saltandlimesd.com; 11:30am-9pm Mon-Thu, 11:30am-9:30pm Fri, 10:30am-9:30pm Sat & Sun*

Campfire, Carlsbad $$$
The restaurant version of glamping, Campfire is decked in outdoorsy decor (picnic baskets, tents and lanterns) that complements the charred chicken and s'mores on the menu. *thisiscampfire.com; hours vary, closed Tue*

Petite Madeline Bakery, Oceanside $
Lemon-glazed braids, bear claws and crogels (a croissant-bagel hybrid) pair perfectly with early-morning strolls on the beach. *petitemadelinebakery.com; 7am-2:30pm Mon-Fri, 7:30am-3:30pm Sat & Sun*

Nick's, Laguna Beach $$$
Dive into a seafood-filled bowl of *cioppino* (shrimp, salmon, sea bass, mussels and more) right on PCH. *nicksrestaurants.com; hours vary*

Head to the races!

	Solana Beach		Cardiff
3 miles		2.5 miles	

SAN DIEGO TO LOS ANGELES

Swami's Beach

Downtown Encinitas

Continuing on Hwy 101, you'll soon spot **Swami's Beach**, a legendary surf spot. You'll also come upon **Moonlight State Beach**, a top destination for swimmers and sunbathers. Bathrooms, a playground, snack bar and rental stand (snag a surf or boogie board) make Moonlight especially family-friendly. Lunch spots like the **Encinitas Cafe** *(encinitascafe.com; $)* and the **Taco Stand** *(letstaco.com; $)* are also within walking distance of the beach.

Because this northern area of San Diego County is slightly more affordable than the beach towns of Orange County, it's not a bad idea to also spend a night or two in Encinitas. The rooms at **Brisa Pacific Hotel** *(brisapacifichotelencinitas.com; $)* are basic, but there is a pool. Or hold out for unique options just a few minutes to the north in Leucadia.

Leucadia

With a name that means 'place of refuge' in Greek, Leucadia is a fitting place for a stopover. The beach community – which, like Cardiff, is part of the city of Encinitas – has sublime seaside stays. **Surfhouse** (p51), a boutique hotel founded by locals, sits right on Hwy 101 and offers surf rentals and lessons, along with rooms named after local breaks. Or splurge on **Alila Marea Beach Resort** *(alilahotels.com;*

Swami's is for surfers, while Moonlight Beach is one of the best for a swim and snack on the shore

Cardiff — 1.5 miles — Downtown Encinitas — 2 miles

$$$), perched on bluffs above **Ponto Beach** and packed with luxe amenities, like a full spa and guest rooms with personal fire pits (ideal for romance-seeking road-trippers).

Whatever your plans, consider a pit stop at one of the area's secluded swaths of sand: **Grandview Beach**, **Beacon's Beach** or **Stone Steps Beach**. All three are accessed via stairways along Neptune Ave that lead down the bluffs. These neighborhood access points are what keep the beaches relatively secluded.

Carlsbad

North of Ponto Beach, Hwy 101 changes names yet again to Carlsbad Blvd. Cruise right into **Carlsbad Village** for a bit of shopping (a surf tee at **Carlsbad Pipelines** makes a great souvenir) and a bite. **Knockout Pizza** (kopizza.com; $) is quick and casual but impressive with its selection of slices. American fare–serving **Campfire** (p47) has fun with a theme, down to the tabletop s'mores, accompanied by a teeny pile of red-hot coals. Save room for a shake at the **Strawberry Shack** (thestrawberryshack.com; $) right on Carlsbad Blvd (Carlsbad is known for its strawberries). And save energy for the town's biggest draw: **LEGOLAND California** (p50), a theme park where everybody's favorite multicolored building blocks come to life.

Oceanside

When Carlsbad Blvd becomes South Coast Hwy (just north of the Buena Vista Lagoon), that's your first sign you've entered Oceanside. The second is when you notice an uptick in breweries and taprooms. This is still San Diego County, after all, and SD is known as the Craft Beer Capital of the World. Stop for a pint at **South O Brewing** (southobrewingco.com), **Bottlecraft Oceanside** (bottlecraft.com) or **Stone Brewing Tap Room** (stonebrewing.com) – all right off South Coast Hwy. Then do your best Tom Cruise/Maverick

continues on p51

Along the Way We Met...

GRACE DOLAN I love to travel and explore new places, but the best part is always coming home to Encinitas. When I'm away, I miss the perfect weather (most days it's between 60°F and 70°F), the food (tons of healthy options, craft beer and amazing tacos) and most of all Moonlight Beach. I love to walk the beach with a friend in the morning, spend the afternoon boogie boarding with my family, then return with a book and blanket at sunset.

Grace is a world traveler and Encinitas local.

GRACE'S TIP: *Don't miss the Taco Stand, Fish 101 or Duck Foot Brewing.*

Leucadia — 8 miles — **Carlsbad** ★ — 3.5 miles — Oceanside

It's famous for its flower fields and strawberries – get a shake at the Strawberry Shack

EXPERIENCE

Play at LEGOLAND

An amusement park based on plastic bricks? LEGOLAND California is so much more than that. It's a dreamscape of rides, games and marvels.

HOW TO

Nearest stop: Carlsbad

Getting here: From Carlsbad Blvd, take Cannon Rd to Legoland Dr. Parking can be purchased ahead of time (from $35) – you'll get a QR code to scan at the entrance.

When to go: Tickets are cheaper on weekdays.

Cost: From $119 per person (ages two and up) when purchased at the front gate.

Tip: Buy your tickets ahead of time online for discounts, especially if you'd like a multipark bundle.

More info: *legoland.com/california*

Mickey might get most of the attention with amusement-park goers, but don't sleep on LEGOLAND, 60 minutes south of Anaheim and 30 minutes north of San Diego. The park is perfect for younger kids (and their parents) who might be overwhelmed by Disneyland. Among its 60 rides and attractions, LEGOLAND has at least a dozen suitable for kids as young as two. Attractions include LEGO building activities, playgrounds and splash pads – all of which can be done without lengthy waits.

LEGOLAND California also has an attached water park, making it a convenient one-stop amusement destination. Open from late May through October (note: it shifts to weekends-only after August), LEGOLAND Water Park has raft slides, body slides, a lazy river and a wave pool among its refreshing attractions.

If that's not enough to keep you busy, SEA LIFE Aquarium – home to more than 5000 marine creatures (including, yes, sharks) – is also on the grounds. You can buy tickets to each park individually, or buy one-day or two-day park-hopper passes (giving you access to LEGOLAND, the water park and the aquarium) and save up to 40% on admission.

Right: LEGOLAND California

FROM LEFT: JR IMAGES/SHUTTERSTOCK, LEGOLAND CALIFORNIA

continued from p49

impression and head to the **Top Gun House** *(250 N Pacific St)*, a local cinematic landmark, for a shameless photo op.

San Onofre State Beach

Leaving Oceanside, things get a little tricky for those adamant about sticking to the scenic PCH. This is where you will have to hop on I-5 because Camp Pendleton, a major Marine Corps base, keeps drivers from hugging the coast. But thanks to the base, **San Onofre State Beach** *(parks.ca.gov; vehicle day-use from $15)*, technically part of Camp Pendleton, remains totally undeveloped and prime for a short hike and swim.

Once you get to San Onofre, you may notice a long line of cars waiting. This is for the **Surf Beach**. It's a legendary spot to ride the swell, but if you're just hoping to stretch your legs and take a dip (and avoid a lengthy wait to park – sometimes two hours on weekends), keep driving to **San Onofre Bluffs**, a separate area that has camping and day-use access. Here you'll find a series of roughly quarter-mile trails (six total) that lead down the bluffs to a sublimely secluded beach. Wear water shoes if you have 'em – the shoreline is rocky.

San Clemente

Breathe easy because in San Clemente you can get back on PCH, called El Camino Real here. You've also finally left San Diego and are now officially in Orange County. Celebrate with a pier-side seafood feast at the **Fisherman's Restaurant & Bar** *(thefishermansrestaurantsanclemente.com; $$)*, or take yet another dip at **T-Street Beach**. Surfers should have a go at renowned break **Trestles** – technically part of San Onofre State Beach, but accessed from San Clemente. Or enjoy a ride on two wheels on the **San Clemente Beach Trail**, a bikeable 2.3-mile route easily accessed from the parking lots at North Beach, San Clemente Pier or Calafia State Park.

Capistrano Beach

Continuing north, just before you hit the heart of Dana Point, you'll come across

BEST PLACES TO SLEEP

Hotel Joaquin, Laguna Beach $$$
Design-centric stay with individually decorated rooms, a pool, bikes and body boards to borrow, and weekly outdoor movie screenings. *hoteljoaquin.com*

El Caminante Bar & Bungalows $$
Located right across from the beach with rooms that have private patios and chimineas so you can cozy up to a fire while stargazing. *elcaminantehotel.com*

Surfhouse, Leucadia $$
The ultimate hotel for aspiring surfers, it offers lessons plus all-inclusive packages in addition to the beach-inspired rooms and complimentary cruisers. *surfhouse.com*

San Onofre Bluffs Campground $
Camp on the bluffs overlooking San Onofre State Beach and stroll down the short trails to the shore for swimming and surfing. *parks.ca.gov*

a curious stretch where PCH hugs the beach especially close, except for the moments when a train comes barreling between you and the Pacific. This is Capistrano Beach, or Capo Beach, as the locals call it. If you need a rest, **El Caminante Bar & Bungalows** (p51) is an ideal spot for either a cocktail or an overnight stay – or both. The bar menu includes mixes so memorable they're called 'liquid journeys,' and the rooms are outfitted with record players and hand-carved Dutch doors that can be left open on top to welcome an ocean breeze. Just up the highway, **Olamendi's** (originalolamendis.com; $$$), which has been serving traditional Mexican meals for half a century, is also worth a stop.

DETOUR: San Juan Capistrano

The tiny mission town of San Juan Capistrano is just a 10-minute detour inland from PCH, but even if it took 10 times that long to get there, it would still be worth the drive. Of course, the 18th-century **Mission San Juan Capistrano** is the city's big attraction, but it's not the only thing to see. Cross the train tracks, where Amtrak's *Pacific Surfliner* makes stops, and explore historic **Los Rios Street**, where you can spot adobe houses dating back to the late 1700s, plus adorable boutiques and the ridiculously charming **Tea House on Los Rios** (theteahouseonlosrios.com; $$$). Not nearly as historic, but equally appealing, the nearby **River Street Marketplace** (riverstreetsjc.com) has more shops, restaurants and even a petting zoo, **River Street Ranch** (riverstreetranch.com; adult/child $16/13).

THE SWALLOWS OF SAN JUAN CAPISTRANO

Browse the gift shops in town and you'll notice a local obsession with swallows. That's because the songbirds are closely associated with Mission San Juan Capistrano. Each October, usually around the 23rd, cliff swallows leave Capistrano for the winter and migrate to Argentina. They then return every March, on or around the 19th, which is St Joseph's Day. Legend says the birds began doing this to seek refuge at the mission after an innkeeper destroyed their nests. To this day, the return of the swallows is one of the biggest celebrations of the year, commemorated with ringing bells, mariachi music and Native American storytelling.

Dana Point

After passing Doheny State Beach and crossing over the San Juan Creek River, be prepared to stop. On the right side of the road, a **monument to PCH** is easy to miss but makes for a great road-trip photo. This is the southern terminus of Hwy 1 (part of PCH), which runs all the way up to Leggett in Mendocino County. While you're stopped, pop into **A's Burgers** (asburgersrestaurant.com; $), which has been grilling patties since the '70s and also has scrumptious chocolate shakes.

continues on p54

Capistrano Beach

2.5 miles

Head inland from here to the storybook town of San Juan Capistrano

Dana Point

Step Back into 1700s California

Mission San Juan Capistrano, the seventh of 21 missions statewide and the birthplace of Orange County, is a landmark, museum, botanical gardens and reminder of California's history.

HOW TO

Nearest stop: San Juan Capistrano

Getting here: From PCH, take Camino Capistrano about 3 miles inland, then take a right on Old Mission Rd. Parking is available on the surrounding streets.

When to go: The mission is closed on Mondays.

Cost: adult/student $18/10

Tip: Grab a device for the self-guided audio tour. It's included and you can tune in for fun facts when you like.

More info: missionsjc.com

Not interested in Catholicism? Visit for the state history. Not into history at all? Come for the architecture and gardens. Still not impressed? At the very least, stop by to spin the wheel of mission jobs and find out what your role would've been back in the day. Corn grinder, candle maker...fingers crossed you don't get latrine digger.

Ruminate on your role as you walk the grounds and explore centuries worth of California history. The mission's Native American Museum and Interpretive Room give a glimpse into the lives of the Indigenous Acjachemen people, who lived here long before the Spanish arrived. You can also see what soldiers' barracks looked like in the 18th century (once the Spanish did land), wander a garden with crops from that same era, and visit a chapel where Junípero Serra, the head of the mission when it was founded in 1776, once gave Mass. It was Serra who also built the very road you're traveling – Hwy 101, or El Camino Real (the Royal Road) as it was called back then.

EXPERIENCE

FROM LEFT: OKSANA2010/SHUTTERSTOCK, MATT GUSH/SHUTTERSTOCK

Right: Mission San Juan Capistrano

continued from p52

Also in Dana Point, the **Ocean Institute** (*oceaninstitute.org; adult/child $16/12*) is a unique maritime museum with live animals plus whale-watching tours and adventures on a replica 1770s schooner. In the same cove, **Baby Beach** is beloved by families for its calm waters, protected by a jetty.

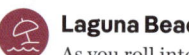 Laguna Beach

As you roll into Laguna Beach, heading north on PCH, you'll probably be expecting gorgeous beaches. And you'll get them, including **Thousand Steps Beach** (it's actually more like 220 steps down a staircase to reach it), **Aliso Beach** and **Treasure Island Beach** – all on your way into town. But what you might not expect is an exceptional modern art outpost, **Laguna Art Museum** (*lagunaartmuseum.org; adult/child $15/free*), just north of the main shopping area. After admiring the collection by primarily California artists, walk to nearby **Heisler Park**, which has a clifftop trail with stunning coastal views.

If you're finding it difficult to leave Laguna (you wouldn't be the first), grab seafood and a seat overlooking PCH at **Nick's** (p47), then check into **Hotel Joaquin** (p51), a design-lover's dream, tucked above Shaw's Cove.

Crystal Cove State Park

Just as you're thinking it'll be tough to outdo Laguna Beach, you'll see signs for **Crystal Cove State Park** (*crystalcovestatepark.org; vehicle day-use from $15*). It might not look like much from the highway, but brace yourself for another charm offensive, featuring a collection of historic cottages, a cute seaside shop and beachfront dining. The area, called the **Crystal Cove Historic District**, is best accessed via the park's Los Trancos entrance. After admiring the 1920s and '30s architecture, climb the stairs to the cliffside **Crystal Cove Shake Shack**.

Along the Way We Met...

VANESSA MORGAN Forget Virginia – Dana Point is for lovers. My favorite date night is to eat at Bourbon Steak in the Waldorf Astoria Monarch Beach Resort & Club. Aside from filets, they've got an extensive wine list with plenty of California pours. The hotel is also one of the best places to see a Dana Point sunset. Catch one on the deck after your meal.

Vanessa is a relationship therapist and Dana Point local.

VANESSA'S TIP: *Get the flight of duck-fat fries – they'll change your life.*

Kayak the harbor or catch a sunset cruise on a replica 1770s schooner

Dana Point — 8 miles — **Laguna Beach**

Newport Beach

Newport Beach

Next up is Newport Beach, famous for the multimillion-dollar yachts docked in its harbor. Even if you don't have a high-priced vessel on the high seas, you can still get time on the water. Follow PCH around Newport Bay to the **Balboa Peninsula** to rent an electric boat at **Newport Harbor Boat Rentals** *(newportharborboatrentals.net; per hr from $105)*. Or take the five-minute ferry to **Balboa Island** *(balboaislandferry.com; adult/child $2/1)* for shopping and an albacore tuna melt at **Wilma's Patio** *(wilmaspatio.com; $$)*.

WHERE TO RENT A BIKE

Pedal through coastal communities and along beach trails with the help of one of these SoCal bicycle rental shops.

Bicycles San Clemente, San Clemente
Take your pick of single-speed cruisers ($15 per hour), electric bikes ($25) and even tandems ($35) – each available by the hour, day or week. *bicyclessanclemente.com*

RIDE Cyclery Bicycles & Service, Encinitas
A family-owned shop that rents road bikes by the day (from $100), and electric bikes by the hour ($20) or day ($120). *ridecyclery.com*

Board Members, Huntington Beach
Electric bike rentals ($70 per day) in downtown that include a helmet, lock, extra-comfy seat and basket. *boardmembersurf.com*

SAN DIEGO TO LOS ANGELES

Visiting the first week of the month? The town does a First Thursdays Art Walk all year

Crystal Cove State Park — 4 miles — 2 miles — **Newport Beach**

See a setting from the 1988 film Beaches – Cottage №13

DETOUR: Anaheim

Huntington Beach is next on the route, but before really diving into Surf City USA, consider a detour inland to Anaheim, home of **Disneyland Resort** (p58). The drive is under an hour from the coast (about 30 to 55 minutes depending on traffic), and leaving from Huntington Beach, you can take CA-39 N to CA-22 E to I-5 N. Beyond mingling with Mickey Mouse, catch a baseball game at **Angel Stadium** *(mlb.com/angels/ballpark)*, or see the Anaheim Ducks skate at the **Honda Center** *(hondacenter.com)*.

Huntington Beach

No need to ask 'Where's the beach?' when you roll into the next town north on PCH. The ocean spray, sand and beach volleyballs practically smack you in the face as you drive parallel to **Huntington State Beach** *(parks.ca.go; vehicle day-use from $15)* toward downtown. This 121-acre swimming, surfing and strolling paradise has all the amenities to let you linger for the day, including bathrooms, volleyball courts, basketball courts and on-site restaurants such as the **Huntington Beach House** *(thehbhouse.com; $)*, serving burgers, wraps and tacos, and **Sahara Sandbar & Pizza** *(saharasandbar.com; $)*. The area also has a paved trail, **Ocean Strand**, that runs for 8.5 miles between Huntington and Bolsa Chica State Beaches. Bike, jog or take a leisurely stroll. The beach is also equipped with fire rings for bonfires, so you can stick around well after sunset.

If you fancy yourself something of a surfing scholar (and honestly, anyone who embarks on a multiday PCH journey could), check out downtown's **Huntington Beach International Surfing Museum** *(huntingtonbeachsurfing*

Huntington Beach

museum.org; suggested donation $2), with its odes to iconic board shapers, lifeguards and athletes.

On the northern side of Huntington Beach, you'll pass stretches with water on both sides of the road. To the right, that's **Bolsa Bay** and the **Bolsa Chica Wetlands**.

Seal Beach

Continue past the Huntington Harbor and Anaheim Bay (on your left) and you'll soon enter Seal Beach, the last OC town on your journey north. Make a pit stop to walk the **Seal Beach Pier** and say hi to Slick – the bronzed sea lion (not a seal, surprisingly) at the entrance. Roll out a towel on the surrounding sands and take a dip at the actual Seal Beach. There are three public beach parking lots nearby ($3 per hour, daily max $15) on 1st, 8th and 10th Sts. On Main St, within walking distance, **Taco Surf** *(tacosurf.com; $)* makes a mean margarita and tasty tacos al pastor.

Newport Beach — 9 miles — Huntington Beach — 15 miles — Long Beach — 25 miles — Los Angeles (Downtown)

Cut inland from here to go to Disneyland, less than an hour away

Long Beach

Hwy 1 takes you right across the San Gabriel River and into Long Beach – and a whole new county. Welcome to LA (p62)! Long Beach has recently earned a rep for its culinary scene: in 2023, its restaurant **Heritage** *(heritagerestaurantlb.com; $$$)*, serving American/California cuisine from a converted craftsman house, was the sole SoCal establishment to get a Michelin star. The brother-sister duo behind that restaurant also has **Olive & Rose** *(oliveandroselb.com; $$)*, a French-style bistro with salads and steak tartare set in the ridiculously cool, totally revamped **City Center Hotel** *(sonder.com; $)*.

Pair these new experiences with classic Long Beach attractions, like a historic tour of the ocean liner **Queen Mary** *(queenmary.com; adult/child $45/35)* and a visit to the **Aquarium of the Pacific** *(aquariumofpacific.org; adult/child $45/35)*. Then you're ready for your close-up in LA proper...

BEST SURF SCHOOLS

Memories of catching a wave make for the best souvenirs. All of the places listed include instruction, plus a wetsuit and board to borrow.

Encinitas Surf Lessons, La Jolla/Cardiff/Encinitas/Carlsbad/Oceanside
A 90-minute private lesson is $145, with savings for adding more people. Bringing four people, for example, would cost $95 per person for 90 minutes. *encinitassurflessons.com*

Laguna Beach Surf School, Laguna Beach
Affiliated with the local board shop Laguna Surf & Sport; offers 90-minute group ($100 per person) or private ($125) lessons. *lagunabeachsurfschool.org*

HB Surf School, Huntington Beach
Private lessons for one person are $180 for 90 minutes and go down in price the more people you add – for example, it's $120 per person when you bring a group of four. *hbsurfschool.com*

Queen Mary

Head to the Magic Kingdom

Immerse yourself in Walt Disney's original amusement park from 1955.

HOW TO

Nearest stop: Huntington Beach

Getting here: Once in Anaheim, take I-5 N to S Harbor Blvd, where the closest lot is the Toy Story Parking Area. Alternatively, head to the Mickey & Friends or Pixar Pals parking structures, both accessed via Disneyland Dr. Standard one-day parking is $35.

When to go: Weekdays from mid-September to mid-November, as well as mid-January to mid-March, have smaller crowds.

Cost: From $104 for a single-day, single-park ticket

Tip: Download the Disneyland app. You can use it to order food, locate characters and check attraction wait times.

More info: *disneyland.disney. go.com*

Disneyland Park

This is the park that started it all, though it has certainly changed in the last 70-plus years. After walking through the gates, you'll enter **Main Street, USA**, the setting for a number of electrifying parades. From there, **Tomorrowland** (home to futuristic roller-coaster Space Mountain) is to your right, **Fantasyland** (with classics like It's a Small World and Peter Pan's Flight) is straight ahead, **Frontierland** (and Big Thunder Mountain Railroad) is next to that, and **Adventureland** (the Jungle Cruise is a must) is directly to your left. Further afield, check out the Pirates of the Caribbean ride in **New Orleans Square**, the wildly popular Star Wars: Rise of the Resistance ride in the **Star Wars: Galaxy's Edge** land and the toddler-friendly **Mickey's Toontown**.

Disney California Adventure Park

Across the plaza, Disney California Adventure is a newer, totally distinct park (that requires separate admission). Here you'll find a focus on thrill rides plus attractions based on newer Disney themes, like Pixar and Marvel movies. Fans of the former will appreciate **Cars Land**, which recreates the world of Radiator Springs, while Marvel devotees should head to **Hollywood Land** for a ride on Guardians of the Galaxy – Mission: Breakout!, a tower attraction with heart-pumping drops. The park is also filled with nods to the Golden State, such as **Grizzly Peak**, a land inspired by California's national parks.

Where to Stay

Disneyland Resort has three official hotels: **Disney's Grand**

DISNEYLAND RESORT

ALSO VISIT... KNOTT'S BERRY FARM

Haven't had your fill of theme parks? Another classic California attraction is **Knott's Berry Farm** *(knotts.com; from $62)* in Buena Park, right next door to Anaheim. Like Disneyland, much of the park is inspired by the state's history and culture, and it also has roller coasters, shows and themed areas. But instead of a mouse, this park's main mascot is a beloved beagle – Snoopy! In addition to the year-round park, Knott's also has a summer-only water park called **Knott's Soak City** *(from $49)*.

Left: Pixar Pier, Disney California Adventure Park; Below: Knott's Berry Farm

Californian Hotel & Spa *(disneyland.disney.go.com; $$$)*, **Disneyland Hotel** *($$$)* and **Pixar Place Hotel** *($$$)*. The advantages of staying at these properties include a 30-minute-early entry to the parks, proximity and special Disney experiences, like themed meals and character sightings. To save money, though, stay outside the resort. **Castle Inn and Suites** *(castleinn.com; $$)* and **Park Vue Inn** *(parkvueinn.com; $$)* are both substantially cheaper per night and still walking distance (about a half-mile) to the parks.

KNOTT'S BERRY FARM

INSIGHT

The Happiest Place on Earth

Mickey is one lucky guy. He lives in Disneyland, dubbed by Walt Disney himself as the 'Happiest Place on Earth.' It's an 'imagineered' hyper-reality where the streets are always clean, employees – called 'cast members' – are always upbeat, and there are parades every day.

WORDS BY **ANDREW BENDER**
Andrew's dozens of Lonely Planet titles include California and Japan

SINCE OPENING ON July 17, 1955 on former orange and walnut groves in Anaheim, Disneyland (aka the Magic Kingdom) has been an irresistible magnet for its combination of wholesome Americana, adventure, fantasy and just plain fun.

Disneyland's opening day didn't bode well. Temperatures over 100°F melted asphalt underfoot, there were plumbing problems, Hollywood stars showed up late, and more than twice the number of expected guests – some 28,000 total – crowded through the gates. But none of this kept eager fans away for long: more than 50 million visitors in the first decade alone, and it's never looked back.

Even more visitors arrived in 2001 with the opening of a sister theme park, Disney California Adventure, and Downtown Disney, offering shopping and dining for before, during or after the parks. Together with three hotels offering a combined 2400 hotel rooms, collectively the campus is called the Disneyland Resort.

So what if every ride seems to end in a gift store, prices are sky-high and there are grumblings that management could do more for its workers? For the legions of wide-eyed kids, doting parents, honeymooners and high schoolers from around the world – all sporting Mickey Mouse ear hats – the Disney experience remains magical.

...and an economic juggernaut

A study by Oxford Economics showed that in 2023 the Disneyland Resort collectively had an economic impact of $16.1 billion throughout Southern California. The resort was Orange County's largest employer (some 36,000 employees), with an additional 65,000 jobs gen-

Sleeping Beauty's Castle

erated outside the parks in restaurants, hotels and related industries.

That same year, according to the site Mickey Visit, the Disneyland Resort received 27,250,000 visitors – an average of 74,675 per day.

Add in Disney's Florida resorts, and the study found a total impact to the US economy of nearly $67 billion.

Disneyland's Greatest Hits

'Disneyland will never be completed,' proclaimed Walt at Disneyland's opening in 1955. 'It will continue to grow as long as there is imagination left in the world.'

'Uncle Walt' passed away in 1966, but his ambitious vision still remains – and evolves. Here are just some historical highlights – and examples of how stories have become theme-park attractions and vice versa.

Disneyland's earliest attractions like Peter Pan's Flight, the Mad Tea Party, Jungle Cruise, Dumbo and Autopia are still instantly recognizable – and eminently rideable – and the Mark Twain Riverboat continues to ply the Rivers of America. Centered around Sleeping Beauty's Castle, they all seem to embody Walt's belief that fantasy, when convincing, can be timeless.

It wasn't long before the Matterhorn Bobsleds and the Monorail introduced new ride technologies. By the 1960s, the Enchanted Tiki Room and Great Moments with Mr. Lincoln showcased audio-animatronics that would redefine theme-park entertainment, and It's a Small World became Earth's most famous earworm. Immersive storytelling came to New Orleans Square with Pirates of the Caribbean and the Haunted Mansion.

Technological optimism reigned supreme in the 1960s and '70s Tomorrowland, although the once futuristic PeopleMover and Carousel of Progress have since given way to the likes of Star Wars and Buzz Lightyear. The Main Street Electrical Parade arrived with nighttime entertainment that continues to enchant. By the late 1970s, thrillseekers' dreams were fulfilled with the roller coasters Space Mountain and Big Thunder Mountain Railroad.

As the Walt Disney Company transformed ever more into an entertainment conglomerate in the mid-1980s, the park introduced non-Disney franchises like Star Wars and Indiana Jones, while Mickey's Toontown sprinkled in family-friendly whimsy.

In 2001, Disney California Adventure hit the ground running with immersive attractions like Cars and Buena Vista Street, and took to the skies with the simulated hang-glide Soarin' over California (now Soarin' Around the World). The Grand Californian Hotel, modeled after classic national park lodges, ushered in a new era – and a higher price point for those willing to spend it.

And for its most recent decade, Disney has embraced immersive lands and cultural sensitivity. Star Wars: Galaxy's Edge and the Avengers Campus ushered in ambitious, story-driven environments including the thrilling Guardians of the Galaxy - Mission: BREAKOUT! And, finally, Pirates of the Caribbean got its first female pirate.

And somehow it seems fitting that for Disneyland's 70th birthday, the new Walt Disney – A Magical Life took its place alongside Abe Lincoln on Main Street USA.

Beyond the Mouse

If you're seeking all Disney all the time, by all means, have at it. If not, the resort's hometown of Anaheim could provide a welcome break. Almost under the radar, Anaheim has developed some of the OC's most interesting dining, especially in the area around the Packing District and Center Street, both near Anaheim City Hall.

Disney may be the most famous of Southern California's theme parks, but it's hardly the only one. Other parks in the region include **Universal Studios Hollywood** (p66), **Knott's Berry Farm** (p59) and **LEGOLAND** (p50). For an even more old-school experience of retro rides, arcade games and snacks by the ocean, visit San Diego's **Belmont Pier** or the **Santa Monica Pier** (p66).

CITY GUIDE:
Los Angeles

View of Hollywood and Downtown Los Angeles (p70)

You're passing through LA, so you owe it to yourself to spend a few days exploring America's second-largest city: at once glamorous, tawdry, demure, frenetic and serene – and full of top-flight art and architecture, inviting beaches and hikes, alluring shopping and world cuisines.

WORDS BY **ANDREW BENDER**
Andrew's dozens of Lonely Planet titles include California and Japan

Getting Around

Driving Most Angelenos drive around LA (and have learnt when to avoid the soul-crushing traffic) or take transit.

Public transportation Most of LA City and County is served by Metro *(metro.net)* subway and light rail trains (generally the easiest for visitors) plus buses and bike shares. Local municipalities also offer their own transit, including Santa Monica's Big Blue Bus *(bigbluebus.com)*. Ride with a TAP Card, available at transit stations or in the Apple Wallet.

Metro fares Fares on LA Metro are $1.75, covering transfers to other Metro transit for up to two hours. Transfers between Metro and municipal buses cost $0.50. Metro fares are capped at $5 per day or $18 per seven days when paid with the same TAP card.

HOW MUCH FOR A

Celestial sip at Spire 73
$24

Sandwich at Eggslut, Grand Central Market
$10

Warner Bros Studio Tour
$76

Arriving

For many PCH drivers, LA is a stop rather than the beginning or end, but if your trip here includes a plane or train, here are some tips.

By air LA's main gateway is Los Angeles International Airport (LAX; *flylax.com*), one of the world's busiest airports and served by all major US carriers and dozens of international airlines. All major car rental agencies have LAX locations, alongside access to buses and light rail. You could bed down in airport-area hotels, but with a little more time and money, Santa Monica (p66), about 7 miles northwest on PCH, or Manhattan Beach (p66), about 5 miles south, offer infinitely more charming stays.

By rail Amtrak trains arrive at the lovely Spanish Colonial Union Station *(unionstationla.com)* at Downtown LA's eastern edge. Connect to LA's Metro subway beneath the station.

For information about subways and light rail trains, go to metro.net.

A DAY IN LOS ANGELES

Wake up easy with a coffee and a stroll, cycle or yoga class along the world-famous beachfront boardwalk in **Venice** and **Santa Monica**. Browse street art and unique fashion along Venice's always-trendy **Abbot Kinney Blvd** *(abbotkinneyblvd.com)*, and maybe ride the solar-powered Ferris wheel at **Santa Monica Pier**.

Explore the history and craft of filmmaking at the **Academy Museum** (p69), then continue north to gawk at the tourists gawking at the concrete handprints and footprints of screendom's biggest stars at the **TCL Chinese Theatre** (p68) in Hollywood.

Spend a summer night with 17,499 of your besties at a concert at the **Hollywood Bowl** (p68), or head to West Hollywood to party the night away at clubs like the **Comedy Store** *(thecomedystore.com)*, or the legendary LGBTQ+ bar the **Abbey** *(theabbeyweho.com)*.

Where to Stay

An LA stay isn't cheap, but, hey, you get what you pay for. Santa Monica and Venice offer varied lodging options and great beachside weather. Eastward, Beverly Hills is synonymous with luxury, and neighboring West Hollywood has solid boutique hotels and front-row seating for shopping, nightlife and SoCal's top LGBTQ+ scene. Hollywood and Downtown LA hotels serve cultural institutions and nightlife, but prepare for a grunge factor.

BEST PLACES TO STAY

Hotel Erwin $$$
Funkified retro lodging, steps from Venice Beach. Fantastic rooftop lounge. *hotelerwin.com*

Beverly Hills Hotel $$$
Hollywood history lives here, lap of luxury since 1912. *dorchestercollection.com/los-angeles/the-beverly-hills-hotel*

Palihotel Melrose $$
Near trendy shops; boutique digs at mere-mortal prices. *palisociety.com*

Hotel Figueroa $$$
A 1926 Spanish Colonial look, DTLA cool. *hotelfigueroa.com*

Where to Eat

Dine on world cuisines and hipster vittles in DTLA, power lunch in Beverly Hills or West Hollywood, soak up showbiz energy (and martinis) in Hollywood, or enjoy beachy fare in Santa Monica and Venice. And, as any Angeleno will tell you, some of the city's best eats come from strip malls and food trucks.

LA'S CUISINE SCENE

LA cuisine spans Michelin-starred extravaganzas, and cultures that have staked their claims to entire neighborhoods: Koreatown (Mid-City LA), Thai Town (East Hollywood), Boyle Heights (LA's Mexican heart, east of Downtown), and West LA's 'Tehrangeles' for Persian and Sawtelle Japantown, just for starters.

And since just about everything grows in California, sample some of the freshest at irresistible farmers markets in Santa Monica (*santamonica.com/experience-santa-monica/farmers-markets*; Wed, Sat, Sun) or Hollywood (*foodaccessla.org/hollywood*; 8am-1pm Sat).

BEST PLACES TO EAT & DRINK

Musso & Frank Grill $$$
Slaking Hollywood honchos with steaks and martinis since 1919. *mussoandfrank.com*; 5–11pm Tue-Sat, 4-10pm Sun

Grand Central Market $
DTLA's gourmet, Beaux Arts food hall: hipster breakfasts to homemade pastas. *grandcentralmarket.com*; 8am-10pm

Butcher's Daughter $$
Airy and vegan-friendly on Venice's buzzy Abbot Kinney Blvd. *thebutchersdaughter.com*; 8am-9pm, to 10pm Fri & Sat

Guisados $
LA's favorite tacos, with locations around town. *guisados.la*; 9am-10pm Mon-Thu, to 1pm Fri & Sat, to 9pm Sun

Santa Monica Pier

LIGHTS, CAMERA, STUDIO TOUR

While **Universal Studios Hollywood** (universalstudioshollywood.com) grabs the spotlight, the experience is more theme park than movie studio, with rides taking center stage. Alternatively, the **Warner Bros Studio Tour** (wbstudiotour.com) offers a fun and (mostly) authentic look behind the scenes of a working film and TV studio. The two-hour tour route changes based on what's shooting, but always includes selfie ops on recreated sets like *Friends* and *The Big Bang Theory*, exhibits about sound design and costumes, and a mind-blowing collection of Batmobiles.

Can't Miss Coastline

Straddling Long Beach and Malibu, LA is defined by its coastline. No visit is complete without taking in the beach scene – Manhattan Beach, Venice and Santa Monica are highlights.

In the South Bay (south of LAX), head to well-to-do Manhattan Beach to marvel at the buff volleyballers and cyclists frolicking in the endless summer.

North of the airport, the Venice Boardwalk is a must-see, often resembling a wacky carnival alive with magicians, jazz combos, solo distorted garage rockers, and artists good and bad.

Easy, breezy Santa Monica's most recognizable feature is its pier, thanks to a massive solar-powered Ferris wheel towering over a mix of carnival rides and games, food vendors, souvenir kiosks and multi-million-dollar coastal views.

To get there take the Metro E Line rail to Downtown Santa Monica, or drive from town to town. Once you've parked, the beach communities are pedestrian-friendly – or connected by a 22-mile beachside bike path (rent a bike and helmet).

Along the Way We Met...

NICOLE BLAINE I feel like in a traditional comedy setting, there's a typical voice: straight, white, cisgender male. I want to make sure that all the walks of life that make up Los Angeles are being seen here. We want every single different type of color, religion, ethnicity, LGBTQ+ spectrum, and even age, so that little kids can see themselves on that stage and know that they can grow up to be that.

Nicole is founder and owner of the Crow Comedy Club, Bergamot Station, Santa Monica

Get Outdoors in Griffith Park

With the Hollywood Hills lined with hiking trails, it's no wonder Angelenos are avid hikers.

HOW TO

Getting here: Take the Metro A Line subway to Vermont/Sunset station. From here, DASH operates the Observatory/Los Feliz shuttle bus service to Griffith Observatory.

Parking: Arrive early or pray for free parking at the observatory. Otherwise, park by the Greek Theatre and hike (about 10 minutes) or take the free shuttle bus up and back.

Five times the size of New York's Central Park, **Griffith Park** (laparks .org/ griffithpark) is LA's communal backyard. It's filled with more than 4300 mountainous acres and 50-plus miles of hiking trails, a zoo, museums and performance venues.

If time is limited, visit the **Griffith Observatory** (griffithobservatory.org; 2800 E Observatory Rd). It offers commanding views from Mt Hollywood across the LA Basin, plus the Hollywood Sign and hiking trails that continue uphill for even grander views. By day, take in planetarium shows or, at night, look into the universe via massive telescopes.

For tastes less outdoorsy and more cultural, the park has you covered with the impressive collection at the **Autry Museum of the American West** (theautry.org; 4700 Western Heritage Way) or an outdoor show at the **Greek Theatre** (lagreektheatre.com; 2700 N Vermont Ave).

Can't make it to Griffith Park? From Hollywood, opt instead for chapparal-draped Runyon Canyon, a 130-acre park famous for its buff runners and the occasional exercising celebrity.

EXPERIENCE ★

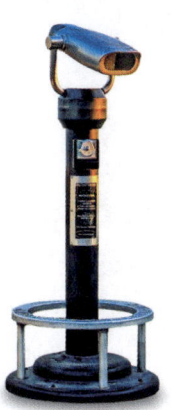

Right: Griffith Observatory

FROM LEFT: CHIZHEVSKAYA EKATERINA/SHUTTERSTOCK, CAMERON VENTI/SHUTTERSTOCK

Stroll the Stars on Hollywood Blvd

Unless you're here for the Oscars, don't expect any actual star-sightings in Hollywood; there's even some grit. But movie glamour is a powerful force, and it shines through.

HOW TO

Getting here: Take the Metro A Line subway to Hollywood & Highland Station.

Parking: Park beneath Ovation Hollywood (*ovationhollywood.com; 6801 Hollywood Blvd*).

Getting around: Hollywood is pedestrian-friendly and generally flat. Hollywood Bowl shuttles (round trip $6) connect from Ovation Hollywood on performance nights.

Tip: Carry lots of $1 bills for selfies with costumed performers on the Walk of Fame.

It's hard not to feel starstruck on the **Hollywood Walk of Fame** (*walkoffame.com*). Some 2600 pink marble stars embedded in the sidewalks salute entertainment industry luminaries, while the handprints and footprints of the biggest stars are cast in concrete outside the **TCL Chinese Theatre** (*tclchinesetheatres.com*). The engrossing **Hollywood Museum** (*thehollywoodmuseum.com*) is jam-packed with props, costumes and memorabilia.

To catch a flick on the Walk of Fame, blockbusters reign at century-old movie palaces like the TCL Chinese Theatre and the **El Capitan Theatre** (*elcapitantheatre.com*), screening Disney magic and live stage shows before the movies.

Summer nights belong to the **Hollywood Bowl** (*hollywoodbowl.com*), the 17,500-seat natural amphitheater. Wide-ranging programming might include anything from Rachmaninoff to reggae to singalong *The Sound of Music*.

Right: TCL Chinese Theatre

POP CULTURE, MEET HIGH CULTURE

Architect Frank Lloyd Wright once said, 'Tip the world over on its side and everything loose will land in Los Angeles.' Indeed, both highbrow and pop cultures thrive here.

LA pop culture goes way beyond Hollywood. Boutiques on Melrose Ave, east of Fairfax Ave, have been outfitting generations of punks, skaters and cool kids. Anime and manga reign in Little Tokyo (around 1st and San Pedro Sts in DTLA). Baseball's **Dodgers** (mlb.com/dodgers), football's **Rams** (therams.com) and basketball's **Lakers** (nba.com/lakers) are all iconic teams.

Beyond the museums of the Miracle Mile and Downtown LA (p70), the 110-acre **Getty Center** (getty.edu) and the cutting-edge **UCLA Hammer Museum** (hammer.ucla.edu) enrich LA culture, alongside world-leading performing arts like the **Los Angeles Philharmonic** (laphil.org).

Dodger Stadium

Miracle Mile Museums

East of the intersection of Wilshire Blvd and Fairfax Ave, LA's Miracle Mile is one-stop shopping for top museums. Fresh off a multi-year facelift, the **Los Angeles County Museum of Art** (lacma.org) shows a breadth and depth of antiquity to modernity unparalleled in the western US. The **Academy Museum of Motion Pictures** (academymuseum.org) salutes showbiz with state-of-the-art exhibitions. Encounter the animal stars of *Ice Age* (or at least their fossils) at **La Brea Tar Pits** (tarpits.org); in-house scientists still unearth bones regularly. And the **Petersen Automotive Museum** (petersen.org) is an awe-inspiring look at motorized transport from concept cars to movie vehicles.

Hollywood Boulevard

Afoot in DTLA

Downtown Los Angeles (DTLA to its friends) is the city's historic hub and cultural capital, studded with museums, restaurants, world-class architecture, music, sports venues and some of the city's best bars. Most of it's easily reached on foot. (No one walks in LA? Kyah, right!)

HOW TO

Getting here: DTLA is the hub of Metro subways and light rail with multiple underground stops. The most central stop is Grand Ave Arts/Bunker Hill, which is close to most sights.

Parking: Driving can be a chore between traffic to and from DTLA, a thicket of one-way streets and expensive parking.

Getting around: To go further afield, take Metro subway or light rail, or DASH buses circulate around Downtown.

Walt Disney Concert Hall

Clad in impossibly undulating, gravity-defying steel panels, Frank Gehry's iconic venue *(www.laphil.com)* is home of the Los Angeles Philharmonic and hosts a full calendar of other acts from jazz to film screenings and a soul-shaking pipe organ. Or just tour the architecture with a free, hour-long audio guide.

Go Broad or Go Home

The **Broad** *(thebroad.org)*, rhymes with 'road', is a must-visit for contemporary-art fans for its world-class (and Insta-friendly) collection of more than 2000 postwar pieces by dozens of heavy hitters. The striking building is shrouded in a white lattice-like shell that lifts at the corners into the lobby. Admission is free (except during special exhibitions), but reserve a timed ticket.

To continue the art adventure, the **Museum of Contemporary Art** *(moca.org)* is right across the street.

Expedition to Exposition Park

A short ride from Downtown on the Metro takes you to Exposition Park, where multiple museums await. The **California Science Center** *(californiasciencecenter.org)* is home to one of just four Space Shuttles. Get your dino on at the **Natural History Museum of Los Angeles County** *(nhm.*

BARS UNDER THE STARS

From rooftops to blacktops, DTLA has plenty of places to enjoy an outdoor drink.

Spire 73
Craft cocktails and small bites on the 73rd floor of the InterContinental, the western hemisphere's tallest open-air bar. *900 Wilshire Blvd*

Perch
City lights twinkle all around, 16 stories up a renaissance revival building in the heart of DTLA. *perchla.com*

Angel City Brewery
Knock back an IPA, sample groovy tunes and enjoy food-truck chow at this microbrew in a former factory in the Arts District. *angelcitybrewery.com*

org) and visit the changing exhibits on African American history, arts and culture at the **California African American Museum** (*caamuseum.org*). The **Lucas Museum of Narrative Art** (*lucasmuseum.org*), founded by *Star Wars* creator George Lucas, is due to open in 2026. Behind it all, the **Los Angeles Memorial Coliseum** (*lacoliseum.com*) has been home to two Olympics and stands to loom large when LA hosts again in 2028.

Above: Walt Disney Concert Hall; Right: Exposition Park

Los Angeles

If the San Diego to LA leg of PCH is like punk music – a frenetic experience of hip beach town after hip beach town – then LA to Santa Barbara is like soft rock or smooth jazz. You'll have more time between towns and longer stretches of isolated coast to take in the views and meditate on your surroundings. But that doesn't mean the towns themselves are any less hip than their southern counterparts. Malibu, Ventura, Carpinteria and more all embody the same surf-driven style of SoCal cool.

Amelia Mularz

PCH near Sycamore Cove, Malibu (p76)
TREKANDSHOOT/SHUTTERSTOCK

Santa Barbara

121 MILES · 3-HOUR DRIVE

THIS LEG:

- Los Angeles
- Malibu
- Leo Carrillo State Park
- Oxnard
- Camarillo
- Ventura Harbor
- Downtown Ventura
- Emma Wood State Beach
- Mussel Shoals
- Carpinteria
- Toro Canyon
- Summerland
- Montecito
- Santa Barbara

Driving Notes

The ocean views start off strong in Malibu, but then PCH veers inland in Oxnard, linking up with Hwy 101. Don't worry, you will get coastal views once more in Ventura. And though you do hug the coast quite a bit on this leg, the terrain is flat, so no need to worry about the kind of tight, clifftop curves you'll find up near Big Sur.

Breaking Your Journey

As stunning as this stretch of PCH is, it's also a multi-lane highway. So you'll want to pull over to absorb the views. The state parks and state beaches have lookout points, and the classic coastal towns of Malibu, Oxnard, Ventura, Carpinteria, Summerland and Montecito have oceanside dining. These towns are also your best bets for lodging.

Amelia's Tips

BEST MEAL I picked Stonehouse (p87) at San Ysidro Ranch for my big honeymoon dinner, and it lives up to the hype.

FAVORITE VIEW Toro Canyon Ridge (p87) offers a 2.5-mile hike with views of Carpinteria and the ocean.

ESSENTIAL STOP Beaches and national park access? Ventura is underrated.

ROAD-TRIP TIP Spend at least one night in a town between LA and Santa Barbara. The best adventures happen in the smaller beach towns.

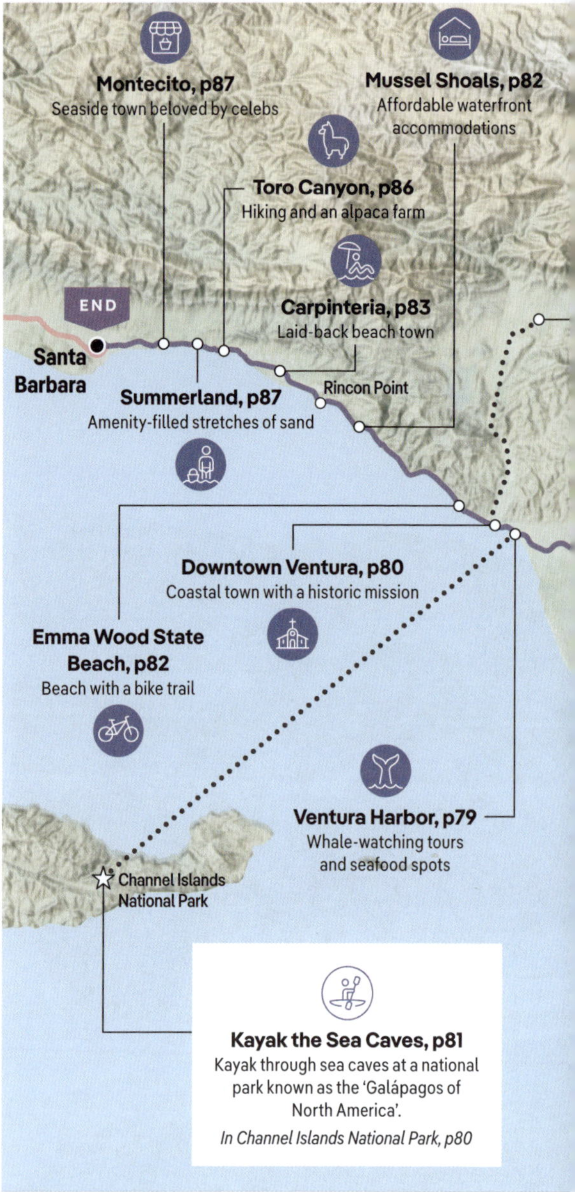

Montecito, p87 — Seaside town beloved by celebs

Mussel Shoals, p82 — Affordable waterfront accommodations

Toro Canyon, p86 — Hiking and an alpaca farm

Carpinteria, p83 — Laid-back beach town

END — Santa Barbara

Summerland, p87 — Amenity-filled stretches of sand

Rincon Point

Downtown Ventura, p80 — Coastal town with a historic mission

Emma Wood State Beach, p82 — Beach with a bike trail

Ventura Harbor, p79 — Whale-watching tours and seafood spots

Channel Islands National Park

Kayak the Sea Caves, p81 — Kayak through sea caves at a national park known as the 'Galápagos of North America'.
In Channel Islands National Park, p80

PREVIOUS STOP Leaving Los Angeles, head to Santa Monica, where you can hop on PCH and follow it into Malibu.

Malibu

If you're hitting PCH on the weekend, especially in the summer, you might get caught in traffic as Angelenos head to the beach (Malibu is still LA County, after all). So if you can't out-drive 'em, join 'em. But before you roll out your towel, consider a stop at the historic **Malibu Pier** *(malibupier.com)*, which will come up first before you hit the major state beaches. The pier has a paid parking lot ($15 for the day), plus organic fare at **Malibu Farm Restaurant & Bar** *(malibu-farm.com; $$$)*.

If you're already feeling the Malibu vibes, check in at the **Surfrider Malibu** (p80), a reimagined 1950s motel that has hosted the likes of Neil Young and members of the Doors. Another

Along the Way We Met...

BRUCE KLUMPH The first stop on your dream Malibu day has to be at the Country Kitchen for a breakfast burrito. Continue up the coast another five minutes and pull over at the Malibu Pier. It's a great place to sit and enjoy your burrito while watching the world-famous Surfrider Beach. Next stop: Point Dume Natural Preserve for a hike around the headland. This mellow 1-mile trek will give you a great view east and west of Malibu, and you might even peep a dolphin or two. After working up a light sweat, make your way up to Kristy's Malibu for lunch and tell 'em Bruce sent ya. Their Kristy's Burger is a must! Zuma beach is directly across the street and a great spot to wind down and catch the sunset.

Bruce is a Malibu local and surf/paddle instructor.

BRUCE'S TIP: *Need a surf instructor? I offer unique Malibu ocean experiences. Feel free to message me on Instagram @bruceklumph.*

Los Angeles (Downtown) — 28 miles — **Malibu**

Watch the surfers from the pier...or take a lesson yourself

Malibu Pier

updated iconic PCH motel, **Hotel June Malibu** *(thehoteljune.com/malibu; $$$)*, is about 8 miles north and also has a musical past – Bob Dylan wrote his album *Blood on the Tracks* in bungalow 13.

As for those beaches, **Malibu Lagoon State Beach** *(parks.ca.gov; vehicle day-use $12)*, closest to the pier, has swimming and surfing at **Surfrider Beach**, bird-watching and nature trails along the lagoon, and the historic **Adamson House** to tour *(adult/child $7/2, cash only)*. Farther north, **Point Dume State Beach** *(2hr parking free)* is known for its cliffs and rocky coves, and **El Matador State Beach** *(day parking free)* has striking rock arches and sea stacks.

Leo Carrillo State Park

If the Malibu motels aren't in your budget, the campground at **Leo Carrillo State Park** *(parks.ca.gov; vehicle day-use/standard campsite $12/45)* is another epic option. Even those who normally would never camp have raved about overnights here, thanks to its proximity to the beach (through a trail that goes under PCH), its sycamore-shaded sites and its charming snack stand/beach store. You do need to plan in advance, as the campground typically sells out, especially on weekends. Reserve a site up to six months in advance at *reservecalifornia.com*. If you don't snag your desired dates, check back, as people cancel frequently.

Enjoy some beachside camping

Leo Carrillo State Park

14 miles

If you're not spending the night, Leo Carrillo is still worth a stop. The park has 1.5 miles of beach for swimming, surfing and coastal cave exploration. Plus, the **Leo Carrillo Beach Trail** (5 miles out and back) is like the PCH of hiking paths, taking you right along the coast.

Point Mugu State Park

Roughly 15 minutes north, **Point Mugu State Park** *(parks.ca.gov; vehicle day-use/standard campsite $12/35)* also has camping. Its two campgrounds include Sycamore Campground (tucked into a leafy grove) and Thornhill Broome Campground, which has sites directly on the beach but no shade. And with over 70 miles of hiking trails, Point Mugu is also a great place to stretch your legs. For a challenge, hit **Mugu Peak Trail**, a 2.8-mile loop with both ocean and mountain views. Alternatively, the **Scenic and Overlook Trails Loop** won't give you the satisfaction of summiting a peak, but it does

BEST PLACES TO EAT

Neptune's Net, Malibu $$
A PCH institution that's been serving clam chowder and fried seafood baskets roadside since the 1950s. *neptunesnet.com; hours vary, open later Mar-Oct*

VenTiki, Ventura $$$
Enjoy a dash of kitsch with kickin' seafood and sliders, plus tropical cocktails (of course), with indoor and outdoor seating. *ventikiloungeandlanai.com; 11am-11pm*

Birria Mi Rancho, Oxnard $
On the Oxnard Taco Trail; pick between crunchy or suave (soft) tacos stuffed with impossibly tender shredded beef. *birriamirancho.com; 9:30am-5:30pm Mon & Wed-Fri, 8:30am-5:30pm Sat, 8:30am-5pm Sun*

Little Dom's Seafood, Carpinteria $$
Breakfast, lunch and dinner, with a raw bar, from the same team behind Little Dom's in LA. *ldseafood.com; 11:30am-9pm Mon-Fri, from 10am Sat & Sun*

Mugu Peak Trail

VENTU PHOTO/SHUTTERSTOCK

have ocean views for substantially less huffing and puffing.

Oxnard

Here's where PCH gets a little unpredictable. As you approach the city of Oxnard, everyone's favorite coastal highway decides to check out the scenery inland before eventually meeting up with Hwy 101, which will take you back out to the coast. But just because our main route doesn't take you to Oxnard's waterfront doesn't mean you should miss it. The city has 7 miles of shoreline, including **Silver Strand Beach** *(parking free)*, which is a favorite spot for beginner and intermediate surfers. If you have little ones in tow, head to the appropriately named **Kiddie Beach** *(parking free)*, which is protected from ocean waves, or check out **Oxnard/Mandalay Beach** *(all-day parking $5)*, with a playground, bike paths and golden dunes.

For Mexican-food lovers, Oxnard might just be your new favorite town. The **Oxnard Taco Trail** *(visitoxnard.com/food-drinks/tacotrail)* is a self-guided collection of the area's many taco spots, including taquerias, food trucks and sit-down Mexican restaurants. Highlights include **Carnitas El Rey** *(carnitaselreyrestaurant.com)*, specializing in Michoacán-style carnitas, and **El 30 Mariscos** *(el30mariscosrestaurant.com)*, with its seafood selection.

Camarillo

Before heading north on Hwy 101 to Ventura, consider taking a right and heading south just a few miles to Camarillo, a small city with a rich agricultural history and a charming **Old Town**. Walk the main drag along Ventura Blvd and flip through stacks of vintage vinyl at

Ventura Harbor

American Pie Records *(americanpierecords.com)*, which doubles as a coffee shop, and pick up some surf or skate gear at **Revolution Board Company** *(www.revosurf.com)*.

Ventura Harbor

From Camarillo, you'll make your way back to the coast, passing over the Santa Clara River before snaking alongside the Ventura waterfront. For boat rentals, whale-watching tours and your pick of fresh seafood spots, head to **Ventura Harbor Village** *(venturaharborvillage.com)*. **Ventura Boat Rentals** *(venturaboatrentals.com; per hr from $40)* is your go-to for fun pedal boats shaped like swans, flamingos and dragons, and **Island Packers** *(islandpackers.com; adult/child $84/69)* leads whale-watching cruises in the Santa Barbara Channel. If you want your seafood in taco form, check out **Baja Bay Surf n Taco** *(bajabay-surfntaco.com; $$)*. Otherwise, feast on fish and chips at **Andria's Seafood Restaurant & Market** *(andriasseafood.com; $$)* or lemon-garlic shrimp and sea scallops served over linguini at **Brophy Bros.** *(brophybros.com; $$$)*.

The water surrounding the harbor isn't just for admiring. Jump in at **Harbor Cove Beach**, beloved for its calm water thanks to protective jetties (it's even nicknamed 'Mother's Beach' because it's so safe). Amenities here include bathrooms and showers, and food (including sandwich-packed lunch boxes to go) is a quick walk away at the nearby **Harbor Cove Cafe** *(harborcovecafe.net; $$)*.

DETOUR: Channel Islands National Park

When it comes to Southern California national parks, Joshua Tree might get all the attention, but that doesn't make **Channel Islands National Park** any less spectacular. Be one of the intrepid adventurers to explore this less frequented park, made up of five islands – San Miguel, Santa Rosa, Santa Cruz, Anacapa and Santa Barbara – only accessible by boat. Island Packers *(islandpackers.com)* is the park's main ferry service, operating out of Oxnard and Ventura harbors, depending on your island destination.

Downtown Ventura

On your way to downtown Ventura, just a few miles north of the harbor along E Harbor Blvd, make a pit stop at the **Ventura Pier**. Built in 1872, it's the oldest pier in California. It also used to be the state's longest wooden pier, but storms over the decades have made it lose some length. At 1600ft, however, it's still substantial and makes for a supremely scenic stroll.

Make your way to Main St, where you'll find the **Museum of Ventura County** *(venturamuseum.org; adult/child $10/free)*, featuring regional fine art as well as exhibits that dig into the area's history. Also on Main St, **Mission Basilica San Buenaventura** *(sanbuenaventuramission.org; tours adult/child $8/3)* – founded in 1782

continues on p82

BEST PLACES TO SLEEP

Surfrider Malibu, Malibu $$$
Rooms have upscale boho vibes, and amenities include a guests-only restaurant with ocean views plus Mini Coopers to borrow (seriously!). *thesurfridermalibu.com*

Leo Carrillo State Park Campground, Malibu $
This is camping with all the comforts: bathrooms, showers, a snack shop and the beach just steps away. *reservecalifornia.com*

Ojai Rancho Inn, Ojai $$
A reimagined retro motel with communal hammocks near the pool and complimentary palo santo for your room. *ojairanchoinn.com*

Cliff House Inn, Mussel Shoals $$
Quite possibly the best deal in SoCal: an oceanfront hotel with a heated pool and breakfast included. *cliffhouseinn.com*

Ventura Harbor
→ Gateway to a national park known as the 'Galápagos of North America'

4 miles

Downtown Ventura
→ Take a detour from here to 'the valley of the moon,' aka Ojai

Kayak the Sea Caves

Putting paddle to water and exploring the sea caves off the Channel Islands National Park's Santa Cruz Island is a once-in-a-lifetime opportunity.

HOW TO

Nearest stop: Ventura Waterfront
Getting here: Take the Island Packers ferry from Ventura Harbor to Santa Cruz island, where you'll meet up with your guide from Channel Islands Adventure Company.
Cost: From $70 adult for round-trip ferry, plus $215 for kayak tour
Tip: In Ventura, stroll through the park's visitor center, which has a nice bookstore and exhibitions.
More info: islandkayaking.com

THE ISLANDS

Santa Cruz The place to go for kayaking sea caves and spotting the island fox.
Anacapa Accessed via ferry from Oxnard, and known for its iconic rock arch.
Santa Rosa Has epic hiking in Lobo Canyon and is one of only two places in the world where Torrey Pines grow.
San Miguel Home to a fossilized forest and a large rookery of seals and sea lions.
Santa Barbara A cliff island with superb diving.

Get a morning greeting from a humpback whale, spot dozens of dolphins and take in the California coastline while sipping your coffee. And that's all before your adventure actually starts. A kayak excursion around Santa Cruz Island – the largest of the five islands that make up Channel Islands National Park – kicks off with a 90-minute ferry ride from Ventura Harbor that often includes wildlife sightings. The humpbacks and blue whales are especially prevalent in the summer (mid-May to mid-September), while winter (mid-December to mid-March) is prime time for gray whales.

Once you dock on Santa Cruz at Scorpion Anchorage harbor, on the northeast side of the island, you'll meet up with your guide from Channel Islands Adventure Company, who will have all your gear, including single and double kayaks, paddles, life jackets and helmets. (Note: there are no kayak rentals on the island, so booking an excursion is the only way to go.) You'll get a quick kayaking tutorial (beginners are welcome), then you'll take off, spending roughly 2½ hours on the water paddling through multiple sea caves, exploring kelp forests and keeping your eyes peeled for more marine wildlife.

Sea kayaking, Santa Cruz Island

BRIAN SWANSON/SHUTTERSTOCK

continued from p80

and the ninth of California's 21 Spanish missions – has self-guided tours, a museum and a shop. About a 10-minute stroll from there up Poli St, the **Ventura Botanical Gardens** *(venturabotanicalgardens.com; adult/child $7/free)* has over 120,000 plants in the ground representing the world's five Mediterranean climate zones: Chile, the Cape of South Africa, Australia, the Mediterranean Basin and California. It also has some of the best coastal views in the area.

DETOUR: Ojai

As you leave Ventura ask yourself, are you interested in another ridiculously charming town? Do you like hiking, massages, staying in boutique hotels and feasting on farm-fresh food? If the answer is no, well, sorry, you'll still run into much of that ahead on PCH (now also called Hwy 101). If the answer is a resounding yes, then take CA-33 inland to Ojai, a name that comes from the Chumash word *awha'y*, meaning 'moon.' That's why you'll often hear the area described as 'the valley of the moon.'

Emma Wood State Beach

After you leave downtown Ventura, it's just a few miles before PCH splits from Hwy 101 once again. Take exit 72 to get on PCH and follow that to State Beach Access Rd. As the street's name suggests, a state beach is in your near future. **Emma Wood State Beach** *(parks.ca.gov; vehicle day-use $10)* is a solid spot for swimming, surfing and fishing (perch, bass, cabezon and corbina have all been caught here). The beach is also home to a section of the **Omer Rains Coastal Bike Trail**, which runs for a total of 4.1 miles, from west of Emma Wood State Beach to San Buenaventura State Beach. But what makes Emma Wood unique is the pair of concrete structures poking out from the surf. These structures are actually remnants of a WWII coastal artillery site.

Rincon Point

Back on the road, you can continue on PCH past a series of beaches – Mondo's, Faria and Hobson – before PCH and Hwy 101 become one again. Technically, you'll pass Mussel Shoals on the left initially, but because of where the exit and beach access roads are, you'll first come upon **Rincon Point** *(parks.ca.gov; vehicle day-use $10)* – take exit 83 to Bates Rd. Called the 'Queen of the Coast,' Rincon Point State Beach is a world-famous surf spot. For swimming and lounging, however, the adjacent **Rincon Park County Beach** *(countyofsb.org; parking free)* has a much wider swath of sand.

Mussel Shoals

For more beach and a somewhat secret, relatively affordable place to stay right on the oceanfront, head to the small coastal community of Mussel Shoals. To get there, hop on Hwy 101 heading south for just over 2 miles and take the Mussel Shoals exit to Old Pacific Coast Highway. There you'll find **Cliff House Inn** (p80), an oceanfront hotel with a private beach and a pool just steps away from the breaking surf. Rooms are basic, but many have direct ocean views, and the nightly rate is a fraction of what you'd pay at other hotels for that kind of access to the beach. The inn is also home to **Shoals Restaurant** *($$)*, specializing in local seafood, with seating both indoors and on a patio by the Pacific.

Downtown Ventura — *3 miles* — Emma Wood State Beach — *8 miles* — Mussel Shoals — *6 miles* — Carpinteria

Carpinteria

Leaving Mussel Shoals, you're just 10 miles from Carpinteria and will officially leave Ventura County and enter Santa Barbara County. For downtown Carpinteria, take exit 86 to Via Real and Linden Ave – the main street that'll lead you past shops and restaurants and right to the beach. Hunt for vintage treasures at both **Homestead Antiques & Trading Co.** and **Murphy's Vinyl Shack**. A few blocks away **Linden Square** *(linden-square.com)* has more modern finds, like California-made candles and easy-breezy dresses at **The Shopkeepers** *(shopkeeperssb.com)*. If you need a quick bite, you can't go wrong with burgers, fries and shakes at **The Spot** *($)*, just steps from the beach. And if you'd like a place to crash, **Carpinteria State Beach** *(parks.ca.gov; campsite from $45)* has a campground.

continues on p86

THE ORIGINAL RESIDENTS OF THE COAST

By at least 13,000 years ago, the Chumash people settled along the water in what is now Southern California. Before the Mission Period, about 150 Chumash towns and villages stretched from coastal Malibu in the south to San Luis Obispo in the north, plus some of the Channel Islands. The name Malibu actually comes from a Chumash word that means 'where the surf sounds loudly.' Other names in the area that have Chumash origins included Point Mugu, Ojai and Port Hueneme. Today, the Chumash population hovers at around 5000 members, with some who can trace their ancestry back to the islands of Channel Islands National Park.

Carpinteria State Beach

CITY GUIDE:

Ojai

Like taking a retreat from your retreat, detouring to whimsical Ojai will leave you reinvigorated and with a new appreciation for California's free-spirited ways. The town, nestled at the foot of the Topatopa Mountains, is known for both its artists and agriculture, and has a stretch of unique shopping as well as restaurants serving locally sourced fare. Spas are also big in town, so kick off your driving shoes and prepare for a soothing side trip.

HOW TO

Getting there: From the Ventura Pier to downtown Ojai, it's less than a 30-minute drive on CA-33N.

Getting around: Downtown Ojai is very walkable, and many of the boutique hotels are nearby. Rideshares are also available, if you're having a cocktail or two.

Sleeping: At Caravan Outpost (*caravanoutpostojai.com; $$*), 11 Airstreams parked around a garden make up the rooms. Ojai Rancho Inn (p80) has a pool and top-notch bar, and Ojai Valley Inn (*ojaivalleyinn.com; $$$*) has all the bells and whistles – a golf course, tennis courts, pools, horseback-riding trails and a spa.

Tip: Eat a Pixie! They're the tangerines grown exclusively in Ojai.

More info: *ojaivisitors.com*

One night in Ojai is plenty of time to explore the downtown, with Ojai Ave as its main drag. But two nights is even better, especially if you want to add on outdoor adventure and soak up as much of the area's spiritual juju as you can. Called the Ojai vortex, the valley has long been celebrated for its calming energy, believed to enhance meditation and inspire creativity. In fact, the spiritual philosopher Krishnamurti used the town as a base for decades, from the 1920s to the '80s.

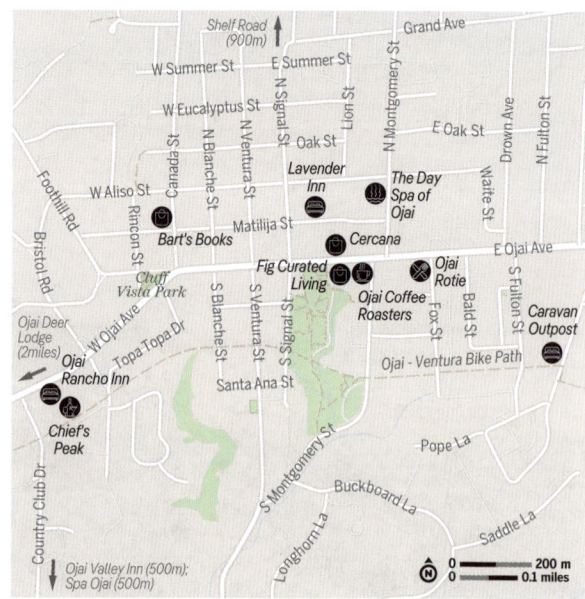

INDULGE IN A DAY AT THE SPA

Ojai has a rep for R&R, and that's in large part because it's home to the legendary **Spa Ojai** *(spaojai.com)* at the Ojai Valley Inn. Even if you're not an overnight guest, you can still book treatments at the spa, a 31,000-sq-ft sanctuary for wellness. Get a relaxation massage (from $285 for one hour) or go for something unexpected, like a meditative sound bath ($300 for one hour), or crystal and reiki energy healing ($275 for 70 minutes). Hey, when in Ojai...

Other top-notch spas in town include the one at the **Lavender Inn** *(lavenderinn.com/spa)*, with its private open-air massage gazebo set in an English garden, and the **Day Spa of Ojai** *(thedayspa.com)*, which has packages that combine multiple treatments for an afternoon or full day at the spa.

Sunset, Ojai

Peep the 'Pink Moment' on a Hike

Ojai is so famous for its captivating, kaleidoscopic sunsets, they have a nickname – the 'pink moment.' These epic minutes at dusk turn the sky a rare rosy hue. Experience it for yourself while hiking the Shelf Road Trail, a relatively easy 3.5-mile out-and-back atop cliffs with views of the whole valley. In spring, you'll even catch the scent of citrus wafting up from the orchards below. You can access the trail on either end: at Signal St and Shelf Rd, or Gridley Rd and Shelf Rd. Both ends have small parking lots.

Browse Totally Unique Boutiques

The most famous store in town is probably **Bart's Books** *(bartsbooksojai.com)*, the world's largest outdoor bookstore. That description, however, sells it short. It's more like a literary labyrinth open to the sky, with shelves holding over 130,000 new and used books. Just a 10-minute walk from there, on Ojai Ave, the town's main drag, **Fig Curated Living** *(figojai.com)* stocks Ojai tea towels and totes, and **Cercana** *(cercanaojai.com)* specializes in fair-trade certified art and goods from around the globe.

EATING & DRINKING IN OJAI

Ojai Deer Lodge $$
A historic restaurant and tavern with roadhouse-style California cuisine and regular live music. *deerlodgeojai.com; hours vary, closed Mon & Tue*

Ojai Rotie $$
Fast, casual rotisserie chicken and freshly baked sourdough gobbled up on a patio in historic downtown. *ojairotie.com; hours vary, closed Mon & Tue*

Ojai Coffee Roasters $
Daily brews and fancy lattes flavored with lavender or golden turmeric, plus bags of beans to go. *ojaicoffeeroasters.com; 6am-5pm Mon-Thu, 6am-6pm Fri-Sun*

Chief's Peak $
The cozy bar at the Ojai Rancho Inn, serving up wine, beer and saké cocktails fireside or poolside. *chiefspeak.com; 3-10pm Mon-Fri, noon-10pm Sat & Sun*

Summerland Beach

HOW MONTECITO BECAME A HOLLYWOOD HIDEAWAY

Long before Oprah, Meghan Markle, Prince Harry and Gwyneth Paltrow took up residence in Montecito, it was a farming area settled by Italian immigrants in the mid-19th century. By the end of the century, wealthy Easterners caught on to Montecito's appeal – with its breathtaking views of both the Santa Ynez Mountains and Pacific Ocean – and transformed it into a residential zone. Then, in the 1920s, Charlie Chaplin got involved in developing the Montecito Inn, solidifying the city as a destination for the Hollywood elite...as well as anyone who appreciates a tranquil escape.

Toro Canyon

Before heading north along the coast, shoot up to the nearby foothills of Toro Canyon, just five minutes from the beach, to hug an alpaca and take a hike. **Canzelle Alpacas** (canzelle.com; adult/child $37/27) is a family-owned farm where you can take a tour and spend time with llamas, sheep, horses, dogs, peacocks, chickens and a Filipino water buffalo (named Archie), in addition to alpacas. Reservations are required, so plan ahead. Afterward, swing by the farm's shop to browse hats, scarves, gloves, throw blankets and toys made from alpaca fiber.

About 10 minutes away (west on Foothill Rd, then north on Toro Canyon Rd), **Toro Canyon Park** (countyofsb.org; parking free) has picnic

Carpinteria

4 miles

Get the chili cheese fries at The Spot

Toro Canyon

2 miles

Summerland

tables, a playground and hiking trails. Toro Canyon Ridge is a popular trail. It's about 2.5 miles out and back, and includes hilltop views of Carpinteria and the ocean.

Summerland

You're only about 8 miles from downtown Santa Barbara, but you'll pass a couple more cute beach towns before you get there. Summerland, a two-exit town off Hwy 101 has enchanting shops and irresistible restaurants on Ortega Hill Rd and Lillie Ave. Shop and eat in one stop at homegoods boutique **Field + Fort** *(fieldandfort.com)*, which is also home to sandwich and salad spot **Feast Café** *($)* – try the chicken tarragon salad sandwich. On the water, **Summerland Beach at Lookout Park** *(countyofsb.org; parking free)* has all the amenities: bathrooms, barbecues, volleyball courts and a playground. It's also the backdrop for beachfront horseback riding with **Los Padres Outfitters** *(lospadresoutfitters.com; private beach ride from $195)*.

Montecito

You're so close to Santa Barbara you can practically smell the chowder wafting from the restaurants on Stearns Wharf Pier. Before you get there, though, you'll come upon Montecito, just a few minutes north of Summerland on Hwy 101.

In Montecito, famous for its celebrity residents, treat yourself to an indulgent day without breaking the bank. Start by wandering an extraordinary estate at **Lotusland** *(lotusland.org; adult/child $60/25)*, a botanical garden spread across 37 acres in the Montecito hills. Then hit the **Hot Springs Canyon Trail** *(sblandtrust.org; parking free)* a 2.6-mile out-and-back route that ends at an actual hot spring.

If you'd like to dig into your wallet a bit, **Montecito Country Mart** *(montecitocountrymart.com)* has upscale clothing, accessory and gift shops, as well as spots for grabbing a coffee, a snack or a full meal. Stop by **Oat Bakery** *(oatbakery.com; $)* for superseed cookies to take on the road, or have a full pizza feast at **Bettina** *(bettinapizzeria.com; $$)*.

Now, if you'd *really* like to dig into your wallet, one of the most legendary hotels in all of California is in Montecito – **San Ysidro Ranch** *(sanysidroranch.com; $$$)*. It's here that John and Jackie Kennedy honeymooned in 1953, so, as you can imagine, it's no run-of-the-mill roadside motel. Even if you don't spend the night, consider an unforgettable meal of California cuisine at the hotel's **Stonehouse** *($$$)* restaurant.

Well rested, well fed and well versed in SoCal's unbelievable beauty, you're now ready to continue on Hwy 101 into Santa Barbara.

San Ysidro Ranch

Shop vintage Mexican folk art at Summerland Antique Collective

See where Jackie and John F Kennedy honeymooned

PHOTO ESSAY

Surf Culture

CALIFORNIAN SURF CULTURE can be traced to the turn of the 20th century, when the sea sport – which traces its origins to Polynesia – was introduced to the West Coast by Hawaiian surfers. However, it was during the post-WWII rise of youth culture in the 1950s and 1960s that the California surf scene really began to take root. Soon, pop culture was flooded with surf references, from the California-centric tunes of the Beach Boys to SoCal surf films such as *Gidget*. Even bikinis, which were previously considered indecent, went mainstream.

While contemporary perceptions of surf culture in the US carry a certain vintage appeal, the sport is still going strong on the Pacific Coast, especially in surfing hotspots such as Huntington Beach (p56), Malibu (p76) and Santa Cruz (p160).

From left:
There's something magical about heading into the sea with your board, prepared to harness the quick thrill of waves.

Die-hard surfers will tell you "dawn patrol" – the early morning surf before the world wakes – is especially enjoyable along this stretch of coastline (in Santa Barbara, p94).

Surfing isn't just about the thrill of catching the perfect wave; it's a way of experiencing nature and understanding your place in it (in San Francisco, p168).

From top:
Surf culture at Huntington Beach (p56) dates back at least a century. It is believed to have held its first local surf contest back in 1933. California's impact on surfing is seen in foam and fiberglass surfboards, which began to replace wooden ones in the 1950s (in Malibu, p76).

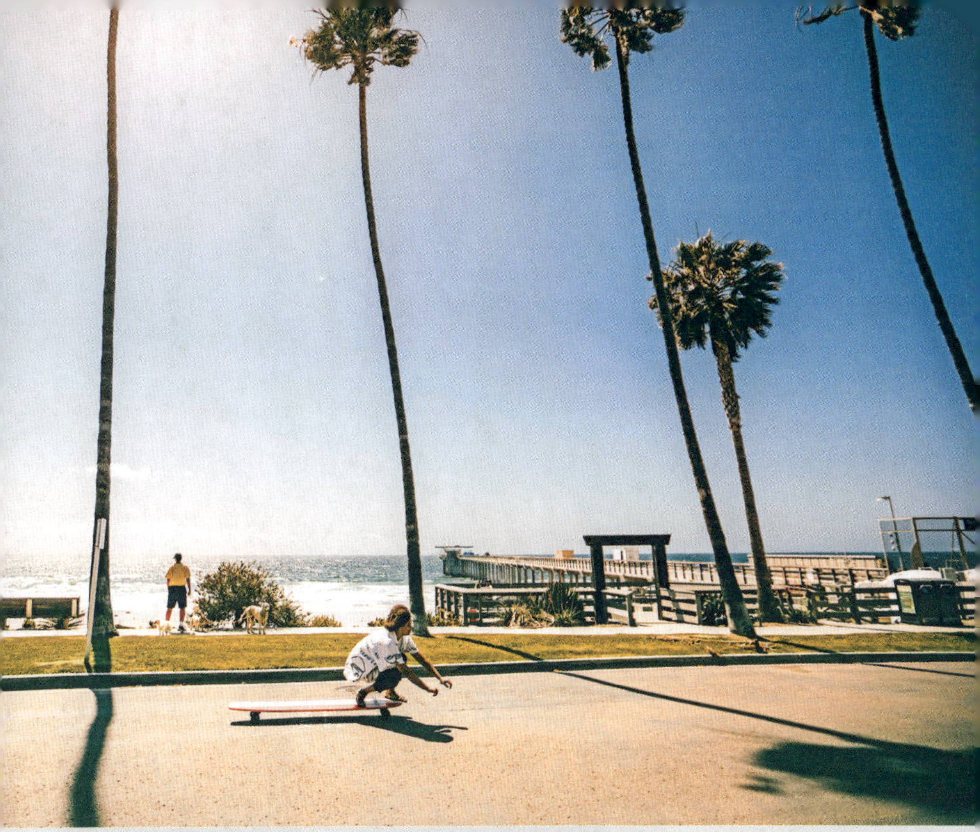

TOP: CAVAN IMAGES/KATHLEEN CARNEY/GETTY IMAGES,
RIGHT: BRANDON COLBERT PHOTOGRAPHY/GETTY IMAGES

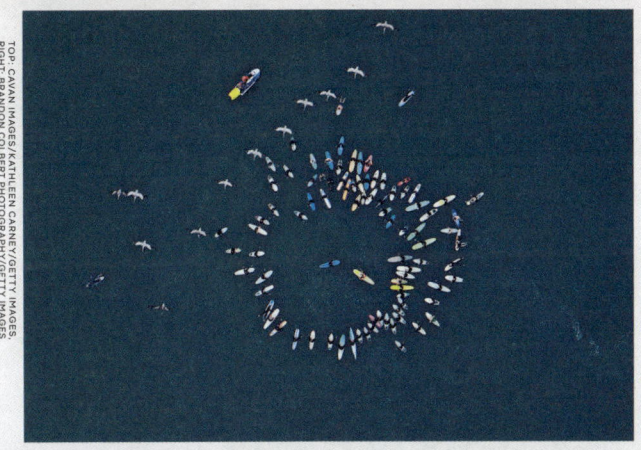

From top:

No waves? No problem! Skateboarding originated in '50s California too, driven by a need for adrenaline when waves were flat (at UCSD Scripps Pier in San Diego, p34).

Paddle-out is a floating memorial with Hawaiian roots where surfers gather on the water to honor late surfers (in San Diego, p34).

Pfeiffer Big Sur State Park (p132), Big Sur
UVL/SHUTTERSTOCK

CENTRAL CALIFORNIA

California's Central Coast delivers some of the Pacific Coast Highway's most iconic views. This region starts in the seaside city of Santa Barbara, winds through the coastal redwoods of Big Sur, passes through the artist enclave of Carmel-by-the-Sea, and ends with views of the Golden Gate Bridge in San Francisco. This rugged coastline is dotted with beach towns, historic missions and monarch butterflies. It draws writers and artists seeking inspiration, provides solitude among tower trees and expansive beaches, and attracts outdoor enthusiasts and naturalists eager to explore the wild.

CITY GUIDE:

Santa Barbara

Say goodbye to sunny Southern California and hello to the California Central Coast. Your first stop on this leg of the journey is the seaside city of Santa Barbara. It's known as the 'American Riviera' for its Mediterranean climate, Spanish Colonial Revival architecture, vibrant wine scene, scenic coastline and upscale, yet laid-back, lifestyle.

WORDS BY **SHARAEL KOLBERG**
Sharael Kolberg is a native Californian who has written about the state from top to bottom

Arriving

By road Most visitors arrive in Santa Barbara by car, especially since Hwy 1 (that merges with Hwy 101 through Santa Barbara County) runs right through the city. There are four exits that lead to Downtown/State St.

By plane You can fly in to the Santa Barbara Airport (SBA; *flysba.santabarbaraca.gov*) right off Hwy 1, only about 10 miles west of Downtown. It offers rental car services.

By rail The *Pacific Surfliner* and *Coast Starlight* stop at Amtrak's (*amtrak.com*) Downtown station – close to the beach, shops, restaurants, hotels and State St's Santa Barbara Visitor Center (*santabarbaraca.com*).

HOW MUCH FOR A

Danish from Andersen's
$5.75

Wine tasting at Deep Sea
$24

Trolley tour
$35

Getting Around

Driving Entering Santa Barbara on Hwy 1, you'll leave the small-town charm of Montecito for the bustling beach city atmosphere. Stay on Hwy 1 to drive through the heart of the city, or take E Cabrillo Blvd to pass by the scenic beaches.

Parking There are several city-managed parking lots and structures, and street parking is available – some are free for the first 75 minutes.

Public transportation Hop on the city bus (*sbmtd.gov; per trip/day $2.50/6*) for an easy and inexpensive way to get around. The Santa Barbara Metropolitan Transit District (MTD) has 30 routes to choose from, so you can get just about anywhere. In summer, there's a shuttle between downtown and the waterfront area ($0.50). Utilize the SBMTD BusTracker app for routes and schedules. Amtrak ticket holders ride for free.

Rideshare Uber, Lyft and taxis are available.

Cycling Santa Barbara is bike-friendly. Rent an e-bike (*wheelfunrentals.com*) for an ecofriendly and fun way to explore the beaches and city. There is an oceanfront bike path, as well as bike lanes throughout the area.

For information about city buses, go to sbmtd.gov:

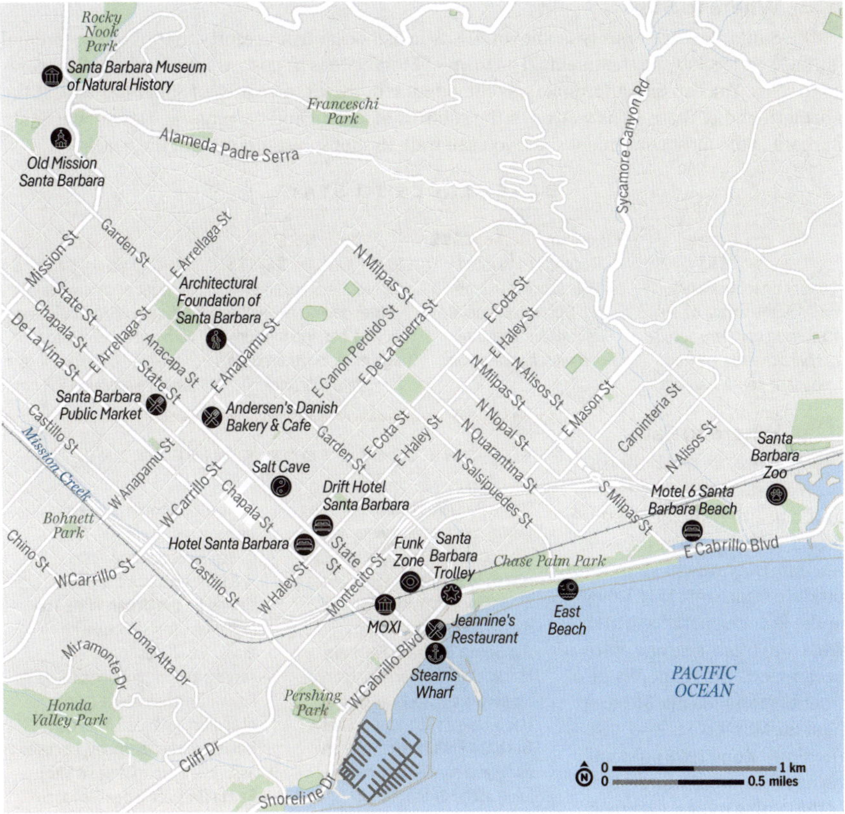

A DAY IN SANTA BARBARA

 Start at the 30-acre **Santa Barbara Zoo** (sbzoo.org), home to more than 500 animals. Soak up some rays, play volleyball or take a dip in the ocean at **East Beach** (E Cabrillo Blvd). Cruise the mile-long beach to **Stearns Wharf** (p98) for waterfront dining and shopping.

 Get your bearings on a 90-minute narrated **Santa Barbara trolley tour** (p97) or learn about the city's history on a two-hour **Architectural Foundation of Santa Barbara** walking tour (afsb.org/santa-barbara-architecture-walking-tours). Kids will love the interactive exhibits at **MOXI, the Wolf Museum of Exploration & Innovation** (moxi.org).

 Head north to the iconic **Old Mission Santa Barbara** (p97), founded in 1786, then to the **Santa Barbara Museum of Natural History** (p97), featuring a planetarium. End with a 45-minute meditation in a pink Himalayan **Salt Cave** (saltcavesb.com), followed by wine tasting in the **Funk Zone** (p98), along the Urban Wine Trail.

Where to Stay

Santa Barbara County is known for its lavish oceanfront resorts that offer exceptional dining, service and spa treatments. The town of Montecito is as posh as it gets, where celebrities go to relax. You can find affordable accommodation in the Uptown area of Santa Barbara, at the northern end of State St, as well as in the suburbs of Goleta and Carpinteria. Downtown Santa Barbara is the most convenient since you can walk to shops, restaurants and the beach.

BEST PLACES TO STAY

The Ritz-Carlton Bacara $$$
Luxury beachfront resort on 78 acres with a 42 spa. ritzcarlton.com/en/hotels/sbarz-the-ritz-carlton-bacara-santa-barbara

Hotel Santa Barbara $$$
Recently renovated 1876 downtown icon with Spanish Colonial Revival architecture. hotelsantabarbara.com

Drift Hotel Santa Barbara $$-$$$
Contactless, minimalist hotel downtown, with coffee bar and in-room yoga mats. drifthotels.co/santabarbara

Motel 6 Santa Barbara Beach $
Budget accommodation featuring retro furnishings, with ocean views. motel6.com/en/home/property/santa-barbara-beach.html

Where to Eat

Dine at a Michelin-starred restaurant in Montecito, have a health-conscious, plant-based meal or fresh-pressed juice in Downtown, shop for produce from Santa Ynez Valley at the farmers markets (p104), feast on fresh seafood with ocean views along the Waterfront, or grab authentic Mexican food on Milpitas St. Also, visit the Funk Zone (p98) to taste regionally sourced wines. Many of the tasting rooms serve food.

THE LOCAL FOOD & WINE SCENE

Santa Barbara is surrounded by farms, ranches and vineyards, making it easy to enjoy locally grown food and regional wines at restaurants, wine-tasting rooms and markets. Stroll the **Santa Barbara Farmers Markets** (sbfarmersmarket.org) for seasonal produce, pick up fresh-caught fish at the **Santa Barbara Fish Market** (sbfish.com) and sip cold-pressed juice at the **Juice Ranch** (juiceranch.com). Chefs create menus that change with the season at restaurants such as **Barbareño** (barbareno.com), **Scarlett Begonia** (scarlettbegonia.net) and **Goat Tree** (hotelcalifornian.com/goat-tree.htm). It's also the perfect setting for the **Urban Wine Trail** (urbanwinetrailsb.com) with more than 20 tasting rooms serving locally produced wines. Pair with a charcuterie made of sourdough bread from **Oat Bakery** (oatbakery.com), cheese assortment from **Cheese Shop Santa Barbara** (cheeseshopsb.com) and gourmet snacks from **Santa Barbara Company** (santabarbaracompany.com; closed Thu).

BEST PLACES TO EAT & DRINK

Andersen's Danish Bakery & Cafe $$
A State St landmark serving authentic Danish pastries and European cuisine. andersenssantabarbara.com; 8:30am-6pm Mon-Thu, to 8pm Fri-Sun

Santa Barbara Public Market $
Upscale food hall with craft beverages downtown. sbpublicmarket.com; 7:30am-11pm Mon-Fri, 8am-11pm Sat, 8am-10pm Sun

Jeannine's Restaurant $$
Iconic restaurant and bakery, popular for breakfast, across from Stearns Wharf. jeannines.com; 7:30am-2pm

Manor Bar, Rosewood Miramar Beach $$$
Library-themed Montecito bar with cocktails. rosewoodhotels.com/en/miramar-beach-montecito/dining/the-manor-bar

Tour by Trolley

Hop on an open-air trolley for a 90-minute narrated tour of some of the top attractions in Santa Barbara, with a short stop at the historic Old Mission Santa Barbara.

HOW TO

Getting here: From Hwy 1/Hwy 101, take exit 96B for Garden St and turn left.

Cost: Adults $28 to $35, children $10 to $15; not suitable for five years and younger.

Tip: Book tickets in advance online.

More info: Tours run at 10am, noon and 2pm; daily mid-June to Labor Day, Thursday to Monday other times of year.

Taking an open-air trolley is a fun, convenient way to see Santa Barbara's sights. The **Santa Barbara Trolley Company** *(sbtrolley.com)* offers a 90-minute tour narrated by a knowledgeable guide that provides insightful information about the history and relevance of the sights, plus how and why to visit them after the tour. Breeze past 14 attractions as the trolley winds its way through the city and neighboring Montecito. The tour departs from the **Santa Barbara Visitors Center** *(santabarbaraca.com)* and includes historical landmarks, shops, restaurants, beaches and hotels. Get a glimpse of the Biltmore Hotel and Montecito Inn, the Santa Barbara Zoo, the Hilton Santa Barbara Beachfront Resort, Santa Barbara Harbor, Butterfly Beach and Andrée Clark Bird Refuge.

Some notable sights include the **Santa Barbara County Courthouse** *(sbcourthouse.org)*, **Santa Barbara Museum of Natural History** *(sbnature.org)*, the **Funk Zone** (p98), **Stearns Wharf** (p98), and **Santa Barbara Museum of Art** *(sbma.net)*. Around the halfway point the trolley stops briefly at the historic **Old Mission Santa Barbara** *(santabarbaramission.org)*.

Santa Barbara trolley

State Street Stroll

You'll find everything you need along vibrant State St, which begins at the ocean and runs through a 10-block pedestrian-only section downtown. From wine-tasting rooms and high-end boutiques to historic buildings and al fresco dining, this is the hub of the city.

HOW TO

Getting here: Take 101 N, exit 96A for Garden St, turn left onto E Gutierrez St until you hit State St. Turn left for Stearns Wharf or right for dining and shops.

Getting around: The best stops are in the 2 miles between Stearns Wharf and Arlington Theatre, which include the car-free State St Promenade. Walk or rent a bike (wheelfunrentals.com).

Parking: There are several city-run parking lots and structures near State St, some offering 75 minutes' free parking.

Tip: Visit 8am to 1pm on Saturday to catch the farmers market with local produce and artisan goods.

More info: See Visit Santa Barbara (santabarbaraca.com).

Sip Local Wines

Santa Barbara County is home to seven wine regions, also known as American Viticultural Areas (AVAs), which means there are many locally produced wines to choose from. State St is host to a number of wine-tasting rooms. Start at the Deep Sea Tasting Room on Stearns Wharf. Head north to J. Wilkes, Melville Winery Tasting Lounge and Barbieri & Kempe Wines – some are part of the Urban Wine Trail. From State St east to Garden St, between Montecito St and Cabrillo Blvd, is the **Funk Zone**, with about a dozen tasting rooms just steps from each other.

Shop Unique Boutiques

Start your shopping spree on **Stearns Wharf** (stearnswharf.org) with a visit to **Old Wharf Trading Company** for souvenirs, nautical gifts and beachwear, and **Nature's Own Gallery** with jewelry and gems. The outdoor **Paseo Nuevo** shopping center on State St has chain stores like GAP and Sephora, vintage finds at Urban Flea Market, and locally made gifts at Seaside Makers. Continuing north, charming La Arcada Plaza (in the ARTS District) features clothing and home interior shops, art galleries, restaurants, the **Museum of Contemporary Art Santa Barbara** and a famous fountain with live turtles.

Stroll Through History

Take a self-guided walking tour along State St to see the Santa Barbara Museum of Art, the 1825 Hill-Carrillo Adobe historical landmark, Arlington Theatre – for films and concerts

1ST THURSDAY ART WALK

Plan your schedule to visit Santa Barbara on the first Thursday of the month to attend the lively **1st Thursday Art Walk** *(sbac.ca.gov/1st-thursdays)*. This free evening event, in the Downtown area, highlights the city's commitment to promoting art and culture, with a focus on local artists. Many times you can meet artists at participating galleries, listen to live music, get free admission to museums or live performances, and enjoy discounts on bites and drinks. It's a wonderful way to immerse yourself in the local culture, mingle with residents, and appreciate many forms of art.

– featuring Mission-style architecture, and the 1924 ornate Granada Theatre. Just off State St, visit the historic Lobero Theatre for performing arts, the Santa Barbara Public Library, Santa Barbara County Courthouse and Casa de la Guerra historical site – all stops on the **Red Tile Walking Tour** *(santabarbaraca.com/itinerary/red-tile-walking-tour)*. End at the free **Santa Barbara Historical Museum** *(sbhistorical.org)*.

Above: State Street; Below: Santa Barbara Historical Museum

Santa Barbara

This stretch of PCH starts in red tile–roofed Santa Barbara and hugs the coast through small towns and past ocean vistas worth stopping for. Along the way, explore massive sand dunes, visit historic missions and see thousands of butterflies. Pause in Pismo Beach for clam chowder, and take a hike followed by a soak in hot springs as you head north. End on a Thursday to catch the lively San Luis Obispo farmers market.

Sharael Kolberg

Santa Barbara (p104)

San Luis Obispo

134 MILES — 2-HOUR DRIVE

THIS LEG:
- Santa Barbara
- Goleta
- Monarch Butterfly Grove
- Gaviota State Park
- La Purísima Mission
- Lompoc
- Vandenberg Village
- Guadalupe
- Nipomo
- Oceano
- Oceano Dunes State Vehicle Recreation Area
- Pismo Beach
- Avila Beach

Driving Notes

This scenic Central Coast section of Pacific Coast Highway will provide endless views of the Pacific Ocean, take you past picturesque flower fields and artistic street murals, offer chances to experience state parks and state beaches, and allow you to slow down as you drive through small towns. Foggy mornings add to the mystique of the journey.

Breaking Your Journey

Whether you're looking to overnight at an oceanfront campground, a luxury resort or a retro motel, this route has a variety of accommodations to offer. For dining or snacks, take a side trip to Buellton or a stop in Pismo Beach. The area around Vandenberg Space Force Base is a bit of a dry patch for amenities.

Sharael's Tips

BEST MEAL Pastries at the Andersen's Danish Bakery & Restaurant (p96) in Santa Barbara.

FAVORITE VIEW High atop a sand dune at Oceano Dunes State Vehicular Recreation Area (p112).

ESSENTIAL STOP Relaxing soak at Sycamore Mineral Hot Springs Resort & Spa (p112).

ROAD-TRIP TIP Stock up on seasonal produce at the Santa Barbara farmers market (p104).

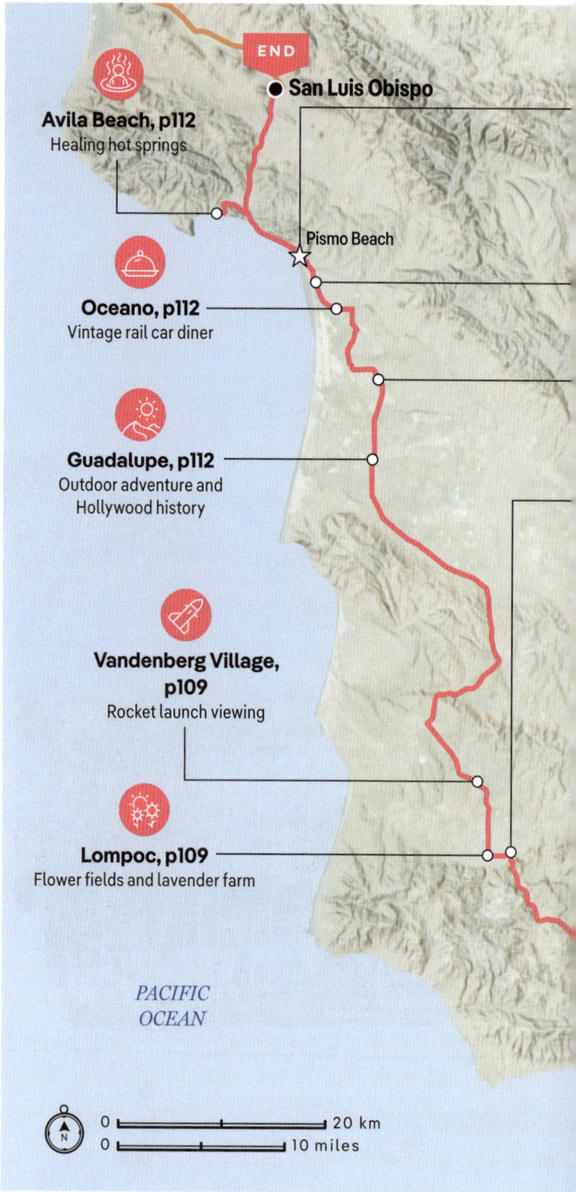

END
● San Luis Obispo

Avila Beach, p112
Healing hot springs

Pismo Beach

Oceano, p112
Vintage rail car diner

Guadalupe, p112
Outdoor adventure and Hollywood history

Vandenberg Village, p109
Rocket launch viewing

Lompoc, p109
Flower fields and lavender farm

PACIFIC OCEAN

0 — 20 km
0 — 10 miles

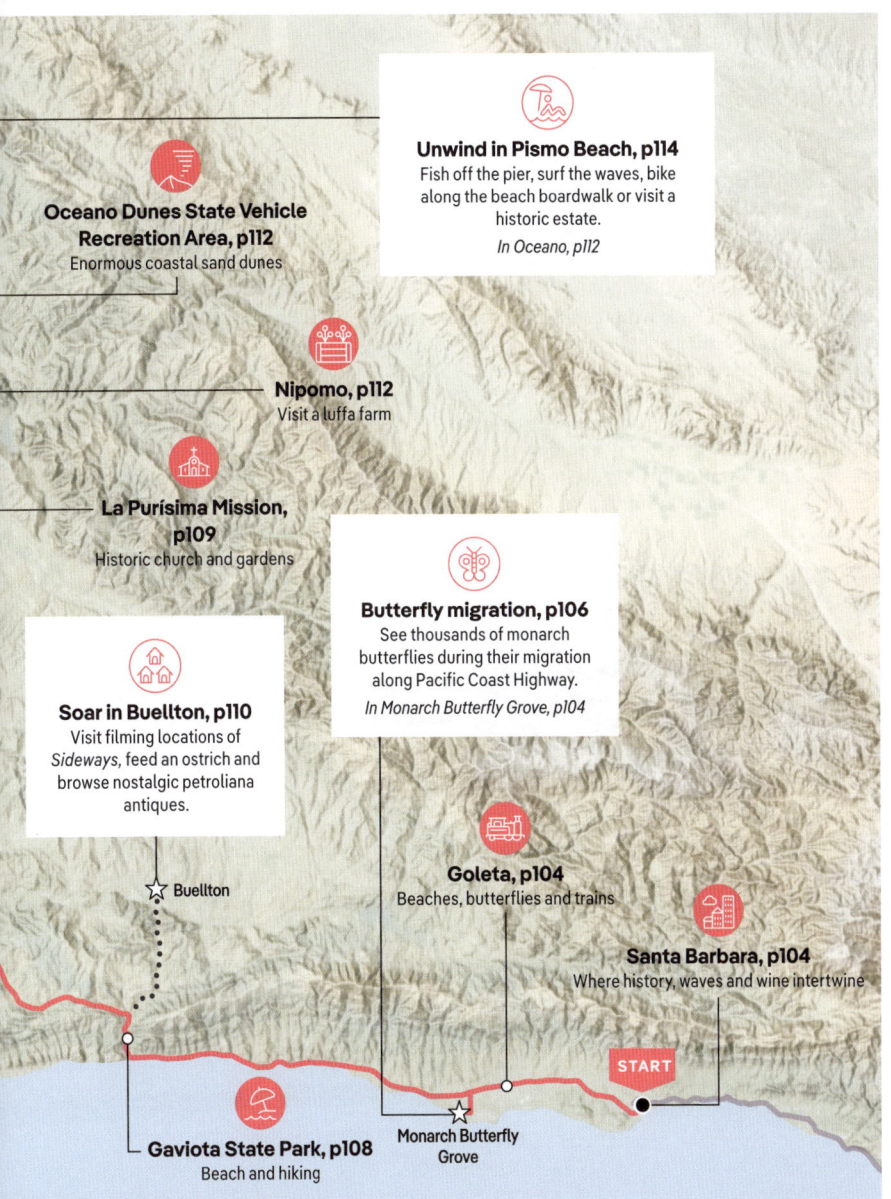

PREVIOUS STOP Go from the luxury boutiques and resorts in upscale town Montecito to laid-back coastal charm in bustling Santa Barbara.

Santa Barbara

Arriving in Santa Barbara (p94) on Hwy 101, you'll pass by the 42-acre **Andrée Clark Bird Refuge**, the **Santa Barbara Zoo** (p95; keep your eyes open for the giraffes), the **Funk Zone** (p98) dotted with wine-tasting rooms, eateries and art exhibits, and cross over State St – the shopping and dining hub (stop at the Andersen's Bakery for pastries). Exit onto Cabrillo Blvd for ocean views and the iconic **Chromatic Gate** – a 22ft-tall rainbow arch sculpture at **Cabrillo Park**. Pause for a walk along historic **Stearns Wharf** (p98).

With fresh, locally grown produce from the **Santa Barbara farmers markets** (sbfarmersmarket.org), this leg of the trip will be off to a delicious start. Swing by the **Downtown** (8am-1pm Sat) or **Old Town** (3-7pm Tue) locations. Stock up on seasonal fruit, veggies, nuts, eggs, honey and made-from-scratch delicacies. Additional locations in Goleta, Solvang, Carpinteria and Montecito.

Goleta

Leave the city behind as you roll into the small town of Goleta, home to the **South Coast Railroad Museum** (goletadepot.org). This 1901 train depot is a remnant of Southern Pacific Railroad's Coast Line route from Los Angeles to San Francisco that led to the development of towns like Goleta. Kids will love the nine-minute ride on the miniature Goleta Short Line train. You can also tour the adjacent historic **Rancho La Patera** (goletahistory.org).

Monarch Butterfly Grove

Driving along the Central California Coast from October through February, you can witness the annual monarch butterfly migration as thousands of butterflies flitter through the air, making their way south for warmer weather. Make time to stop at the Monarch Butterfly Grove at Ellwood Mesa (p106), where an enormous number of these colorful flying insects seek refuge and sustenance in the eucalyptus

Stearns Wharf

FROM LEFT: TUPUNGATO/SHUTTERSTOCK, WILL ARONSON/SHUTTERSTOCK

Fuel up with farmers market snacks

Santa Barbara farmers markets

trees. Exit Hwy 101 north towards Hollister Ave, where the 137 acres of open space also features trails that lead to the beach.

Timbers Roadhouse

You won't mind getting barbecue sauce on your fingers while indulging in classic American comfort food at **Timbers Roadhouse** (*timbersgoleta.com; $$$*) in Goleta. Serving everything from saucy ribs and juicy burgers to oxtail mac and cheese, and pie baked with fresh, seasonal fruit, this classic diner dates back to the 1950s. The name is a nod to the materials from which it was built – wood from a pier that was destroyed during World War II. After numerous

continues on p107

BEST PLACES TO EAT

AJ Spurs, Buellton $$$
This cowboy-themed restaurant looks like the set of a Western movie. The barbecue sauce will make your taste buds tingle. *ajspurs.com; from 4:30pm*

Splash Cafe, Pismo Beach $
Don't let the long line at this casual beachside spot deter you. The clam chowder, fish and chips, and burgers are worth the wait. *splashcafe.com; 9am-9pm Mon-Thu, to 8pm Fri & Sat*

Madonna Inn, San Luis Obispo $
Stop by the bakery for a slice of the world-famous, decadent pink champagne cake made with white cake and Bavarian creme, and topped with pink chocolate curls and shavings. *madonnainn.com/bakery; 7am-10pm*

See thousands of butterflies at Monarch Butterfly Grove

Monarch Butterfly Grove

Dine on American barbecue at Timbers Roadhouse

Butterfly Migration

Goleta is just one of many places along the Central Coast to see the butterflies come south for the winter.

HOW TO

Nearest stop: Start in Goleta

Getting here: They are all located just off Hwy 1. Some locations have parking lots; others have street parking.

When to go: The western monarch butterflies migrate to California October through February.

Cost: Free

More info: For detailed information and an interactive map of the migration route, visit *westernmonarchtrail.org*

The air comes alive with orange-winged butterflies during the winter migration season (October to February). They conserve energy, stay warm and protect themselves from predators by hanging in large clusters in the eucalyptus trees. There are many places to see these impressive clusters – with thousands of butterflies – during this leg of the trip. Visit in mid-December for the highest concentration. In Goleta, the **Coronado Butterfly Preserve** *(blandtrust.org/land/coronado-butterfly-preserve)* is located in a residential neighborhood. It can be reached by taking Hwy 101 N and Hollister Ave to Coronado Dr. Take the trail to reach Goleta's Monarch Butterfly Grove at Ellwood Mesa (p104) or continue to the beach.

About an hour and a half north on Hwy 1, exit Concha Rd, turn right on Eucalyptus Rd to arrive at Monarch Butterfly Grove at Trilogy in Nipomo (p112). Heading north towards Pismo Beach (p114), you'll pass right by **Pismo State Beach Monarch Butterfly Grove** *(parks.ca.gov/?page_id=30273)*, which makes it an easy stopping point. Read the educational signage to learn the process of the monarch butterfly life cycle, from caterpillar to butterfly.

Above: Monarch butterflies; Right: Monarch Butterfly Grove at Ellwood Mesa

Madonna Inn

continued from p105
owners and a long hiatus, the restaurant is back to serving guests hearty meals.

Sun Outdoors

Hike the 5-mile round-trip **Bill Wallace Trail** (named for environmentalist and former Santa Barbara County supervisor), take a dip in a heated outdoor swimming pool, purchase snacks, camping gear or beach supplies at the market, visit a llama and goat farm, watch an outdoor movie, and camp in a tent or RV – all at **Sun Outdoors** *(sunoutdoors.com; $$)* near Goleta. This dog- and family-friendly resort is a great place

BEST PLACES TO SLEEP

Sun Outdoors, Santa Barbara $-$$
Sun Outdoors is a budget-friendly tent and RV campground with a pool, general store, laundry facilities and playground, near El Capitán State Beach. *sunoutdoors.com*

Sideways Inn, Buellton $$
Inspired by the film *Sideways*, this boutique hotel sits in the heart of Buellton. There is no elevator at this two-story property. *sidewaysinn.com*

Madonna Inn, San Luis Obispo $$$
No two of the 110 rooms are alike at this iconic, kitschy hotel with themed suites such as safari, caveman, love nest and floral fantasy. *madonnainn.com*

Monarch Butterfly Grove

9 miles

Sun Outdoors

> **STREET MURALS**
>
> Lompoc's history and culture can be seen through about 40 street murals on buildings throughout town. In Old Town, park near the **Lompoc Museum** (lompocmuseum.org) to stroll this outdoor gallery. The **Lompoc Mural Society** (lompocmurals.com) has been commissioning and restoring the murals since 1990. The first mural, titled *Flower Industry* by Santa Monica artist Art Mortimer, depicts flower-seed growers, which is appropriate since Lompoc was formerly the 'Flower Seed Capital of the World.' These days, its focus is on cut flowers.

for some R&R as you meander north. There's a playground for the kids and a park for the dogs. Plus, it's only a short walk to **El Capitán State Beach** *(parks.ca.gov/elcapitan)*. If glamping is more your style, check out the cabins, yurts, suites and new cottages at **El Capitan Canyon Resort** *(elcapitancanyon.com; $$$)* next door. Guests can borrow a beach cruiser bicycle, enjoy wine tasting at the market, and listen to free live music concerts in the summer.

Gaviota State Park

This coastline is dotted with state beaches that are beautifully rugged and offer a refreshing – think *cold*! – way to experience the Pacific Ocean. As you make your way along Hwy 1, slow down so you don't miss the left-hand turn-off to **Gaviota State Park** *(parks.ca.gov/gaviota)*. The 2712 acres include a beach, as well as hiking trails and a campground. The pier is closed due to structural damage. Veer right at

Along the Way We Met...

MICHAEL RODRIQUE I love everything about La Purísima Mission. Besides being in my hometown, Lompoc, it's the most restored California mission. You can truly step back in time to the early 1800s. There are great hiking trails, including my favorite [Vista de la Cruz] up to the cross, with amazing views of Lompoc and the mission.

Michael is a senior park aide at La Purísima Mission (lapurisimamission.org) in Lompoc.

MICHAEL'S TIP: *Wear comfortable shoes, bring water, and visit the visitor center and gift shop.*

- Sun Outdoors
- 13 miles
- Gaviota State Park
- Detour to Buellton
- 23 miles
- La Purísima Mission

the park entrance to reach the trailhead for the **Gaviota Wind Caves** via Hollister Ranch Rd. Campers can book a standard site for tents, motor homes or trailers (no hookups available) There are also hike- and bike-in sites. On your way north from Gaviota, consider a detour up Hwy 101 to **Buellton** (p110).

La Purísima Mission

Wander through history at **La Purísima Mission State Historic Park** *(lapurisima mission.org)*. Founded in 1787, the 900-acre site features restored buildings showcasing life in the 1820s, a church and garden, and 25 miles of hiking trails in the surrounding area. No matter how hot it is outside, the 4½ft-thick adobe walls keep it cool inside. And the natural light is magical against the whitewashed walls. Time your visit on a Demonstration Day Saturday to try hands-on mission-era activities.

Lompoc

Take exit CA 246 W into the small town of Lompoc, the original homeland of the Chumash people. From Hwy 1, take W Ocean Ave to see the **Lompoc Flower Fields** *(explorelompoc.com/flower-fields)*, which burst with color from April through September. Although you cannot walk through the fields, you can stop for photos in front of the rainbow-hued blooms. To taste locally grown wines, turn left off Hwy 1 onto N 12th St and Industrial Way, home to the **Lompoc Wine Ghetto** *(explorelompoc.com/lompoc-wine-ghetto)* with about a dozen boutique tasting rooms.

Vandenberg Village

East of Lompoc, much of the land is occupied by **Vandenberg Space Force Base**,

Lompoc Flower Fields

which encompasses approximately 99,000 acres, including 42 miles of coastline. Its remote location makes it ideal for launching and testing intercontinental ballistic missiles and satellites. To catch a live launch, sign up for alerts *(vandenberg.spaceforce.mil)*, then head to a viewing spot, such as at the end of Moonglow Rd in Vandenberg Village, where there's also a trailhead for **Burton Mesa Ecological Reserve** with 5368 acres to explore. The Space Launch Complex 10 – a National Historic Landmark – is located on the base, as is an ancient Chumash rock art site at Chumash Honda Ridge. However, it is a closed military base, so you cannot access those areas. There is public access to Surf, Wall and Minuteman Beaches, but restrictions are in place March through September to protect the endangered snowy plover during its nesting season.

continues on p112

Soar in Buellton

Veer off Hwy 1 and head to the small town of Buellton, with quirky attractions and outdoor adventures. From zip lining to Hollywood nostalgia, this detour is just minutes from the coast.

HOW TO

Nearest stop: Gaviota or Las Cruces to the south; the Danish Village of Solvang is less than 4 miles east.

Getting here: From Gaviota, take a detour north on Hwy 101 for nearly 9 miles, where it intersects E Hwy 246 and you'll end up in the heart of Buellton.

When to go: Visit in the fall for cooler temperatures, the annual Buellton Fall Festival *(buelltonfallfest.com)* in November, and harvesting activities at nearby wineries of Santa Ynez Valley.

Tip: Watch *Sideways* before you visit since many scenes were filmed in Buellton.

More info: Discover Buellton *(discoverbuellton.com)* is the official source for visitor information.

Take exit 139 from Hwy 101 N and turn left onto Santa Rosa Rd to get to **Vega Vineyard & Farm** *(vegavineyardandfarm.com)*, a family-friendly, 208-acre historic ranch. Start with a glass of wine and charcuterie at the charming tasting room, stroll past the picturesque vineyards, and wander down the dirt path to see the adorable farm animals – sheep, goats, pigs, emu and chickens. There's also a children's play area, the Mercantile shop, a restaurant, farm stand and accommodations in a historic adobe house or modern vineyard house.

Feeding Frenzy

Whether you think these awkwardly large flightless birds are frightening or fabulous, visiting **Ostrichland USA** *(ostrichlandusa.com)* is a unique experience. More than 150 emus and ostriches freely roam the 32-acre property, but aggressively seek food handouts from visiting tourists. The birds are safely contained behind fencing, but peek their heads through feeding holes in search of tasty pellets. Hold the food bowl tightly – the birds have a powerful peck. You'll find souvenirs in the gift shop.

Sky-High Views

Soar high above the Santa Ynez Valley on a thrilling two-hour zip-line experience with **Highline Adventures** *(highlineadventures.com)*. Adventure seekers will traverse three dual zip lines at speeds over 50mph, on lines up to 3360ft long, while dangling about 400ft high. These could be the longest and fastest zip lines in California. For a unique experience, try the moonlight zip-line tour. You can also check out the challenging adventure

GOING SIDEWAYS

Buellton gained notoriety as the filming location for the Academy Award–winning movie *Sideways* (2004), starring Paul Giamatti and Thomas Haden Church. The storyline of this dramedy features two single guys bonding during a road trip through California wine country, before one of them ties the knot. As you can imagine, chaos ensues. Fans of the movie visit Buellton to see the spots were scenes were shot, including the Sideways Inn (p107), Hitching Post II, Ostrichland USA, AJ Spurs Saloon & Dining Hall (p105) and Zaca Creek Golf Course.

Ostrichland USA

park course or take a mellow protea farm tour.

Lavender Fields

As you drive west on Hwy 246, you can't miss the sprawling purple field at **Lavender Fields Forever** (lavenderfieldsforever.org; Jul & Aug). The distinct scent is familiar and calming. Pick your own lavender, take photos with the stunning backdrop, or shop the farm stand for lavender oil or dried lavender bundles. Although you are allowed to walk though the fields, they are buzzing with bees. Keep some lavender in your car to keep it smelling nice while on the road.

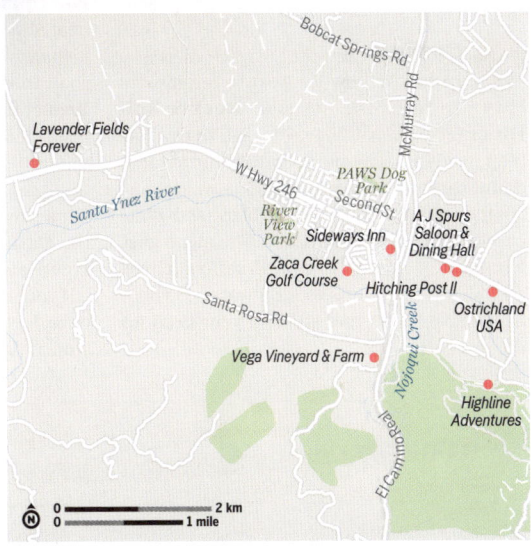

Guadalupe

Passing through Guadalupe, look for the **Dunes Center** *(dunescenter.org)* on your left-hand side, just past 9th St. The staff provides information on how to access and enjoy the 22,000-acre **Guadalupe-Nipomo Dunes Complex**, the world's largest intact coastal dune ecosystem that includes 18 miles of coastline. In 1923, Cecil B DeMille filmed *The Ten Commandments* here and the Dunes Center has relics from the set, including a large headless sphinx. There's also a large collection of sand samples from around the world – red, white, black, brown, green, coarse, fine and rocky.

Nipomo

In Nipomo, exit right from Hwy 1 onto Via Concha Rd, then right on Eucalyptus Rd, and left on Kingston Dr to reach the Monarch Butterfly Grove at Trilogy. For a quirky side stop, visit the **Luffa Farm** *(theluffafarm.com)* nearby. From Kingston Dr, turn left on Center Point Pl, right on Willow Rd, and follow the signs on your right. Book a tour with the 'Luffa Lady' to see luffas growing on the vine.

Oceano

Follow Willow Rd west to rejoin with Hwy 1 to reach the nostalgic **Rock & Roll Diner** *(rockandrolldiner.com; $$)* in Oceano. Step inside the vintage train cars turned into dining cars to step back to the 1950s, where vinyl booths, laminate tabletops and black-and-white checkered floors set the scene. The menu goes beyond burgers and shakes, with seafood, Greek and Mexican options too. Be warned: you'll likely have Elvis tunes stuck in your head for the rest of the day.

Oceano Dunes State Vehicle Recreation Area

To explore the vast area of the coastal sand dunes, drive your 4WD at the only California state park that allows driving on the beach and dunes – **Oceano Dunes State Vehicle Recreation Area** *(ohv.parks.ca.gov/oceanodunes; 7am-10pm; $5)*. Traverse 8 miles of shifting sand on this unique adventure. A variety of 4WD rentals are available on-site *(sunbuggy.com)* for self-guided tours. Discover more about the area at the **Ocean Dunes District Visitor Center**. After exploring the dunes, head north on Hwy 1 to **Pismo Beach** (p114) for fishing on the pier or a stroll along the bluffs.

Avila Beach

From Pismo Beach, it's back on the road, which means hours in the car, which can lead to tight, aching muscles. Luckily, on this stretch of the journey just before San Luis Obispo you'll encounter healing hot springs to soothe your tired body and mind. Turn left off Hwy 1 onto Avila Beach Dr to reach **Avila Hot Springs** *(avilahotsprings.com)* with a heated freshwater pool, two water slides and a shallow mineral pool. Continue down the road to reach **Sycamore Mineral Springs Resort & Spa** *(sycamoresprings.com)*, a luxury resort featuring a lush hillside with 24 private mineral hot tubs accessible via steep stairs. Book a ground-level tub to avoid the climb. For a private soak for up to 20 people, reserve the Oasis Waterfall Lagoon. Book ahead to secure a spot.

If you like farm animals, freshly picked produce, hay rides and fried-chicken sandwiches, stop at **Avila Valley Barn** *(avilavalleybarn.*

Eat in a train car at Rock & Roll Diner

SANTA BARBARA TO SAN LUIS OBISPO

Oceano Dunes State Vehicle Recreation Area

com), next door to Avila Hot Springs. At this family-owned farm, you can interact with goats, sheep, cows, alpacas and Elmo the emu. You won't leave hungry with the opportunity to pick your own seasonal fruit, grab a roasted corn on the cob, order a smoked tri-tip sandwich or chili dog from the Chicken Shack & Smoke House, or shop for produce grown on the property. And why not finish it all off with a milkshake from the Sweet Shop or a piece of hot apple pie from the bakery, à la mode, of course. Every season there is something different to experience.

CALIFORNIA MISSIONS

Follow the footsteps of the Spanish missionaries who influenced the state's culture, along the **California Mission Trail** (californiamissionstrail.org). Thirteen of the 21 missions are located in this region between Santa Barbara and San Francisco, with seven just off Hwy 1. Learn about the history, architecture, culture, religion and impact on Indigenous peoples at these historic sites. Starting in 1769, Father Junípero Serra – the patron saint of California – founded the first nine missions. He died in 1784 and is buried at Carmel Mission Basilica.

3.5 miles — Pismo Beach
7 miles — Avila Beach
10 miles — San Luis Obispo

Ride a 4WD at Oceano Dunes State Vehicle Recreation Area

Unwind in Pismo Beach

Visitors flock to this coastal town to explore the expansive beaches, state parks and iconic pier.

HOW TO

Nearest stop: Pismo Beach is located between Oceano and Avila Beach.

Getting there: Hwy 1 passes through Pismo Beach. Take Amtrak's *(amtrak.com) Pacific Surfliner* to the Grover Beach station. San Luis Obispo is only about 8 miles away.

Getting around: Rideshare services, or public transportation through SoCo Transit *(sctlink.com)* buses and dial-a-ride service, and San Luis Obispo RTA *(slorta.org)* buses. Metered street parking downtown.

When to go: Fall brings warm temperatures, less fog, fewer crowds and the clam festival in October.

More info: Experience Pismo Beach *(experiencepismobeach. com)* or Visit SLO CAL *(slocal.com).*

The beaches, bluffs and butterflies are just a few reasons to visit this laid-back coastal town. You can surf the waves, sip local wines or shop the boutiques on Pomeroy Ave. It is a popular destination – expect crowds during the busy summer months. A novel activity to try while you're in town is clamming. Pismo has been known as the 'Clam Capital of the World' and the Pismo clam is one of the largest along the California Coast. Visit in October for the annual Pismo Beach Clam Festival.

Scenic Beaches & Bluffs

Ccean views and beaches draw tourists to Pismo Beach. Pismo State Beach stretches about 17 miles across Pismo, Grover Beach and Oceano, with budget accommodation at **Pismo Coast Village RV Resort** *(visitpcv.com; $).* On the northern end sits 11-acre **Dinosaur Caves Park** with a playground and a flat 1.1-mile round-trip bluff-top trail running along Ocean Blvd. Spot whales through the public binoculars at Ocean Blvd and Morro Ave. Beach access is via the staircase at the north end of Ocean Blvd.

Iconic Pismo Beach Pier

Make time to visit the renovated historic Pismo Beach Pier, where you'll find vintage airstreams providing visitor information, fish bait, and bites and drinks. Walk to the end to look for breaching humpback whales or playful bottlenose dolphins. Pose for a photo in front of the large Pismo Beach sign at the lively Pismo Beach Pier Plaza. There's metered parking on Pomeroy Ave, where you'll find a variety of shops and restaurants. The new **Pismo Beach Club** *(thepismobeachclub. com; $$$)* nearby offers boutique accommodation with mid-century modern design

BEST PLACES TO EAT

Splash Café $
Popular eatery, with long lines, near Pismo Beach Pier, known for its clam chowder. *splashcafe.com; 9am-8pm Mon-Thu, 9am-9pm Fri & Sat*

Oyster Loft $$$
Upscale seafood with indoor and outdoor seating offering views of the Pacific. *oysterloft.com; 5-9pm Wed-Sun*

Giuseppe's Cucina Italiana $$$
Pizza cooked in a wood-burning oven, pasta and gelato, and local seafood dishes. *giuseppesrestaurant.com*

Cracked Crab $$
Wide variety of seasonal, locally sourced crab creations, plus burgers and salads. *crackedcrab.com; 11am-9pm Sun-Thu, 11am-10pm Fri & Sat*

Historic Sites

The **Chapman Estate** (*chapmanestatefoundation.org*), on Ocean Blvd in Shell Beach, includes an oceanfront 1930 English Tudor-style mansion with an extensive art collection, manicured grounds, a windmill and a lighthouse. Book a docent-led tour or stroll the property on your own during Open Gates Season. **Price Historical Park** (*friendsofpricehouse.com*) features a 7-acre property with Pismo Beach founder John Michael Price's 1893 home, Price Anniversary House, and hiking and biking trails.

Above: Pismo Beach

INSIGHT

A Cultural History of the Coast

A living gallery of California design, Hwy 1 has it all. From the space-age Googie cafes in Los Angeles to the coast's neon-lit motels and art-deco bridges, and the salt-weathered inns of the far north, every mile is framed in style.

WORDS BY **CHRISTABEL LOBO**
Christabel is a writer and illustrator based between Abu Dhabi and wherever her next flight lands

MOST PEOPLE THINK of the Pacific Coast Highway as a perfect stretch of asphalt, nestled between cliffs and the ocean. But look closer, and it's also a stage set.

From the Googie drive-ins of Los Angeles to the neon motel signs of Northern California, the road's visual language is what sold the quintessential Californian dream: bold, bright and built for the driver's eye.

This is the story of how architecture, signage and roadside design have long decorated the Pacific Coast Highway, transforming a simple highway into an icon of freedom and the open road.

Southbound Style

In the postwar boom, the highway became both commute and catwalk. Its shoulders were lined with service stations shaped like space-age sculptures and diners that looked like rocket ships ready to blast off. This was the birthplace of Googie architecture, where glass walls, futuristic angles and neon signs grabbed the attention of families cruising past at 50 mph.

Few original Googie buildings survive intact, but you can still pull off at Pann's near LAX or the retro-styled Mel's Drive-in in Santa Monica's restored Penguin building for a taste of that futurist optimism. Inside, you might spot a row of chrome stools lined up under a low-slung roof, with sunlight bouncing off plate-glass windows. Menus promise breakfast all day, and the neon outside doubles as a beacon for drivers long after the lunch rush ends.

The style's mix of modernism and roadside kitsch helped cement the image of California as

Pann's

a place where the future was not just coming – it had already arrived, and you could order it with a side of fries and a milkshake.

Selling the Shore

By the early 1900s, the coastal route north of Santa Monica hit a hard stop at Malibu. The land there belonged to May Rindge, the formidable owner of the 17,000-acre Rancho Topanga Malibu Sequit, who had already outmanoeuvred the Southern Pacific Railroad to keep its tracks off her property. When Los Angeles County floated plans to extend a coastal road through Malibu, she countered with locked gates and armed guards.

It wasn't until the early 1920s – when the project was folded into the new Roosevelt Hwy, a Mexico-to-Canada route meant to unite the entire West Coast – that momentum shifted. In 1923, the US Supreme Court sided with the county, affirming its right to take Rindge's land for public use.

The Malibu stretch was the last to open, with a ribbon-cutting in June 1929 presided over by California's governor, flanked by Miss Mexico and Miss Canada, and followed by a parade of more than 1000 cars navigating its new curves.

Mid-Coast Motels and Neon Nights

North of Los Angeles, the highway leaves behind the sprawl and moves through smaller towns where design takes on a more intimate scale. The 1950s saw a boom in roadside motels, each vying for attention with eye-popping neon signs. In Morro Bay (p123), the bright red Morro Crest Inn sign still blinks to life at dusk; in Pismo Beach (p114), retro script still curls across stucco walls.

Pulling in at dusk, you'd hear the buzz of the sign before you saw it, the letters flickering to life against the coastal fog. The typography, color schemes and sign shapes told you who they were trying to attract: honeymooners, surfers, road-tripping families.

Even the gas stations joined in. Many were built in the streamlined programmatic style – whimsical shapes like ships, shells or futuristic pavilions that were popular at the time – that made fuel stops part of the coastal road-tripping adventure.

The Central Coast

From San Simeon to Big Sur, the highway plays like its own film reel. The road's most photographed stretch – between Bixby Bridge (p134) and Pfeiffer Canyon Bridge – owes as much to engineering as to scenery. Built in 1932, Bixby Bridge was an art-deco feat of its time, its graceful concrete arch turning a once isolated coastline into a drivable fantasy.

By the 1960s, Big Sur attracted a different crowd. The back-to-the-land artists, writers and architects came looking for wild edges and nature to inspire their work. Post-and-beam cabins and cliff-side lodges, like the original Nepenthe restaurant (p131), paired modernist lines with redwood beams and stone hearths.

Northern Icons

Further north, the design language shifts again. In Santa Cruz, the iconic Giant Dipper coaster marquee still flashes above the Santa Cruz Beach Boardwalk (p161), while neon seafood signs glow over the Wharf at dusk. These designs weren't meant to be glimpsed at 50 miles an hour. Instead, they require lingering – the typography reads as easily from a Ferris wheel as from a car window.

By the time the highway enters redwood country near Mendocino, the palette changes. Neon gives way to weathered shingles, clapboard inns and hand-painted signs. But even this restraint is part of the California road trip's promise. The idea that the further you drive, the more you leave behind.

To travel the Pacific Coast Highway is to move through layers of visual storytelling. Some of it is deliberate – a sign designed to catch your eye, a building meant to look like it could fly – and some of it is purely accidental. But together, they keep selling the California dream. One curve at a time.

San Luis Obispo

Hwy 1 from San Luis Obispo to Carmel-by-the-Sea winds along the Big Sur Coast—home to plunging sea cliffs and towering coastal redwoods—some dating back more than 1,500 years. Travelers from around the globe come to experience this rugged coastline with its ethereal fog sometime masking the epic views. American author and beatnik Jack Kerouac was drawn to the remote area for solitude, silence, and as a respite from life's woes. The curvy road with unmatched landscape can be hypnotic.

Sharael Kolberg

Bixby Bridge (p134)
PANDORA PICTURES/SHUTTERSTOCK

Carmel-by-the-Sea

139 MILES · 3-HOUR DRIVE

THIS LEG:

- San Luis Obispo
- Morro Bay
- Cambria
- Hearst Castle
- Ragged Point
- Limekiln State Park
- Julia Pfeiffer Burns State Park
- Loma Vista
- Pfeiffer Beach
- Bixby Bridge
- Garrapata State Park
- Point Lobos State Natural Reserve
- Carmel-by-the-Sea

Driving Notes

Hwy 1 in Big Sur is often touted as the most scenic route in California, and maybe even the US. Drive from north to south to easily pull off at scenic overlooks. The Big Sur section is prone to landslides, especially in rainy winter, so be sure to check for road closures *(roads.dot.ca.gov)* before you set out on your drive.

Breaking Your Journey

For the best views, stop for a bite and a break at Nepenthe (p131) or Ragged Point (p126), or kick back in an Adirondack chair with your toes in the river and a beer in hand at the Big Sur River Inn (p133). For an overnighter, book a rustic room in the redwoods at the historic Deetjen's Big Sur Inn (p130).

Sharael's Tips

BEST MEAL Cacio e pepe pasta at Nate's on Marsh (p125), San Luis Obispo.

FAVORITE VIEW Watching a colony of massive elephant seals plop on shore at the Elephant Seal Vista Point (p127) in San Simeon.

ESSENTIAL STOP Pfeiffer Big Sur State Park (p132) for hiking.

ROAD-TRIP TIP In Big Sur, travel mid-morning through afternoon, to avoid the morning and evening fog that can shroud the views.

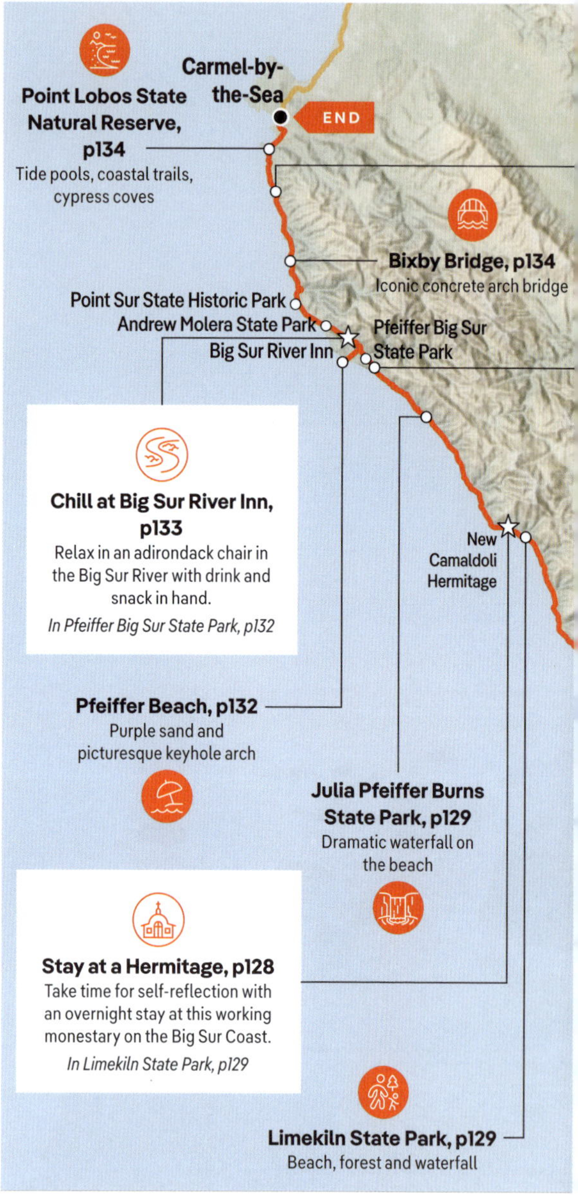

Point Lobos State Natural Reserve, p134
Tide pools, coastal trails, cypress coves

Carmel-by-the-Sea
END

Bixby Bridge, p134
Iconic concrete arch bridge

Point Sur State Historic Park
Andrew Molera State Park
Big Sur River Inn
Pfeiffer Big Sur State Park

Chill at Big Sur River Inn, p133
Relax in an adirondack chair in the Big Sur River with drink and snack in hand.
In Pfeiffer Big Sur State Park, p132

New Camaldoli Hermitage

Pfeiffer Beach, p132
Purple sand and picturesque keyhole arch

Julia Pfeiffer Burns State Park, p129
Dramatic waterfall on the beach

Stay at a Hermitage, p128
Take time for self-reflection with an overnight stay at this working monastery on the Big Sur Coast.
In Limekiln State Park, p129

Limekiln State Park, p129
Beach, forest and waterfall

PREVIOUS STOP Leave Avila Beach's farms and hot springs as you head north to the lively college town of San Luis Obispo.

San Luis Obispo

As you wind your way up the Central Coast, San Luis Obispo (p124) is a destination that you'll want to spend a couple of days exploring. Be prepared for scenic hiking, eclectic dining and art in various formats. The **San Luis Obispo International Film Festival** *(slofilmfest.org)* is a six-day event held every April to celebrate independent cinema. Filmmakers from around the world descend on the city to show thought-provoking, educational and inspiring films that span a variety of topics. The festival debuted in 1993. Film screenings are held at various venues around town, including the independently owned **Palm Theatre** *(thepalmtheatre.com)* – home to the **SLO Film Center**, the 1942 art-deco **Fremont Theater** *(fremontslo.com)* featuring impressive murals adorning the walls and ceiling, and the **Downtown Centre 7** *(themovieexperience.com)* movie complex. Various film screenings and events are also held throughout the year.

For an interesting outing that combines architecture, history and hiking, head to **Poly Canyon** on the **California Polytechnic State University, San Luis Obispo** (Cal Poly SLO) campus, where you'll find the **Architecture Graveyard** *(polycanyon.calpoly.edu/history)*. A roughly 3-mile round-trip hike will take you past more than 20 permanent, large-scale structures built by the university's architectural engineering students, dating from 1964 to 2022. Many of them are in disrepair, but a few have been renovated. The College of Architecture and Environmental Design holds an annual Design Village competition *(designvillage.framer.website)* during which seniors design and construct experimental shelters based on a designated theme. They have to carry their

Morro Bay

building materials to Cal Poly Canyon, spend the weekend in their shelters, then deconstruct and remove them. Check with the Cal Poly parking office for permits and directions *(afd.calpoly.edu/parking)*.

Morro Bay

Leaving San Luis Obispo, you'll head back toward the coast to arrive at Morro Bay. Its most prominent landmark is the 576ft-tall **Morro Rock**, situated at the entrance of **Morro Bay Harbor**. Sea lions often congregate in the area. The rock is part of the 'Nine Sisters' chain of volcanic peaks. Climbing it is not allowed, as it is a protected marine reserve and bird sanctuary. Get an up-close view by parking in the lot off Coleman Dr. In the opposite direction, you'll see three concrete smoke stacks looming 450ft high – part of a defunct 1950s power plant that closed in 2014.

It's worth a stop at the small but interesting **Morro Bay Maritime Museum** *(morrobaymaritime.org)* nearby. From Morro Rock, take Coleman Dr and turn right on Embarcadero. You can't miss it on your left – just look for several large marine vessels displayed outdoors. Get a close look at things like a two-person submersible, a 19th-century fishing boat and a Coast Guard rescue boat. Continue down Embarcadero, then turn left onto Beach St until you reach Main St where you'll find lots of restaurants and motels.

Harmony

Driving north, make a pit stop at the **Brown Butter Cookie Company** *(brownbuttercookies.com)* on S Ocean Ave

> ### HWY 1 ALIASES
>
> A highway by any other name, is still a highway. Hwy 1 goes by many names, most notably and interchangeably, the nickname Pacific Coast Highway or PCH. Alternatively, it is labeled CA 1 (California 1) or SR 1 (State Route 1), the official name it was given in 1939. The entire route is a Blue Star Memorial Highway, in honor of the men and women of the US armed forces. This stretch, from San Luis Obispo to Carmel-by-the-Sea, which includes Big Sur, is a National Scenic Byway (also an All-American Road) due to its unique geography and landmarks, outdoor recreation opportunities and abundance of marine life.

in **Cayucos** to fuel up your trip. Down the highway, you'll see the sign for Harmony *(harmonytown.com)*, population 18. This quirky unincorporated area is worth a stop. The master craftsmanship at **Harmony Glassworks** *(harmonyglassworks.com)* is impressive, and you can watch them in action or take a class to try glassblowing. Grab lunch at Harmony's **Tiny Kitchen** *(tinykitchenharmony.com; 10am-4pm Thu-Mon)* food truck, but leave room for hand-crafted ice cream from **Harmony Valley Creamery** *(harmonyvalleycreamery.com)*, the reason the town began.

continues on p126

See historic sea vessels at the Morro Bay Maritime Museum

15 miles

Harmony

CITY GUIDE:
San Luis Obispo

San Luis Obispo lives up to its nickname SLO as a slow-travel destination with a laid-back vibe, and a focus on sustainability and cultural experiences. It's also home to Cal Poly SLO, a respected public university. Here you can visit a museum, hike one of the peaks or catch a football game

HOW TO

Getting there: Hwy 1 runs right through San Luis Obispo. To get downtown, take exit 202A to merge onto Marsh St, then turn left on Chorro St to reach Higuera St. Amtrak *(amtrak.com)* also stops here.

Getting around: There are parking garages and lots downtown ($2 per hour), as well as pay stations for on-street parking ($2.25 to $2.75). SLO Transit *(slotransit.org)* runs buses ($1.50) and the Old SLO Trolley ($0.50, weekends July to September).

Sleeping: The **Madonna Inn** *(madonnainn.com; $$$)* is an iconic hotel with nostalgic themed rooms. Downtown, **Hotel San Luis Obispo** *(hotel-slo.com; $$$)* offers bright modern rooms, a rooftop bar and a full-service spa, while while budget-friendly options such as **La Quinta** *(wyndhamhotels.com; $$)* can be found along Monterey St in MoJo.

More info: visitslo.com, slocal.com

This small cowboy city offers inspiration at the **San Luis Obispo Museum of Art** *(sloma.org)*, history at **Mission San Luis Obispo de Tolosa** *(missionsanluisobispo.org)*, founded by Father Junipero Serra in 1772, and novelty at the Instagram-famous **Bubblegum Alley**. Every Thursday from 6pm to 9pm, the **Downtown SLO Farmers' Market** *(downtownslo.com/farmers-market)* draws a crowd seeking produce, artisan goods and live music. Situated in wine country, there are several wineries and tasting rooms to choose from. Take 277 S to Edna Valley for award-winning, cool-climate wines, especially Chardonnay and Pinot Noir. Outdoor enthusiasts can hike one of the 'Nine Sisters' peaks.

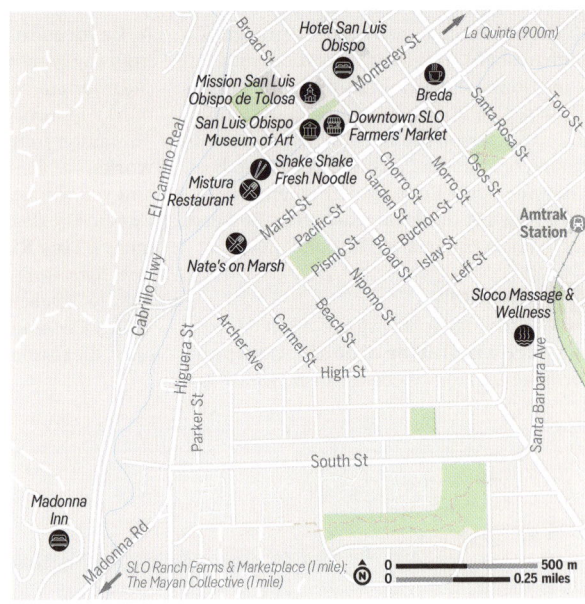

San Luis Obispo

SAN LUIS OBISPO: MADE FOR ROAD TRIPS

Historians widely acknowledge that the 'motel' – a portmanteau of 'motor hotel' – took root in San Luis Obispo in the 1900s. As cars became more mainstream and more people took to open roads, San Luis Obispo's convenient location, midway between Los Angeles and San Francisco, made it the perfect spot to break journeys for a night. Right off Hwy 101, the Spanish mission-style Mo-Tel Inn was in business from 1925 to 1991. Mo-Tel Inn was quite the stop in its prime, and most notably, newlyweds Joe DiMaggio and Marilyn Monroe lunched at the Motel Inn in 1954, after honeymooning in the nearby wine town of Paso Robles. In its heyday, it also offered hot showers, carpeted interiors, plus parking (a must-have included in the US$1.25 back fee when the motel opened). The Mo-Tel Inn became known for its generous cocktail menu and eats, including freshly barbecued steaks and spare ribs. And so popular was the house salad that its dressing was sold in jars.

SLO Ranch Farms & Marketplace

Entering the city from the south, you'll see the **SLO Ranch Farms & Marketplace** (*sloranchfarms.com*) on your left. This new development is a gathering place to dine, shop, and play. Stop by the food hall for pizza, sushi, sandwiches or charcuterie snacks, kick back by a firepit and listen to live music, or take a candle-making class at the **Mayan Collective** (*themayancollective.com*). The Corral is a popular place for kids to interact with farm animals, take a tractor ride or hit the bounce house.

Sloco Massage & Wellness

Taking care of your wellness while traveling is essential. Get a massage, take a fitness class, visit a juice bar. **Sloco Massage & Wellness** (*slocomassage.com*) offers a wide range of services to keep you feeling your best while on the road. For an individualized experience, combine a variety of services, such as massage, infrared sauna, red light therapy, Somodome meditation, cryotherapy, dry salt therapy or an AmpCoil journey. Staying hydrated and getting enough sleep will also help you feel your best to make the most of your trip.

BEST PLACES TO EAT & DRINK

Breda $
Satisfy your sweet tooth with gourmet chocolates and desserts by a Michelin-starred pastry chef. *breda-slo.com*

Shake Shake Fresh Noodle $
Newcomer causing quite the buzz over its hand-pulled noodles. *ssfreshnoodle.com*

Mitsura $$$
Upscale place dishing up authentic Peruvian cuisine. *misturarestaurants.com*

Nate's on Marsh $$$
Enjoy casual Italian and American cuisine, and California wines. *natesonmarsh.com*

Cambria

Approaching Cambria, turn right onto Main St to experience this charming coastal town. In the East Village, visit the **Cambria Historical Museum** *(cambriahistoricalsociety.com)* to learn about the pioneer families that founded the town in the 1860s and wander through the storybook garden at **Spellbound Gift Shop & Garden** *(spellboundherbs.com)*. Continue down Main St for one-of-a-kind shops, casual restaurants and art galleries. At the end of the road, cross the highway and turn left onto Moonstone Beach Dr. Park at Santa Rosa Creek to access **Moonstone Beach Boardwalk**, a flat wooden walkway that parallels the ocean, with benches and viewing platforms.

Hearst Castle

The opulent **Hearst Castle** *(hearstcastle.org; $35; 9am-3pm)* sits perched on a hilltop on the 127-acre San Simeon property. Guided tours are offered daily. Wander through the grand rooms, upstairs suites, cottages and kitchen. Allow two hours for tours. Next up…wildlife viewing at San Simeon's **Elephant Seal Vista Point.**

Ragged Point

Stop at the **Ragged Point Inn** *(raggedpointinn.com)* area to enjoy fine dining at the restaurant, a burger from the snack bar, nibbles and drinks from the market, or a latte and dessert from the coffee shop – a pick-me-up for the drive. There are also picnic tables to use if you packed your own food. Take the tree-covered dirt path past the restaurant to see the *Portal to Big Sur* art piece that perfectly frames the dramatic coastline. Adventurers can take the steep hike down the Ragged Point Cliffside Trail to the black beach below where you can see Black Swift Falls. Too tired to continue the drive? Stay the night in an ocean-view room at the inn. According to Cal Poly scholars, this area is the ancestral home of the traditional lands of the yak tiṭʸu tiṭʸu yak tiɬhini Northern Chumash Tribe of San Luis Obispo county and region.

continues on p129

BEST PLACES TO EAT

Vintage Cheese Company, San Luis Obispo $-$$
Visit the Build Your Own Cheese Box Bar for fresh cheese, dried fruit and nuts – perfect for a picnic. Located in the **SLO Ranch Farms + Market** food hall. *sloranchfarms.com; hours vary*

Big Sur River Inn Restaurant, Big Sur $$
Order the portobello-mushroom sandwich and your favorite drink from the restaurant and take it down to the Big Sur River to eat while seated in an Adirondack chair. *bigsurriverinn.com; 8am-9pm*

Village Corner California Bistro, Carmel $$$
Savor chunky avocado toast made with ciabatta – a house specialty – on the sunny outdoor patio at this Carmel staple. *carmelsvillagecorner.com; 8am-4pm Fri-Wed, to 9pm Thu*

Hike Past Seals

See hundreds of elephant seals from a raised platform at the rookery, as you hike from the Elephant Seal Vista Point to Piedras Blancas Light Station in San Simeon.

HOW TO

Nearest stop: Hearst Castle and San Simeon to the south. Ragged Point is 10.5 miles to the north.

Getting here: Take Hwy 1 north 4.5 miles from Hearst Castle. The parking lot for the Elephant Seal Vista Point is on the left.

When to go: December through March, birthing and breeding season.

Cost: Free-$10

More info: *elephantseal.org, piedrasblancas.org*

One of the best wildlife-viewing experiences on California's Central Coast is seeing the enormous elephant seals in San Simeon – males can weigh up to 5000lb. Park in the dirt lot off Hwy 1. From the free **Elephant Seal Vista Point** *(elephantseal.org),* you look down on hundreds to thousands of these pinnipeds strewn across the beach, flicking sand on themselves to stay cool. The **Elephant Seal Boardwalk & Trail** includes wheelchair-accessible platforms and a half-mile boardwalk that extends north and south of the parking lot.

Piedras Blancas Light Station

The **Piedras Blancas Light Station** *(piedrasblancas.org ; $10)* is a historical landmark, wildlife sanctuary and research station. It's about a 4-mile round-trip hike from the Elephant Seal Vista Point to the entrance gate of the light station. Start on the boardwalk, then take the Boucher Trail to the lighthouse road and turn left. Reservations are required to visit the light station via a docent-led tour, including the Fog Signal Building. During the Hike In Open House dates, you can hike to the light station and tour it for free.

EXPERIENCE ★

Above: Elephant seal; Right: Elephant Seal Vista Point

FROM LEFT: PAUL TESSIER/SHUTTERSTOCK, ARTYART/SHUTTERSTOCK

Stay at a Hermitage

Decompress through meditation while embracing nature and reflecting on spirituality at New Camaldoli Hermitage, a peaceful monastery high above the Pacific Ocean.

HOW TO

Nearest stop: Located between Limekiln State Park to the south and Lucia Lodge slightly to the north.

Getting here: Almost 2 miles past Limekiln State Park, you'll see the sign on the right for the New Camaldoli Hermitage. Turn right onto the steep and windy 2-mile road to get there.

Cost: $145 to $350 per night (two-night minimum), including meals.

More info: contemplation.com

For travelers seeking silence, solitude and self-reflection, New Camaldoli Hermitage offers basic accommodation in a serene setting with expansive ocean views. It is a working Camaldolese Benedictine monastery where Roman Catholic monks lead a life of seclusion while working together as a community. This is not a place to come to chit-chat.

The hermitage offers rooms to visiting guests of any faith who want to disconnect (no cell service or wi-fi) and make time for contemplation and connection with God. Retreat House rooms have shared showers, while guest houses have full private bathrooms. There are also some private hermitages with kitchenettes. All food is provided on a self-serve basis. The property includes a church, a bookstore, a communal kitchen, picnic tables and hiking trails. Travel writer Pico Iyer writes about his time spent in solitude at the hermitage in his book *Aflame: Learning from Silence*. He discovered that taking a break from his hectic lifestyle to 'just sit and watch' had a profound effect on him. Visitors can also participate in retreats that are offered throughout the year.

New Camaldoli Hermitage

Limekiln State Park

As you drive from Ragged Point to **Limekiln State Park** *(parks.ca.gov/limekiln)*, pull over at the **Willow Creek View Point** to see views of San Martin Rock. Time permitting, take the road down to **Willow Creek Beach** for a scenic stop with a black pebble beach, big boulders and striking cliffs. If you're in the mood for a hike through the redwoods or a stroll along the beach, make a stop at Limekiln State Park. The site is known for its historic limekilns that were used in the 1800s for lime calcining. Hike the half-mile **Limekiln Trail** to see the kilns (check for trail closures). At the time of research, the campgrounds here were closed until further notice. Between here and the next stop, you can turn right to visit **New Camaldoli Hermitage**.

Lucia Lodge

A midway point on this journey is **Lucia Lodge** *(lucialodge.com; $$$)*. You may recognize it as the fictional Sealight Inn from the Netflix show *Ratched*. It has been in operation since the 1930s, but in 2021 the store and restaurant were destroyed in a fire – so bring your own food. The rustic accommodations are perched on a cliff, in a remote location overlooking the Pacific. There are no TVs or phones, and typically no cell service, but guests can access wi-fi. It's a great place to disconnect from your devices, embrace nature and finally read that book you packed.

Esalen Institute

Since 1962, the **Esalen Institute** *(esalen.org; $$$)* has been fostering self-discovery and growth through a variety of workshops focusing on things like empowerment, healing, self-love,

McWay Falls

tranquility and manifesting. Classes can include yoga, meditation, hiking, dancing, journaling or drumming. It was an early proponent of the Human Potential Movement. The expansive oceanfront property features hot springs, meditation hut, organic gardens, a swimming pool, an orchard, a bookstore and a spacious lawn area. Visitors attending multiday events can choose to stay in accommodations such as a shared bunk-bed dorms, a standard room with private bathroom, a yurt or a guest house. Access is by reservation only. Day passes are available for spa treatments and access to the hot springs, and allow attendance to open classes.

Julia Pfeiffer Burns State Park

One of the most photographed landmarks in Big Sur is **McWay Falls**, which cascades 80ft down onto the beach

Along the Way We Met...

NIKO MALKOVICH The library is such a magical place for people to come together. We get people from all over the world, but it's also maintained its roots, which is what Henry Miller would have wanted. We've done a really good job of bringing the arts to Big Sur and keeping the creative spirit going.

Niko is a board member and treasurer at the Henry Miller Memorial Library in Big Sur.

NIKO'S TIP: *Big Sur is a place for you to slow down. Our motto here is 'Where nothing happens'.*

in **Julia Pfeiffer Burns State Park** *(parks.ca.gov/?page_id=578)*. The McWay Waterfall Trail leads hikers to an epic view of the falls (there is no beach access). Unfortunately, the trail is closed for long-term repairs. There is a tiny lookout point 200yd north of the park entrance, on the ocean side of Hwy 1. The park does offer two hike-in camp sites, a picnic area and hiking on Ewoldsen Trail. Day use is $10 through self-registration.

Deetjen's Big Sur Inn

In Big Sur you can overnight in a rustic room at a historic hideaway that has been welcoming guests since the 1930s. **Deetjen's Big Sur Inn** *(deetjens.org; 831-667-2377; $$$)* is set among the redwoods with original handcrafted buildings that offer a cozy escape from the cool climate. Rooms can be viewed online, but you have to call to book. No TVs, cell service or wi-fi – just the sights and sounds of nature. For dining, step out of the fog and into the warm and welcoming restaurant, serving breakfast and dinner. There are four dining areas, with fireplaces, candles and string lights creating a cozy, home-like atmosphere.

Henry Miller Memorial Library

Literary, art and history buffs will enjoy visiting the **Henry Miller Memorial Library** *(henrymiller.org)* with its extensive bookstore carrying works by authors such as Henry Miller, Jack Kerouac, Hunter S Thompson and Kurt Vonnegut. Upon entering the property, visitors walk through and past intriguing art pieces constructed from reclaimed and recycled materials. The library regularly hosts events such as poetry readings and concerts.

Nepenthe

A trip to Big Sur wouldn't be complete without a visit to **Nepenthe** *(nepenthe.com; $$$)*. Open since 1949, it draws travelers from around the world not only for the food, but also for the spectacular views of the Big Sur Coastline. Dine on the outdoor patio or by the roaring indoor fireplace. Make reservations in advance since it is a popular stopping point. For a casual breakfast or lunch with outdoor dining, head to Café Kevah. The Phoenix Shop carries everything from fine jewelry and books to home goods and clothing. Across the street from Nepenthe, browse the **Hawthorne Gallery** *(hawthornegallery.com)*, where the artwork and architecture are impressive.

BEST PLACES TO SLEEP

Hotel San Luis Obispo $$$
Enjoy a glass of local wine at the rooftop bar, a refined steak dinner on the patio, or a relaxing spa treatment at this luxury hotel in Downtown San Luis Obispo. *hotel-slo.com*

Pfeiffer Big Sur State Park $
Camp among the redwoods along the Big Sur River. The park features a nature center, restaurant and lots of hiking trails. Booking six months ahead is recommended. *parks.ca.gov/?page_id=570*

La Petit Pali $$$
With two locations in Carmel, these boutique hotels are cozy and quaint, with in-room fireplaces, free champagne breakfast, and bicycles for cruising around town. *lepetitpali.com*

Café Kevah

Keyhole Rock

Loma Vista

As you wind your way north, you will pass by **Post Ranch Inn** and **Alila Ventana Big Sur**, both of which offer ultra-luxury, all-inclusive accommodations. **Ventana Campground** offers tent sites and glamping cabins surrounded by the redwood forest with Big Sur River running through it. About a half-mile north, you'll come across Loma Vista. Fill up with gas here since the next station is 40 miles away. The deli makes fresh sandwiches to order and the market has the largest selection of goods in Big Sur.

For a beer and a bite, the **Big Sur Taphouse** (bigsurtaphouse.com) is a good call – don't miss the hidden patio. Meet and support local artists at **Big Sur Artworks** (bigsurartworks.com) and buy products from local vendors at **Mother Botanical & Shop**.

Pfeiffer Beach

The next sight is the world-famous **Pfeiffer Beach** (fs.usda.gov; 9am-8pm; per vehicle $15), known for its patches of purple sand (not the entire beach) caused by manganese garnet washed down from the surrounding hillsides. The other point of interest is **Keyhole Rock**, which is popular with photographers. There is no sign for the turn-off. About a half-mile past Point Loma, turn at the yellow 'Narrow Road' sign on your left to drive 2.2 miles to the beach. As it is a federal beach, you can't use your state park pass. Go early – there is usually a line of cars and the parking lot fills up fast.

For information about where to go, what to do and what to see in Big Sur, stopping at **Big Sur Station** (lpforest.org/big-sur-station; 9am-4pm) is essential. The park rangers there will provide free maps, directions and advice for making the most of your time in this part of the Central Coast.

Pfeiffer Big Sur State Park

Drive a half-mile north on the scenic wooded highway and turn right at the signs for **Pfeiffer Big Sur State Park** (parks.ca.gov/pfeiffer). This often crowded 1348-acre park is an outdoor enthusiast's dream. Hikers can explore the 8 miles of trails, including the wheelchair-accessible 0.45-mile River Path and the 2-mile round-trip Valley View Trail to the base of **Pfeiffer Falls**. There is no beach access. Bring your gear to overnight at the campground, in a canopy of redwoods with the river lulling you to sleep. For more creature comforts, stay at the **Big Sur Lodge** (bigsurlodge.com; $$$) with a restaurant, coffee bar and fully stocked market. Dip your toes in the water at **Big Sur River Inn**.

continues on p134

Chill at Big Sur River Inn

Relax in the Big Sur River in an inviting Adirondack chair to take in the sights and sounds of Big Sur.

HOW TO

Nearest stop: Pfeiffer Big Sur State Park to the south; Andrew Molara State Park to the north.

Getting here: From Pfeiffer Big Sur State Park, continue north on Hwy 1. The Inn will be on your left.

When to go: Go in the fall or spring to avoid the summer crowds and the wet winter.

Cost: $$–$$$ (lunch menu $14 to $38)

More info: bigsurriverinn.com

Take a break from the road at Big Sur River Inn. The must-do activity is to sink into an Adirondack chair in the Big Sur River, shaded by trees, with your toes in the refreshing water. Breathe in the fresh air and let the rippling current relax you. Bring your suit if you want to get more than your feet wet. If your tummy is rumbling, grab a burger or salad at the restaurant (or order a picnic lunch to eat in the river), head to the burrito bar at the General Store, or get a scoop at the Ice Cream Bus. To rest up from the drive, spend a night or two in a riverside suite at the Inn, which also has an outdoor swimming pool. A portion of the fee supports the Big Sur Health Center, as part of the Kind Traveler *(kindtraveler.com)* network. It's also a good base camp to spend some extended time exploring the miles of hiking trails in the nearby state parks.

Big Sur River Inn

Andrew Molera State Park

From the Big Sur River Inn, cruise along Hwy 1 for about 2.5 miles to reach **Andrew Molera State Park** *(parks.ca.gov/?page_id =582)*. You'll leave the dense redwood forest behind as you embark on this relatively undeveloped swath of land. Spreading across nearly 5000 acres, it has a vast network of hiking trails and access to the broad, barren beach. From the Creamery Meadow Trailhead parking lot, take the 2.2-mile round-trip trail to **Andrew Molera Beach** (swimming not recommended), passing near the **Molera Ranch House Museum** and **Ventana Wildlife Society's Discovery Center** *(ventanaws.org)*. If you're up for it, you can also bed down at the hike-in campground. Reservations required.

Point Sur State Historic Park

Next up is **Point Sur State Historic Park** *(parks.ca.gov/?page_id=565)*, which includes the **Point Sur Lightstation** and the Cold War–era **Point Sur Naval Facility**. This historic lighthouse has remained in continuous operation since it was built in 1889, first by lighthouse keepers and then via automation starting in 1974. Docent-led tours *(pointsur. org)* are available for both, but are on a first-come, first-served basis. Reservations are not accepted. Plan your road trip to arrive at this remote location on specific tour days and times. You'll get to explore the area, climb the stairs to the top of the lighthouse, learn about the once top-secret mission at the naval facility, and take in the dramatic ocean views from the 361ft-high volcanic rock that the park is perched on. Dress in layers, as it can be windy.

Bixby Bridge

The concrete arched design of the 1932 Bixby Bridge (or Bixby Creek Bridge), with the rugged coastline as a backdrop, makes it one of the most photographed bridges in California – and a very popular selfie spot. The lookout point is on the left after you cross the bridge, which can be tricky since you'll have to cross Hwy 1. Be forewarned, fog can occasionally block the view.

Garrapata State Park

Hwy 1 runs parallel to the ocean along this stretch, and you'll see several pull-offs with trail markers for **Garrapata State Park** *(parks .ca.gov/garrapata)*. The coastal bluff-top trails are mostly flat and offer picturesque views of the ocean, sandy beaches and rocky seashore, which are part of the **Monterey Bay National Marine Sanctuary** *(montereybay.noaa.gov)*. Bring binoculars to watch for whales, sea lions, sea otters and pelicans. The park also extends inland and features hiking through canyons and forests. The access point is Gate 8/Soberanes Canyon Trailhead. From here, you can hike inland on the Soberanes Canyon Trail as an out-and-back hike or along the bluffs on the Soberanes Point Trail that leads to Painters Point and Soberanes Creek Falls. The Rocky Trail Ridge was closed at time of research.

Point Lobos State Natural Reserve

As you get closer to Carmel-by-the-Sea, **Point Lobos State Natural Reserve** *(parks.ca.gov/ pointlobos)* provides myriad ways to interact with the natural environment. Spot sea lions from the bluff on the **Sea Lion Point Trail**. After

Bixby Bridge

you pass Carmel Highlands General Store – a great place to stop for water and snacks before or after a hike – take the Point Lobos road, off Hwy 1 on your left. The road leads to the Cypress Information Center, where you can get ideas on how to maximize your time at the park. Along the road, there are a number of places to park to access trails with ocean views, beach access or groves of shady trees. Legendary landscape photographer Ansel Adams captured the essence of the area through his surreal photographs.

LANDSLIDES & ROAD CLOSURES

Heavy rain in winter can saturate the soil of the steep slopes along Hwy 1, causing notorious landslides, which can lead to closures of the two-lane highway. In February 2024, the Saint Regent's slide caused a 6.8-mile segment of the road to collapse. Since then, Cal Trans has been working tirelessly to reopen the road, but at the time of publication there was no set date for reopening. Check for road closures (roads.dot.ca.gov) before your trip. With the Saint Regent's closure, visitors from the south can drive as far north as Lucia; from the north, you can drive all the way down to Esalen. The PCH is expected to reopen in Big Sur in March 2026.

- Bixby Bridge — 6.5 miles
- Garrapata State Park — 4.5 miles
- Point Lobos State Natural Reserve — 4 miles
- Carmel-by-the-Sea

Henry Miller Memorial Library
SHARAEL KOLBERG/LONELY PLANET

INSIGHT

Big Sur: A Creative's Muse

For decades, Big Sur has drawn writers, artists and musicians seeking a quiet and inspiring space to create enduring works of art and literature, with nature as their muse.

WORDS BY **SHARAEL KOLBERG**
Sharael Kolberg is a native Californian who has written about the state from top to bottom

THE THICK REDWOOD forest, jagged cliffs, breaking waves and misty fog have provided a serene backdrop for creative minds to embrace their imagination. The remoteness allows space for ideas to take form, away from the chaotic or mundane day-to-day tasks and responsibilities. It was the original homeland of Indigenous people, including the Esselen Tribe, dating back nearly 6000 years.

In 1937, the Big Sur stretch of Hwy 1, spanning roughly from Ragged Point (p126) to Carmel Highlands, opened to the public, using prisoners from San Quentin for hard labor. The route allowed city dwellers to escape the hustle and bustle and immerse themselves in the natural world. Due to its stunning coastal beauty, it's one of the most scenic drives in the US, and in 1966 it was designated as California's first official State Scenic Highway by then First Lady, Lady Bird Johnson.

Writing in Solitude

One of the most influential and controversial writers associated with Big Sur was American author and artist Henry Miller. His unconventional and provocative writing caused some of his works, such as *Tropic of Cancer* (Obelisk Press, Paris, 1934), to be banned in the US. He moved to Big Sur in 1944 and spent nearly two decades there, writing several books. In *Big Sur and the Oranges of Hieronymus Bosch* (New Directions Publishing Corporation, 1957), he writes, 'One's destination is never a place but rather a new way of looking at things.' For Miller, Big Sur seemed to embody a philosophical freedom that allowed him to compose raw literature portraying life in an untamed landscape.

Miller's unconventional lifestyle, removed from societal norms, inspired the Beatniks to journey to Big Sur in the 1960s, for introspection and refuge among a community of kindred spirits. In contrast to Miller's uplifting account of the area, Beatnik author Jack Kerouac penned *Big Sur* (Farrar, Straus, Cudahy, 1962) in strife. Initially retreating to the solitude of Big Sur to escape fame, he found the isolation had a profoundly negative impact on his state of mind.

Around the same time, up-and-coming journalist Hunter S. Thompson (later known for his *Fear and Loathing* books) published an article entitled 'Big Sur: The Tropic of Henry Miller' (*Rogue* magazine, 1961). He is said to have been living and working at what is now the Esalen Institute (p129), which was established in 1962 and was the birthplace of the Human Potential Movement that pushed the boundaries of untapped human abilities through personal growth workshops and coaching.

Painting the Landscape

Henry Miller also used painting as a creative outlet, and created thousands of rudimentary watercolor paintings during his time in Big Sur. Due to his literary fame, his artwork has been exhibited worldwide, and original pieces sell for thousands of dollars.

His dearest friend, Emil White, worked casually as Miller's assistant. The two developed a deep kinship over shared interests, which led Miller to dedicate *Big Sur and the Oranges of Hieronymus Bosch* to White. Inspired by Miller, White took up painting, capturing the surrounding Big Sur environment through what's been called a folk-art style. He sold his oil paintings throughout the local community and to visitors to the area.

Shortly after Miller's death, in 1981 White converted his small cabin in the woods into the Henry Miller Memorial Library (p130), as a tribute to his friend and as a resource and venue for promoting the arts in Big Sur. The nonprofit library is less of a memorial, which Miller was against, and more of a bookstore celebrating his work. It carries Miller's books, as well as literature from other Big Sur authors, and regularly hosts events such as open poetry nights, concerts, writing workshops and lectures.

Just north of the library, you'll find Nepenthe restaurant (p131), perched between the Pacific and the Santa Lucia Mountains, which has been

> '"One's destination is never a place but rather a new way of looking at things." [– Henry Miller] For Miller, Big Sur seemed to embody a philosophical freedom that allowed him to compose raw literature portraying life in an untamed landscape.'

welcoming locals, tourists and creative types since 1949. The property, which started with a log cabin built in 1925, was expanded to include the restaurant, Café Kevah and the Phoenix Shop – designed by Rowen Maiden, an architectural student of Frank Lloyd Wright. The original cabin, where Miller briefly stayed with novelist Lynda Sargent in 1944, still stands above the restaurant. The indoor-outdoor restaurant and open-air cafe offer some of the most outstanding views of the Big Sur Coast.

The Phoenix Shop features a wide variety of carefully curated products – many made by local artists – such as books, clothing, jewelry, housewares, paintings, bath products, toys and games, and garden decor. Some of the merchandise is created by featured artists who are relatives of Nepenthe founders, Lolly and Bill Fassett. Their children include quilter Kaffe Fassett, knitter Holly Fassett, quilter Dorcas Owens née Fassett, and grandchildren fabric artist Holly Kristina Rose and painter Erin Lee Gafill, who founded the Big Sur Arts Initiative in 1998.

Across the street, the Hawthorne Gallery (p131) showcases work from seven members of the multi-talented Hawthorne family – ranging from paintings and jewelry to glass and sculpture – as well as pieces from other accomplished artists. A relative newcomer to Big Sur, the two-story gallery opened in 1995, and the architecture itself is a work of art. On the 2nd floor, there is a deck featuring an outdoor sculpture gallery and expansive views of the vast ocean and rugged coastline, which has been a muse for artists for decades.

As you continue north on Hwy 1, the Loma Vista area is home to Big Sur Artworks (p132), a collective of local artists whose work mainly features the colorful landscape of Big Sur, in various mediums and styles, including plein air painting. They also offer occasional painting workshops. The gallery includes paintings by artist Leslie Drew, who captures the natural environment in oil on canvas. 'It's an endless supply of vistas,' says Drew. 'Never a shortage of inspiration.'

Singing to the Sea

Like other artists, musicians also retreated to Big Sur to make time for self-reflection and to focus on songwriting. In the 1960s, the area drew those who shared counterculture values, and 1964 kicked off the annual Big Sur Folk Festival at Esalen. The intimate concert venue drew big names, including Joan Baez, Joni Mitchell and Crosby, Stills, Nash & Young. Johnny Rivers' 1968 song 'Going Back to Big Sur,' reflects his time there. Contemporary singer-songwriter Alanis Morrisette mentions many of the influential people of the area in her song "Big Sur," including the Ohlone, the Esselen, the Salinan, Henry [Miller], Jack Kerouac and Julia [Pfeiffer].

Keeping the Muse Alive

To this day, writers are still drawn to Big Sur as a place to concentrate on their work, free of the distractions of everyday life. Travel writer and author Pico Iyer has been sojourning to Big Sur since 1991 to delve into a world of silence, among a community of Camaldolese Benedictine monks at New Camaldoli Hermitage (p128), near Lucia. He recounts his time there in his newest book *Aflame: Learning from Silence* (Riverhead Books, 2025), where he learns, 'It's not just freedom from distraction and noise and rush: it's a reminder of some deeper truths [I] misplaced along the way.'

> 'It's not just freedom from distraction and noise and rush: it's a reminder of some deeper truths he misplaced along the way.' – Pico Iyer

Sign for Nepenthe, Phoenix Shop and Café Kevah (p131)
BP CUFF/ALAMY

Carmel-by-the-Sea

With behemoth redwoods and a rocky coastline in the rearview mirror, the landscape shifts to a concatenation of state beaches lapped at by the ocean in every hue of blue. From Steinbeck Country, the rural road juts north, with no urban sprawl encroaching on the natural landscape – just wild coastline, expansive open spaces and miles of lulling ocean views. Pass through easygoing seaside towns – where a surfboard is a prized possession and waves are for riding, photographing and meditating – and end in the cosmopolitan City by the Bay.

Sharael Kolberg

Pigeon Point Light Station (p152)
MARTINA BIRNBAUM/SHUTTERSTOCK

San Francisco

130 MILES · 3-HOUR DRIVE

THIS LEG:

- Carmel-by-the-Sea
- Monterey
- Fort Ord Dune State Park
- Moss Landing State Beach
- Seacliff State Beach
- Capitola Village
- Santa Cruz
- Wilder Ranch State Park
- Año Nuevo State Park
- Pigeon Point Light Station
- Half Moon Bay
- Moss Beach Distillery
- Devil's Slide
- San Francisco

Driving Notes

The Central Coast can be foggy and crowded in the summer, and wet and desolate in the winter. Build time into your itinerary to stop at attractions, such as the Monterey Bay Aquarium, the Santa Cruz Beach Boardwalk and Pigeon Point Lighthouse. There are ample opportunities for long walks on the beach or hitting the multitude of hiking trails.

Breaking Your Journey

For convenient stopping points with a variety of dining options, overnight accommodations and points of interest, consider spending a day or two at the start of the journey in charming Carmel or bustling Monterey, or further north in vibrant Santa Cruz. Closer to San Francisco, stop in the seaside town of Half Moon Bay for a stroll down historic Main St.

Sharael's Tips

BEST MEAL Kale and quinoa salad at historic Moss Beach Distillery (p151).

FAVORITE VIEW The twinkling lights of the Santa Cruz Beach Boardwalk illuminating the night sky (p150).

ESSENTIAL STOP Scenic 17-Mile Drive from Carmel-by-the-Sea to Pacific Grove (p144).

ROAD-TRIP TIP Pack binoculars to stop at lookouts and scan the ocean for gray, blue and humpback whales.

Walk along a Classic Main Street, p154
Experience the small town charm of a coastal gem while shopping and dining on Main St.

Devil's Slide, p153
Coastal multi-use trail

Half Moon Bay

San Francisco — END

Moss Beach Distillery, p151
Dining on a patio with ocean views

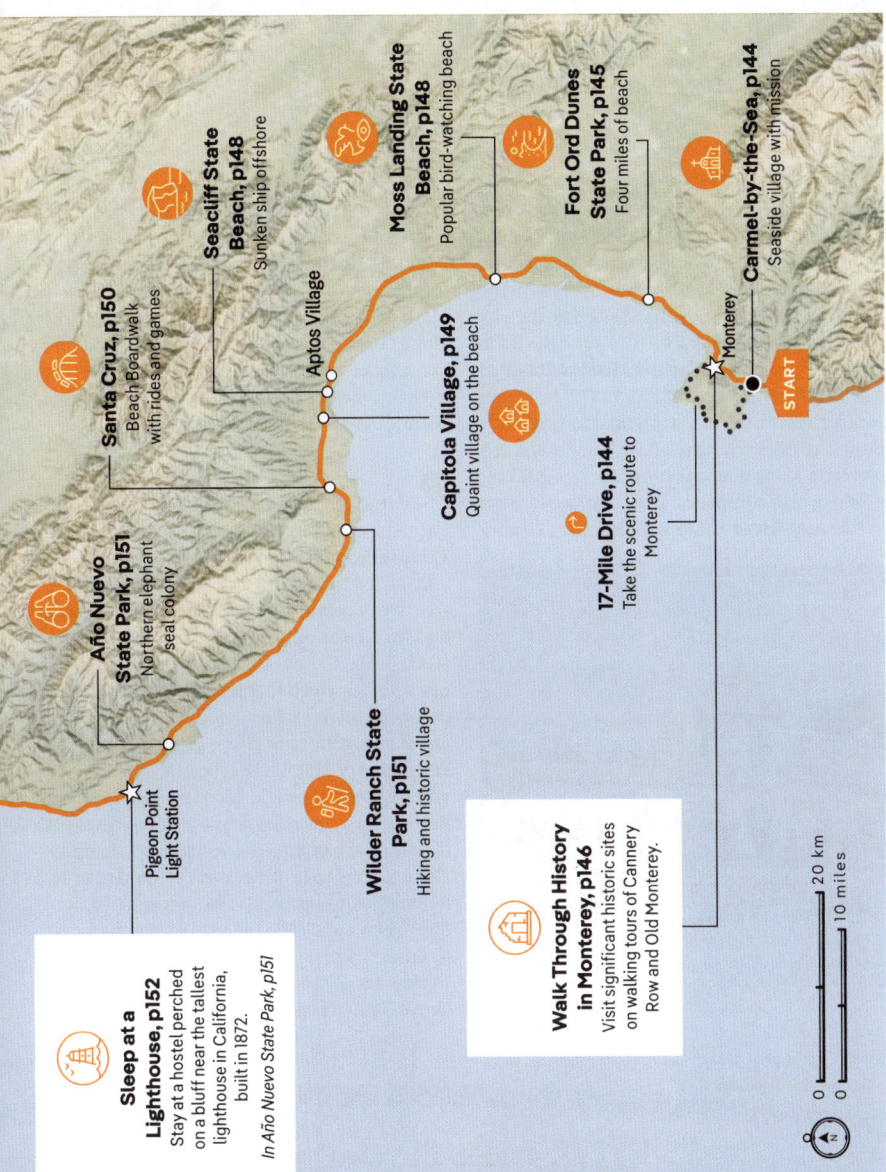

PREVIOUS STOP Leave behind the Big Sur National Scenic Byway as you enter Carmel-by-the Sea, with pretty cottages and a white-sand beach.

Carmel-by-the-Sea

Carmel is known for its storybook cottages, white-sand **Carmel Beach** – where dogs can frolic off-leash – and art galleries galore, showcasing artistic representations of the inspiring natural landscape. Entering the city from the south on Hwy 1, turn left onto Rio Rd to get to the enchanting **Carmel Mission Basilica** *(carmelmission.org)*. Founded in 1771 by Father Junípero Serra, this is also his final resting place. From the mission, turn left on Rio Rd and left on Santa Lucia Ave to connect to Scenic Rd for a loop drive with spectacular ocean views. Stop at **Carmel River State Beach** *(parks.ca.gov/?page_id=567)*, where birds flock to the lagoon, then head to **Ocean Ave** for luxury shopping, gourmet eats and boutique stays. Pop in to the adorable **Cottage of Sweets** *(cottageofsweets.com; 10am-10pm; $)* for fudge, licorice and chocolate delights. See one of the original, quirky Hugh Comstock cottages, the **Tuck Box** *(Dolores St btwn Ocean & 7th Ave)*, just off Ocean Ave. For a quirky souvenir, swing by City Hall to get a free permit to wear heels higher than 2in.

DETOUR: 17-Mile Drive

After cruising Ocean Ave, as you leave Carmel-by-the-Sea, take a detour on the scenic **17-mile Drive** *(pebblebeach.com/17-mile-drive)* – managed by Pebble Beach Resorts. Take Ocean Ave west towards **Carmel Sunset Beach** and turn right onto San Antonio Ave to enter through the Carmel Gate. There is a $12.25 fee per vehicle, which includes a map showing 17 points of interest. Each stop features signage about its significance. Stops include places like Huckleberry Hill, the Restless Sea, Seal Rock and the Lone Cypress – used as Pebble Beach Resorts' logo since 1919. Show your receipt to get discounts at participating shops and restaurants along the way. The drive attracts more than 1.5 million visitors per year, so be prepared to wait in line to enter and exit. The road serpentines past beaches, points, rocks, massive mansions and world-class golf courses. Leave through the Pacific Grove Gate to make your way into **Monterey**.

Carmel Mission Basilica

Carmel-by-the-Sea

Visit the Carmel Mission Basilica, founded in 1771

Take a detour on scenic 17-Mile Drive

4 miles

Fort Ord Dunes State Park

Fort Ord Dunes State Park

This 1000-acre park includes a 4-mile stretch of beach on Monterey Bay and historic ammunition bunkers built into the dunes – remnants of Fort Ord, an army training camp. From the parking lot, it is a quarter-mile walk to the ocean, through a coastal landscape of windswept golden dunes. Look for the self-guided audio-tour signs to use your mobile device to learn about the area. The **Monterey Bay Coastal Recreational Trail** parallels the park. It is an 18-mile paved biking and walking path that runs from Pacific Grove to Castroville, along the former Southern Pacific Railroad line. The closest access point is at the north end of the park, off Imjin Pkwy.

continues on p148

BEST PLACES TO EAT

Zelda's on the Beach, Capitola Village $$-$$$
Beachfront dining with an expansive outdoor patio on the sand, pier and ocean views, and a menu featuring fresh seafood dishes, steak and salads. *zeldasonthebeach.com; from 8am*

Moss Beach Distillery, Moss Beach $$-$$$
A historic landmark (that is not an actual distillery) serving California Coastal cuisine, with a dog-friendly patio and unmatched ocean views. Beware of the 'Blue Lady' ghost. *mossbeachdistillery.com; noon-7:30pm*

Beach Chalet Brewery & Restaurant, San Francisco $$$
Classy 2-story restaurant with house-brewed beer and fresh seafood, at the westernmost tip of Golden Gate Park, overlooking Ocean Beach. Historic murals on the 1st floor. *beachchalet.com; 9am-8pm Mon-Wed, 9am-9pm Thu & Fri, 10am-9pm Sat, 10am-8pm Sun*

Monterey

Take a historic walking tour through Old Monterey

9 miles

Fort Ord Dunes State Park

Walk Through History in Monterey

The town's historic roots can be seen in Old Monterey and beyond.

Nearest Stop: Carmel-by-the-Sea

Getting there: While Hwy 1 does run through the city, the historic sites are in or around Old Monterey. From Pacific Grove, take Lighthouse Ave. From Carmel-by-the-Sea, exit at 399B towards Monterey, turn left on Soledad and Dr, and right on Pacific St.

When to go: Avoid summer months, as they can be hot and crowded.

Tip: Wear good walking shoes. If you visit between Memorial Day and Labor Day, take the free, open-air, electric MST Trolley that runs a round trip between Monterey Transit Plaza and the Monterey Bay Aquarium *(montereybayaquarium.org)*.

More info: *seemonterey.com*

Monterey State Historic Park

Start your trip to Monterey by learning about its past through a visit to the **Monterey State Historic Park** *(parks.ca.gov/mshp)*. The park consists of 11 historic buildings, and secret gardens. Begin at the **Pacific House Museum** *(20 Custom House Plaza)*, where you can browse the interpretive center or take an hour-long tour of the park. For an inside look at the **Robert Louis Stevenson House** *(530 Houston St)* or **Larkin House** *(464 Calle Principal)*, take a 45-minute guided tour. Tours are offered on a first-come, first-served basis. To explore on your own, try the cell-phone audio tour available. Numbers are listed at each site.

Old Fisherman's Wharf

At **Old Fisherman's Wharf** *(montereywharf.com)*, you can shop for nautical-themed souvenirs, dine on fresh seafood such as clam chowder in a sourdough bread bowl, chew on freshly pulled saltwater taffy, or enjoy the view of **Monterey Bay** and its active marine life. Before

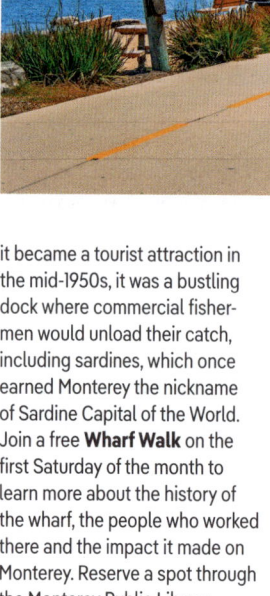

it became a tourist attraction in the mid-1950s, it was a bustling dock where commercial fishermen would unload their catch, including sardines, which once earned Monterey the nickname of Sardine Capital of the World. Join a free **Wharf Walk** on the first Saturday of the month to learn more about the history of the wharf, the people who worked there and the impact it made on Monterey. Reserve a spot through the Monterey Public Library *(monterey.gov/library/events)*.

Walking Tours

As you're walking the streets of Monterey, look for the round

BEST SEAFOOD

Monterey Bay is teeming with fish and shellfish that are caught or harvested daily to create fresh seafood dishes. Beachfront **Salt Wood Kitchen and Oysterette** (saltwoodkitchenandoyster ette.com; 5:30-9pm daily, plus 10am-2pm Sat & Sun; $$$) at Sanctuary Beach Resort serves Monterey Bay Rockfish 'n' chips, Shake's **Old Fisherman's Grotto** (oldfishermansgrotto. com; 11am-9pm; $$$) makes 'Monterey style' clam chowder in a sourdough bread bowl, and the casual **Dock Side Fish Market** (15 Fishermans Wharf; $), on Old Fisherman's Wharf, has crab and shrimp cocktail on ice. Consult Monterey Bay Aquarium's Seafood Watch guide (seafoodwatch.org) for sustainable options.

yellow **Path of History markers** embedded in the sidewalk. These designate a 2-mile, self-guided walking route with 55 historical points of interest. Look for the bronze signs at each stop (shaped like the historic Colton Hall) to read about the significance of the place. Download the Monterey Walking **Tour** app or pick up a printed brochure at the Pacific House Museum. At **Cannery Row** (canneryrow.com), you can navigate 27 sites related to Monterey's fishing and canning industries using the Cannery Row Walking Map app.

Above: Near Old Fisherman's Wharf

Moss Landing State Beach

Whether you want to fish, picnic, horseback ride, view wildlife or walk barefoot on the beach, **Moss Landing State Beach** *(parks.ca.gov/?page_id=574)* – part of the Monterey Bay National Marine Sanctuary – is an easy stopping point. Don't go swimming because there is an aggressive rip tide, although you might see experienced surfers and windsurfers taking advantage of the waves and wind. Heading towards the beach on Hwy 1 is **Moss Landing Wildlife Area**, but the parking is minimal, and there's plenty of wildlife viewing at **Elkhorn Slough**, adjacent to the beach. It's a great place for bird-watching as it's on the Pacific Flyway, a bird migratory path that runs from Alaska to Patagonia. To access the beach, turn left onto Jetty Rd, where you'll find free parking. Looming over the area are the 500ft-tall twin smokestacks, relics of the 1950s Moss Landing Power Plant.

Rancho San Andrés Castro Adobe Park

A little off route, the **Rancho San Andrés Castro Adobe Park Property** *(parks.ca.gov/?page_id=22271)* is an 8000-acre Mexican rancho from the 1800s that features a two-story Castro Adobe hacienda. The property is open to the public via docent-led tours during free Open House days. The docents attempt to recreate what life might have been like living here, through traditional attire, authentic music, vivid storytelling and educational displays. Register for a 15-minute time slot prior to arriving. With further renovations in the works, the site is set to become California's newest state historic park. To reach the property, located in Watsonville, take exit 428 for Buena Vista Dr, then turn left at Old Adobe Rd, and drive about a mile through rural neighborhoods.

Aptos Village

Continuing north, exit 433B and take Soquel Dr into Aptos Village. This small town dates back to the 1800s and features historic architecture, giving it a unique charm. It is situated between the ocean and the beach, and is a gateway to the **Forest of Nisene Marks State Park** *(parks.ca.gov/?page_id=666)*. If your tummy is growling, grab breakfast at **Cat & Cloud Cafe**, a barbecue sandwich from **Aptos St Barbecue**, or casual Italian food at **Mentone**, a Michelin Bib Gourmand restaurant. To head from the village to the beach, take Soquel Dr and turn left onto State Park Dr.

Seacliff State Beach

Wannabe treasure-hunters and archeologists will find **Seacliff State Beach** *(parks.ca.gov/?page_id=543)* fascinating, with the possibility of spotting fossils in the surrounding sea cliffs that could be millions of years old. If you do find one, you are restricted from taking it home with you. From the beach, you can't miss another relic, the 1930s sunken concrete ship, the SS *Palo Alto*, sticking out of the water. Originally built as an entertainment venue, the ship was abandoned due to bankruptcy. A storm in 2023 damaged a pier leading to the ship, as well as the state beach campground. The pier was ultimately removed, and the campground remains closed. This beach is good for swimming, features a visitor center, and is connected to **New Brighton State Beach** *(parks.ca.gov/?page_id=542)*. After a day in the sun, cool down with a housemade scoop of ice

Bring binoculars for spectacular bird-watching

- Fort Ord Dunes State Park
- 13 miles
- Moss Landing State Beach
- 11 miles
- Rancho San Andrés Castro Adobe Park Property

Capitola

cream at **Marianne's** *(mariannesicecream.com; 218 State Park Dr)* in Aptos.

Capitola Village

The quaint beachside town of **Capitola** claims to be the oldest seaside resort town in California, founded in 1874. From Seacliff State Beach, it's only about 3 miles to charming **Capitola Village** *(capitolavillage.com)* – take Hwy 1 north, exit at Park Ave and turn left onto Monterey Ave. Throngs of travelers still flock to the village to relax on **Capitola Beach**, fish off the 855ft, revitalized **Capitola Wharf**, feast on fresh seafood at one of the restaurants along the

BEST PLACES TO SLEEP

Sanctuary Beach Resort $$$
Secluded luxury beachfront resort in Monterey with beach firepits, holistic seaside spa, wellness classes, a dog-stick library, and an oyster bar and sophisticated restaurant serving wood-fired fare. *thesanctuarybeachresort.com*

HI Pigeon Point Lighthouse Hostel $
Private or shared oceanside budget accommodation in Pescadero on a bluff next to a 115ft-tall historic lighthouse with a cliffside hot tub in a dark sky preserve. *hiusa.org*

Ritz-Carlton, Half Moon Bay $$$
Five-star bluff-top resort featuring luxury rooms with private terraces, sustainable cuisine, full-service spa, modern fitness center and two championship golf courses. *ritzcarlton.com/en/hotels/hafrz-the-ritz-carlton-half-moon-bay*

8 miles	1 mile		3.5 miles	
Aptos Village	Stop for homemade ice cream at Marianne's	Seacliff State Beach		Capitola Village

Swings, Santa Cruz Beach Boardwalk

Esplanade, such as **Zelda's on the Beach** (p145), or shop at the boutiques carrying swimwear, beach toys and seaside souvenirs. Book a stay in one of the highly photographed, brightly colored suites on the beach through **Capitola Venetian Vacation Rentals** *(capitolavenetian.com)*.

Roadside Farm Stands

A highlight of this region is the rich agricultural industry. Inland from the coast, Salinas Valley is known as the 'Salad Bowl of the World' for its fresh produce. While road-tripping through the area, you'll see farmlands blanket the landscape with a patchwork of colors, and local farmstands, such as Pezzini and Redoni, providing freshly picked, nourishing treats, like strawberries, lettuce, broccoli and artichokes, to sustain you while you meander up the coast.

Santa Cruz

While visiting Santa Cruz, popular activities include going to the **Santa Cruz Beach Boardwalk** (p161) and the **Santa Cruz Wharf** (p161). It's also well known as a surfing spot. For something less frequented, make a stop at **Natural Bridges State Park** to hike through thousands of butterflies. The monarchs migrate to California for the winter, seeking shelter in the eucalyptus groves mid-October through mid-February. Take the **Natural Bridges Monarch Trail** *(8am-8pm; park $10)* through the **Monarch Grove** to see them hanging in large

Capitola Village — 6.5 miles — Santa Cruz — 4 miles — Wilder Ranch State Park — 17 miles — Año Nuevo State Park

clusters. They can also be found in the groves at **Lighthouse Field State Beach** (p161).

Wilder Ranch State Park

Spreading across 7000 acres, **Wilder Ranch State Park** *(parks.ca.gov/?page_id=549; 8am-sunset; $10)* offers 35 miles of trails, from the mountains to the sea, which can be explored by hiking, mountain biking or horseback riding. For those who are more into history than hiking, from the parking lot, take the wheelchair-accessible path through an Archeological Resource Area, then cross Coast Rd to reach the Cultural Preserve area. The site, which was originally home to the Indigenous Ohlone people, features a well-preserved dairy ranch from the 1800s. Take a self-guided tour of 13 designated landmarks, including an adobe, a machine shop, a Victorian home and barns. Download the guide – which is also a great coloring book for kids – or pick one up at the visitor center. Free guided tours are available at 1pm on Saturdays and Sundays. No reservation required.

Año Nuevo State Park

About 17 miles to the north is **Año Nuevo State Park** *(parks.ca.gov/?page_id=523)*, one of the best places to learn about and view thousands of elephant seals banked on the beach. Swing by the **Marine Education Center** and gift shop, housed in a converted 1800s dairy barn, to see educational displays about marine life in the area and to pick up a free hiking map and free permit (required for elephant-seal viewing April through November). There is also a short film about the elephant seals in the historic horse barn. Take the 1.6-mile (one way) **Año Nuevo Point Trail** to reach the viewing area. At the center, there are picnic tables overlooking the ocean and free mounted binoculars. Save room for pie on your way to **Pigeon Point Light Station State Historic Park**. **Pie Ranch** *(pieranch.org)*, just up the road from Año Nuevo State Park, is a must-stop for freshly made pies with fruit sourced from local farmers. The shop also carries fresh produce, flowers and gifts.

A String of State Beaches

The tantalizing ocean beckons you to stop and gaze at its splendor as you continue up the coast in San Mateo County, past several state beaches *(californiabeaches.com, parks.ca.gov)*, including **Bean Hollow**, **Pescadero**, **Pomponio**, **San Gregorio** and **Cowell Ranch**. Each has unique qualities worth exploring, from harbor-seal spotting and historical landmarks to massive sandstone bluffs and colorful gemstones.

James Johnston House

Entering **Half Moon Bay** *(visit halfmoonbay.org)*, you'll notice a two-story white house in the distance, on your right. This is the historic **James Johnston House** *(johnstonhouse.org)*, built in 1853, home to San Mateo County pioneers, the Johnston family. After decades of neglect and abandonment, restoration efforts began in the 1970s. Today, visitors can take a free docent-led tour of the restored house on the third Saturday of the month *(11am-3pm Jan-Sep)*.

Moss Beach Distillery

After spending the day or night in Half Moon Bay, there's a hidden landmark about 7 miles north that you won't want to miss. From Hwy 1, also known as Cabrillo Hwy along this stretch,

continues on p153

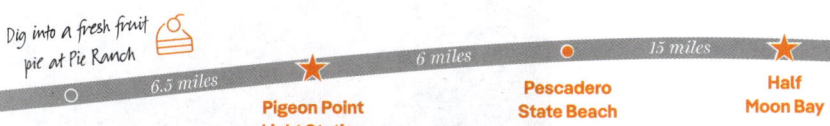

EXPERIENCE

Sleep at a Lighthouse

Budget travelers visiting Pigeon Point Light Station State Historic Park can spend the night in a hostel next to the lighthouse.

HOW TO

Nearest stop: Año Nuevo State Park or Pescadero State Beach; about 28 miles north of Santa Cruz and 21 miles south of Half Moon Bay.

Getting here: From Año Nuevo State Park, drive north about 7 miles and turn left at Pigeon Point Rd.

When to go: Sunrise and sunset for the best photos; April for peak gray whale–watching season. Summer mornings can be foggy.

Cost: Free

More info: parks.ca.gov/?page_id =533

Pigeon Point Light Station State Historic Park includes the Fog Signal Building, which currently displays the original Fresnel lens that was first lit in 1872 to help guide ships navigating the rugged Central California Coast. Now, an automated LED beacon does the same job. There is also a park store housed in the former Carpenter Shop. The historic **Pigeon Point Light Station** has been undergoing renovations since February 2024 and is estimated to reopen in spring of 2026. Explore the park grounds on a guided tour at 2pm on Sundays. Registration is not required. The **HI Pigeon Point Lighthouse Hostel** *(hiusa. org)* is situated in four converted light-station buildings, and offers basic private rooms that sleep up to six or shared accommodation with three bunk beds (towels and sheets included). There are no private bathrooms. Amenities include a shared kitchen, game room and laundry facilities. Dogs, alcohol, smoking and drones are not permitted. Visitors and hostel guests can take advantage of the grounds that feature wooden walkways with lookout points, trails and a stairway leading down to the beach, and plenty of hiking trails in the area. It's also popular for whale-watching and bird-watching.

Pigeon Point Light Station

Along the Way We Met...

ALISON MCGREGOR We bring 40 at-risk youth to Santa Cruz to explore the tide pools with a docent at Natural Bridges State Park, to visit the aquarium [at Seymour Marine Discovery Center], enjoy God's creation, see the ocean life, smell the salt air, and feel the wind on their faces. Some have never been to the ocean. We like to bring them here to see what's beyond their neighborhoods.

Alison is is the executive co-director of faith-based nonprofit One-Eighty Adventures (180lodi.org/adventures) based in Lodi.

ALISON'S TIP: *The tide pools have a lot of what you're looking for, all in one area.*

continued from p151

turn left onto Cypress Ave, and follow the signs for **Moss Beach Distillery** *(mossbeachdistillery.com;140 Beach Way; noon-8:30pm; $$-$$$)*. This historical landmark, which is not an actual distillery, was a popular speakeasy during the height of Prohibition. Rumor has it the 'Blue Lady' ghost haunts the property, trying to relive the glory days. Head straight through the upstairs dining room and take the stairs down to the Seal Cove Patio. This casual open-air patio has 180-degree ocean views (when it's not foggy). With a focus on California coastal cuisine, the menu features items such as clam chowder, crab cakes, seafood pasta, fish tacos and a variety of sandwiches and salads. Walk off your lunch at the nearby **Fitzgerald Marine Reserve** *(smcgov.org/parks/fitzgerald-marine-reserve)*. Park at the north end of Beach Way and take the wooden stairway down to the beach.

Devil's Slide

Inching closer to San Francisco, once you pass **Gray Whale Cove State Beach** and before you go through the tunnels, make a left turn into the south parking lot for the **Devil's Slide Trail** *(smcgov.org/parks/devils-slide-trail)*. This paved 1.3-mile road is the original Hwy 1, completed in 1937. It was closed due to damage by landslides, but was eventually repaired and reopened as a multi-use recreational trail in 2014, and is part of the **California Coastal Trail**. From the parking lot, on your left you can see what's left of a graffiti-covered WWII triangulation station, teetering high atop a dirt peak, looking as though it might tumble off into the ocean below. Once used as a lookout to detect enemy ships, it now sits abandoned on private property. Then it's through **Pacifica** to your next stop – San Francisco, where you'll soon discover why Tony Bennett left his heart there.

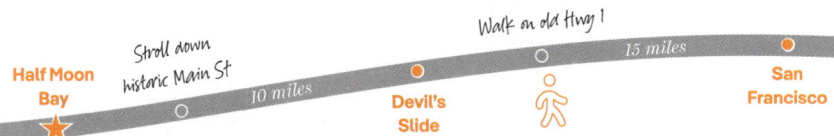

Walk along a Classic Main Street

Walking down Main St in Half Moon Bay gets to the roots of what makes this charming coastal town tick. From quaint coffee shops and trendy thrift stores to impressive art galleries and local wine tasting, you can experience a slower-paced way of life in the bustling Bay Area.

HOW TO

Nearest stop: James Johnston House, at the south end of Main St. Moss Beach is about 7 miles north.

Getting here: From Hwy 1, turn right on Main St. Free 12-hour parking on Johnston St and Purissima St, parallel to Main St; two-hour parking limit on Main St.

When to go: Every October, there is a big Half Moon Bay Art & Pumpkin Festival, with prize-winning pumpkins that can weigh more than 2000lb. It's a fun family event, but the traffic and parking might test your patience.

More info: visithalfmoonbay.org

Maps & Coffee

Half Moon Bay offers a variety of outdoor activities to take advantage of the natural environment, such as surfing (it's home to the big-wave surf spot Mavericks), hiking, mountain biking and exploring tide pools, but the heart of the town lies on Main St. Entering from the south, once you get to Miramontes St, take a left or right for free parking on Johnston St or Purissima St. First stop – the **California Welcome Center** (visitcalifornia.com; 637 Main St) for maps, brochures and souvenirs. Next, grab coffee and a pastry (any time of day) from **Moonside Bakery & Cafe** or **Half Moon Bay Bakery**, established in 1927.

Historic Buildings

You'll notice many nostalgic buildings along Main St, some with facades, such as the oldest retail building in town (built in 1873) at 527 Main St, home to **LuzLuna Imports**. **Half Moon Bay City Hall** (built in 1922) was originally a bank, and still has the vault to prove it. Kittycorner is the landmark terra cotta–colored **Cunha's Country Store** (a great place for sandwiches), founded in 1924, but rebuilt after a 2003 fire. The **Half Moon Bay Feed & Fuel**, established in 1911, carries a range of farm and ranch supplies – stop in to see the fuzzy chicks. Stop in for a beer and a burrito at **Cantina @ San Benito House**, located in the **San Benito House** (built in 1905), or spend the night upstairs at the **San Benito House Historic Inn**.

BELYAY/SHUTTERSTOCK

CRUISING THE COASTAL TRAIL

If you've walked on a trail along the California Coast, you may have noticed markers with a round blue and white swirl emblem designating the path as part of the **California Coastal Trail** (CCT; *californiacoastaltrail.org*). They can also be found in sidewalks in urban areas. It runs along **Half Moon Bay State Beach**. The trail, which is in various stages of development, will span the all of California's coastline once it's complete. The project originated from a 1972 initiative to establish a continuous, nonmotorized, accessible trail system along the coast. The trail stitches together a network of paths, trails and beaches that run through all 15 coastal counties.

EXPERIENCE ★

Art Galleries Galore

Several art galleries line Main St, with local artists showing off their talent through creative works of art. The first Friday of the month is First Fridays, a downtown art walk where galleries invite the community to browse their collections – you might even want to take a piece home. At the northern end of Main St, before hitting the road towards Moss Beach, get your caffeine fix and a sweet treat at **Half Moon Bay Coffee Company**.

Above: Main Street

CITY GUIDE:
Santa Cruz

Sky Glider, Santa Cruz Beach Boardwalk (p161)

With seaside amusements, sandy beaches and whale-rich waters, Santa Cruz is a surfer's paradise. Perched on the northern rim of Monterey Bay, this city of 63,000 has been brewing counterculture rebellion since the 1950s – though today you're just as likely to bump into Silicon Valley royalty as renegade artists.

WORDS BY **ANITA ISALSKA**

Anita is a British-born journalist who splits her time between California, the Pacific Northwest and the French Alps

Arriving
Santa Cruz is between San Francisco (70 miles north) and Carmel-by-the-Sea (45 miles south). Most people rock up by car, but you can also catch bus 17 ($7) from San Jose Diridon station, which has train connections across the San Francisco Bay Area.

Tours
You can generally get lucky with same-day bookings but it's wise to show up with reservations for surf-school and whale-watching tours; even the quirky Mystery Spot gets booked up on weekends and holidays. It's easy to DIY by booking directly with operators but the Santa Cruz Visitor Center *(santacruz.org)* can help with nuanced local information like weather, monarch butterfly sightings and more.

HOW MUCH FOR A

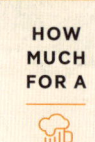

Craft beer $8

Clam chowder in a bread bowl $15

Ride on the Giant Dipper $8

Getting Around
Driving Santa Cruz is an easy exit from Hwy 1 and driving around the city is generally cruisy – though it can be slow going on busy Pacific Ave and Beach St.
Parking There are plenty of places to park downtown, including six free time-limited lots; check the parking map on *cityofsantacruz.com*. Beachside areas tend to have metered parking. Parking at state beaches and parks costs a flat $8 to $10 so plan stops carefully if you intend to beach-hop by car – unless you have a **state parks pass** *(parks.ca.gov; from $125)*. Ideally, park at your accommodation then walk, cycle or bus your way around.
Walking Restaurant-packed downtown Santa Cruz is just 20 minutes' walk from the beach boardwalk.
Bus Santa Cruz has efficient local **buses** *(scmtd.com; per ride $2)*. Useful routes from downtown (Front St and Soquel Ave) are numbers 20 (heading west to Natural Bridges State Beach) and 2 (east through Seabright towards Capitola).
Electric bike Use the local electric **bike-sharing scheme** *(santacruz.bcycle.com; 30min $7)* to get around without parking hassle.

For information about weather, butterfly sightings and more, go to santacruz.org:

A DAY IN SANTA CRUZ

Seize a latte from **Verve** (verve coffee.com; 7am-6pm), one of the originators of Santa Cruz' coffee roasting scene, before strolling south to admire the cresting surf. **Cowell's Beach** (p160) is ideal for surfing lessons or you can treat it as a spectator sport and watch seasoned riders dominate the waves at **Steamer Lane** (p160).

Get raucous on the **Santa Cruz Beach Boardwalk** (p161)! Eliciting shrieks of glee since 1907, this amusement park has retro-style and roller-coaster thrills. Twenty minutes' walk east, the harbor is alive with seals and otters. Tours with **Kayak Connection** (kayakconnection.com; adult/child from $95/70) guide you to cute critters from a distance.

Sunset is magical: families pack up and revelers settle in at breweries. Sip golden glassfuls at **Humble Sea Brewing Company** and guzzle nibbles at **Abbott Square Market**. Or head to Capitola for fish 'n' chips at **Zelda's** (zeldasonthebeach.com; 8am-10pm).

Where to Stay

Serenity, hedonism or family-friendly fun...your choice of neighborhood can transform your stay. **Downtown** is walking distance from the boardwalk, beaches and restaurants, but note that exuberant nightlife can make some areas feel seedy after dark. On the San Lorenzo River's east bank are budget hotels of variable quality stretching into **Seabright**. Escaping the crowds? **Westside** is near beauty spots like Natural Bridges (p161) and 5 miles east of Santa Cruz is **Capitola**, a dainty city with pastel-colored buildings and a small pleasant beach.

BEST PLACES TO STAY

Hotel Paradox $$
Driftwood furniture and pool. Rooms are design-forward and business smart. *thehotelparadox.com*

Pacific Blue Inn $$
Near downtown and boardwalk, solid eco credentials. *pacificblueinn.com*

West Cliff Inn $$$
Cream and nautical blue rooms, many with fireplaces and ocean views. *westcliffinn.com*

Captain's Inn at Moss Landing $
Rustic inn 20 minutes south; ideal for sea dogs and kayakers. *captainsinn.com*

Where to Eat

No one will dissuade you from filling up on funnel cake at the boardwalk. But Santa Cruz' true staples are fish tacos, burritos and clam chowder, easy to find on the wharf and downtown along Pacific Ave. Find a smorgasbord of downtown restaurants and bars (from Thai to Hawaiian to exceptional negronis) along Cedar St and Front St (between Union St and Lincoln St).

> ### LIBATION INNOVATION
>
> The amber ale in your hand isn't just for kicks, it's an emblem of Santa Cruz history. When Gold Rush prospectors turned to farming in the 1850s, the Pajaro Valley (east of Santa Cruz) practically blazed with fields of hops. The most successful was the McGrath hop, named after an Irish farming family and exported far and wide along the West Coast, leading to the very first brewery opening in the 1860s.
>
> The scene has only gotten hipper and hoppier since: try the signature 'foggy' IPAs – fresh, fragrant and fruity – at **Humble Sea Brewing Company** (humblesea.com; 3-9pm Mon-Thu, noon-9pm Fri-Sun). Something even craftier awaits at **Sante Adairius** (rusticales.com; noon-9pm Sun-Thu, to 10pm Fri & Sat) in Seabright, 1.5 miles east of downtown, where Belgian brewing methods yield barrel-aged ales and barley wine.

BEST PLACES TO EAT & DRINK

Abbott Square Market $
Upscale food court with live music. Tables are sought after; move fast. *abbottsquaremarket.com; 8am-10pm Sun-Thu, to 11pm Fri & Sat*

Penny Ice Creamery $
Get in line for zany flavored scoops drowned in marshmallow. *thepennyicecreamery.com; noon-11pm*

Hanloh $$$
Exemplary Thai inside bookstore–wine bar Bad Animals. We dream of the cod. *hanloh.com; 5-9pm Wed-Sun*

Venus Spirits $$
Oak-aged gins wash down European small plates. *venusspirits.com; 5-9pm Mon-Thu, 4-9pm Fri, 11:30am-9pm Sat & Sun*

Surfers, Santa Cruz

Learn How to Catch Waves

The surf's always up in Santa Cruz. Pro surfers hang ten at legendary breaks like Steamer Lane, which attracts a steady stream of onlookers, while absolute beginners can learn to ride waves in gentle, predictable swells at Cowell's Beach. Book a lesson with **Richard Schmidt Surf School** *(richardschmidt; group lesson from $120)* a veteran outfit that guides you from posing on your board on the sand to hoisting yourself up, up and away, buoyed by sheer adrenaline as you ride your first wave and crash triumphantly into the foaming surf.

SILVER SCREEN SANTA CRUZ

You might feel a frisson of déjà vu as you explore Santa Cruz. The **beach boardwalk** has long been a movie A-lister, hitting the big time as a setting in Clint Eastwood's *Sudden Impact* (1983), where Dirty Harry battles bad guys beneath the Giant Dipper. The boardwalk's eerie atmosphere after dark has kept action- and horror-movie directors in thrall for decades, as a backdrop for motorcycle-riding vampire gangs in *The Lost Boys* (1987) and comedy-horror sci-fi in *Killer Klowns from Outer Space* (1988). *Us* (2019), by Oscar-winning writer-director Jordan Peele, imagined sinister clones beneath the boardwalk, while end-of-days thriller *Birdbox* (2018) starred a blindfolded Sandra Bullock staggering around **Henry Cowell Redwoods State Park**.

Palm trees and sandy beaches aside, Santa Cruz has all the ingredients for a spooky atmosphere on camera: just listen to the screams of sea lions beneath the wharf or go hiking in the mist-draped forests. Strange tales are always in rich supply: a freak attack by shearwater birds in Capitola in 1961 inspired Alfred Hitchcock's *The Birds* (1963) and Santa Cruz County has long been a hub for legends of Bigfoot. All isn't as it seems in surf city...

Left: Redwood Forest Train

Ride Through Redwood Forests

Explore the ancient glades surrounding Santa Cruz by driving 6 miles northeast to **Henry Cowell Redwoods State Park** *(parks.ca.gov; $10)*. Walk along trails that weave between gigantic redwoods, the tallest 282ft high, and board the **Redwood Forest Train** *(roaringcamp.com; adult/child $41.95/26.95; 10:30am daily)* for a bumping and jolting 75-minute journey, accompanied by shrieking whistles and clouds of steam.

On your way back to Santa Cruz, the enjoyably silly **Mystery Spot** *(mysteryspot.com; reserve ahead; $10)* is an alleged gravitational oddity amid the redwoods. Leave cynicism at the door of this cult attraction – you'll get memorable photos!

Walk along West Cliff Drive

This 3-mile seaside pathway extends between soul-stirring cliffs and Santa Cruz' boardwalk.

HOW TO

Getting here: Park at Natural Bridges ($10) or get bus 20 from downtown (Front St and Soquel Ave).

When to go: Between mid-October and mid-February you can see migrating monarch butterflies in Natural Bridges' eucalyptus grove.

Hours and admission: Boardwalk and wharf are free to enter; hours vary. The Surfing Museum opens noon to 4pm Thursday to Monday (to 5pm June to August); Vino by the Sea is open 4pm to late Wednesday to Friday, from 2pm Saturday and Sunday.

GIANTS OF THE DEEP

Keep your eyes on the horizon to spot distant whales from West Cliff Drive. Humpbacks are common from March through November, but December to mid-May brings colossal gray whales to the bay. Get closer by joining a tour with **Santa Cruz Whale Watching** (santacruzwhalewatching.com; adult/child $66/48).

Begin at **Natural Bridges State Beach**, where a dramatic arch-shaped sea stack attracts gaggles of cormorants and gulls. Follow the oceanside walking path, West Cliff Drive, heading east. After 1.5 miles you'll reach Lighthouse Field State Beach and at the tip of the headland is Steamer Lane, where gigantic surf breaks beckon to pro surfers. Watch the action and step in the 1967 lighthouse: inside, the **Santa Cruz Surfing Museum** has insights into a century of wave riders, including the Hawaiian princes who popularized surfing in Santa Cruz back in the 1880s.

Another mile along the trail takes you to Cowell's Beach and the wharf; there's a Chardonnay with your name on it at **Vino by the Sea** (vino-by-the-sea.com). You can now hear yelps of joy carried on the breeze from the **Santa Cruz Beach Boardwalk** (beachboardwalk.com). Let them beckon you to vintage thrills like a spin on the ornate Looff Carousel, with its 73 horses and original 19th-century pipe organ, or the Giant Dipper, a century-old wooden roller coaster with high-up ocean views.

Natural Bridges State Beach

Road collapse, PCH at Big Sur
MELINA MARA/THE WASHINGTON POST/GETTY IMAGES

INSIGHT

Surviving Climate Change

Driving the Pacific Coast Highway represents pure freedom – but paving paradise has a heavy cost. Maintaining a highway at the edge of the West Coast, where mudslides thunder from the mountains, is getting harder as anthropogenic climate change accelerates.

WORDS BY **ANITA ISALSKA**
Anita is a British-born journalist who splits her time between California, the Pacific Northwest and the French Alps

WHEN YOU DRIVE the Pacific Coast Highway, you collect vivid mental snapshots along the way: like the royal-blue ocean filling your view as you round a bend. The shimmers of light that bounce off the water, forcing you to flip down the sun visor. Heart-hammering moments when the road edges close – too close! – to a cliff edge.

But some Hwy 1 experiences are less cinematic, like jolting to a standstill in a slow-moving line of cars and waiting for someone in a hi-vis vest to wave you past the traffic cones. Or, even more frustrating, driving right up to the 'Road Closed' and 'Slide Ahead' signs and reluctantly making a U-turn.

For as long as automobiles have trundled across California, landslides have threatened road access – and they're wreaking havoc on parts of Hwy 1. As the impact of human-caused climate change continues to intensify, scientists are scrambling to monitor the increasing threats to the West Coast's most iconic roadway.

A Highway of Blind Optimism

Today, it's hard to picture coastal California without mighty Hwy 1 threading between its towns, cities and beauty spots. But centuries ago there were no shortcuts. Native American people traveled on foot along trading routes that spiraled through the coastland, and paddled rivers and bays in dugout canoes.

For settlers, who lacked deep knowledge of the land, it was agonizingly slow and arduous to navigate wagon trails around the coast. The transcontinental railroad reduced California's isolation and fed population growth, but by the late 19th century, long travel times up and down the coast were weighing heavily on growing settler communities. They wanted to accelerate trade and more easily bring medical help to shipwrecked sailors. Could wild California be tamed by the creation of coastal roads?

Building the roads that would become the PCH was an exercise in colonialist determination. Road surveyors set out to document the coast, ranchers who objected to the use of their land were battled in court, and construction began in earnest in 1919. Initial estimates of $1.5 million in construction costs ballooned to more than $10m – even with prison camps delivering cheap labor. Some 70,000 pounds of dynamite were produced to blast granite and sandstone from the coast, and industrial quantities of steel were hauled in to build bridges.

As the road was completed section by section, settler communities and prisoner laborers – granted shorter sentences for their blood and sweat, along with 35¢ per day – breathed sighs of relief. Completing the road through remote Big Sur in 1937 was a particular feat.

But dramatic weather events go back throughout California's oral and recorded histories, and severe storms have caused major closures and endless expensive repairs – long before the coast roads were designated a single highway in 1964.

Caught Between Fire & Water

The PCH snakes between the wildfire-prone forests cloaking California's mountain ranges and the merciless Pacific Ocean, whose waves thrash away at the cliffs and occasionally claim a chunk of land.

> Building a road here is both a wonder of modern engineering and an act of madness.

Building a road here is both a wonder of modern engineering and an act of madness. Wildfires can clear the land of plantlife that helps maintain the ground's integrity. This leaves the earth vulnerable to sudden wet weather: rainstorms can create mudslides that barrel over the smoothed-out ground and inundate sections of the highway.

The road's early years saw dramatic and deadly events. The Los Angeles flood of 1938 claimed scores of lives, destroyed properties, ravaged railway lines and provoked mudslides that swamped the road. Soon after, the Trippet Ranch Fire leapt across the highway from the Santa Monica Mountains to torch 12,000 acres. Twenty years later, a massive mudslide dubbed the 'Killer Slide' inundated the road with 20ft of mud. With major storms and floods every few years, cycles of major roadway repairs became the norm.

Enter the Fourth Horseman

Three major factors that influence landslides are vegetation-clearing fires, intense rainfall and the impact of infrastructure development, all of which California has in abundance. And that's before you add climate change to the mix.

A study in *Science*, published August 2025, showed that California's fire season is getting longer, afflicted areas are growing in size, and global warming will continue to ignite earlier and earlier fire seasons. Meanwhile, warming oceans create stronger atmospheric rivers, which deliver more extreme rainfall.[1] In a 2025 article, Irasema Alcántara-Ayala, professor of natural hazards at the National Autonomous University of Mexico, projected that landslide severity and frequency were both set to increase because of climate change.

From the fog-clad north to the sunniest corner of SoCal, no part of the Golden State will be immune to worsening landslides. When NASA used satellite data to monitor California's slow-moving landslides in 2022, they found that all were sensitive to the weather volatility brought about by climate change – and California has hundreds of active landslides.[2]

Disasters as Usual

In Big Sur on California's Central Coast, highway closures due to landslides have become painfully routine.

This stretch of the PCH has been immortalized in films and car commercials, not to mention in the hundreds of thousands of Instagram posts of Bixby Bridge and Big Sur's famous valley of calla lilies. It's also where local authorities are losing the battle to keep the highway open.

Landslides blocking the PCH can cut off entire communities for years at a time. When we wrote this, a 6.8-mile section of Hwy 1 from Lime Creek Bridge to Lucia was well into its second year of closure due to Regent's Slide – longer, if you count 2023's closures at the capricious slip zone known as Paul's Slide.

Instead of cruising south all the way through Big Sur to Ragged Point and San Simeon, road-trippers needed to end the trip early or commit to a 200-mile detour to San Simeon (backtracking north, then following the inland Hwy 101 south, before looping west to the coast and back north...until the next set of 'Slide Ahead' closure signs).

An estimated 90% of Big Sur's economy relies on tourism, so inaccessibility to road-trippers imperils people's livelihoods – as well as causing transport misery for workplaces and schools, and delaying access to emergency healthcare services. The long closure spawned many hand-wringing headlines about whether Big Sur will ever recover, and whether the PCH is a failed project. ('The demise of an iconic American highway,' lamented the *Economist* in July 2024.)

To many locals, road closures along California's coast are simply inevitable and community resilience is vital – it's the trade-off for living in paradise. Meanwhile, federal investments in landslide monitoring and warning systems aim to keep track of moving geological targets. Nonetheless, ongoing closures and volatile weather continue to prompt soul-searching about the long-term sustainability of this legendary road.

> To many locals, road closures along California's coast are simply inevitable and community resilience is vital – it's the tradeoff for living in paradise.

---

1 Atmospheric rivers, concentrated bands of water vapor, create as much as 50% of California's rainfall.

2 You can observe California's landslides on *conservation.ca.gov/cgs/landslides*

Mudslide clean-up, PCH at Malibu
MYUNG J. CHUN/LOS ANGELES TIMES/GETTY IMAGES

Golden Gate Bridge (p172)
NOEL V. BAEBLER/SHUTTERSTOCK

NORTHERN CALIFORNIA

It's time to slow down – and pull out your hoodie – because the California of palm trees and sun-drenched beaches is now far behind you. While you might not be unpacking your swimsuit again for the rest of your journey, you're also unlikely to find yourself in a traffic jam, at least once you leave the Bay Area. Ahead of you lies a long and undulating road that passes through untouched beaches and past trees so mighty and humbling that you'll be tempted to pull over again and again just to marvel at it all.

CITY GUIDE:
San Francisco

Lombard Street

San Francisco summons dreamers and restless souls. Art collectives, tech start-ups and modern-day hippies all share the bayside city, where the Beat poets of the 1960s never really went away and the LGBTQ+ community is as vibrant as ever. Come stroll its steep streets and iconic bridges, and be forever changed.

WORDS BY **ANITA ISALSKA**
Anita is a British-born journalist who splits her time between California, the Pacific Northwest and the French Alps

Arriving
By air San Francisco International Airport, with direct connections across the US, Europe and Asia-Pacific, is on Hwy 101, 12 miles south of downtown. Several car-rental operators are inside or near the airport.
By rail The *Coast Starlight* train, which trundles a scenic route from Seattle to Los Angeles, stops in the Bay Area (Oakland and San Jose).
By road The legendary Golden Gate Bridge greets arrivals from the north (and charges them a $9.50 southbound toll). If you're driving from the south, consider staying overnight 'on the peninsula' (which includes areas like Millbrae). There's good-value accommodation and it's connected to San Francisco by regular BART trains.

HOW MUCH FOR A

Good martini **$15**

Mission burrito **$11**

Exploratorium entry adult/youth **$40/30**

Getting Around
City bikes Bay Wheels *(lyft.com/bikes/bay-wheels; per ride from $4)* offers pay-per-ride bikes and e-bikes. Use cycle lanes and be cautious around Market St and anywhere you share the road with buses and trams. BYO helmet.
Cable cars and Muni Cling on for a steep ride on a cable car ($9) and use Muni buses and trams to zip between neighborhoods.
BART and Caltrain BART trains *(bart.gov)* reach the Mission, the airport, Oakland and peninsula neighborhoods. Caltrain *(caltrain.com)* connects SF with San Jose via Silicon Valley.
Tickets Use a Clipper card *(clippercard.com)* for trams, BART, buses and Caltrain. Buy a reloadable card at the station ($3) or download the app.
Parking There are secure paid parking lots downtown. Park streetside with caution and never leave any items visible in your vehicle. Many hotels don't include parking in rates; valet parking is offered in upscale places (worth it).

Self-Driving Cars
Look, no hands...and no driver! San Francisco is a testing ground for driverless cars and you can order a surprisingly serene rideshare through the Waymo One app *(waymo.com)*. Note that robocars are loved and loathed: the experience is novel but there are justifiable fears of the impact driverless cars may have on rideshare drivers' livelihoods. But most San Franciscans agree: driverless cars whooshing along SF's super-steep roads are fascinating to watch.

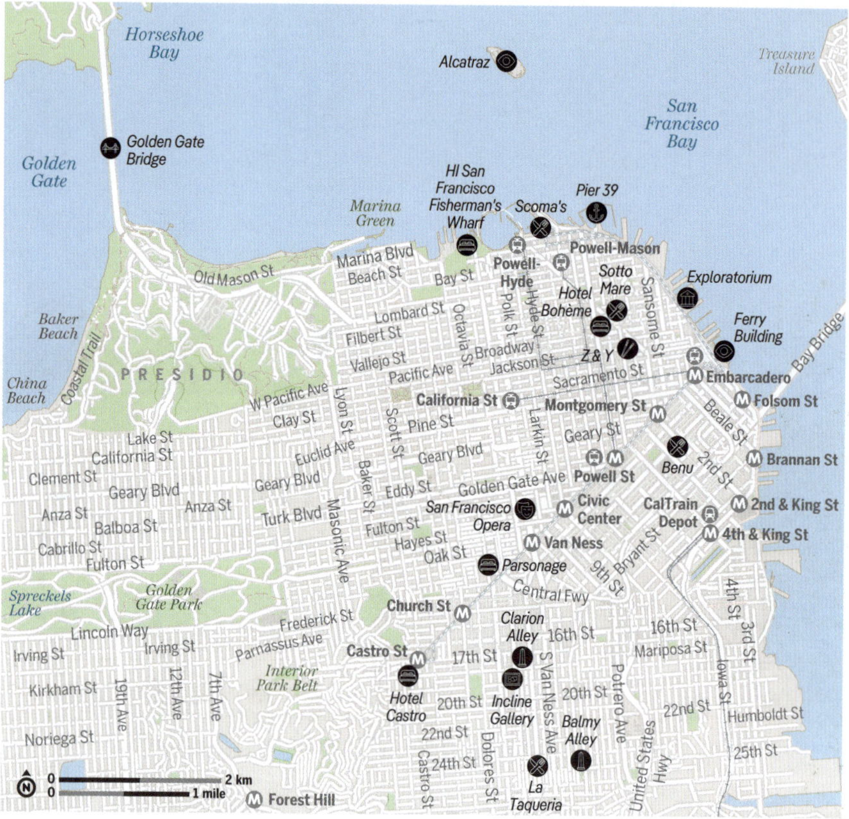

SAN FRANCISCO

A DAY IN SAN FRANCISCO

Stroll beneath the clock tower and into the **Ferry Building** (ferry buildingmarketplace.com) for coffee and baked goodies. Walk north for a big-ticket attraction: the **Exploratorium** (exploratorium.edu; 10am-5pm Mon-Sat, from noon Sun) or a ferry to **Alcatraz** (nps.gov/alca; bookings essential). Don't miss the sea lions at **Pier 39** (pier39.com).

Time to stretch your legs. Cycle or hike to the Presidio for views of the **Golden Gate Bridge** (p172) if it reveals itself from its cloak of fog. Jump in a rideshare to the Mission to admire brightly colored murals on **Balmy** and **Clarion Alleys** (p173), stopping in at alternative galleries like **Incline** (inclinegallerysf.com; 1-5pm Sat & Sun).

You can easily spend the whole evening in the Mission, chomping on burritos, downing killer margaritas, then tumbling onward to the Castro, where the rainbow-colored road points you to endless LGBTQ+ clubs and bars. A gourmet alternative: world-class dining at **Benu** followed by a show at the **SF Opera** (sfopera.com).

Where to Stay

Pick your preferred neighborhood flavor and use public transit to zip around with ease. **North Beach** is a sweet spot with abundant midrange accommodation; it's walkable to piers, Chinatown and buzzy nightlife. Other contenders are vibrant gayborhood the **Castro** (p172); the lively, tourist-friendly **Marina & Fisherman's Wharf**; and central, well-connected **SoMa**. Get local advice if your preferred hotel is downtown or in the Tenderloin, as some areas may feel unsafe.

BEST PLACES TO STAY

HI San Francisco Fisherman's Wharf $
Shared and private rooms in a hostel with glorious bay views. *hiusa.org*

Hotel Bohème $$
Stay where Beat poets once roamed at a quaint 1880s inn. *hotelboheme.com*

Hotel Castro $$
Sleep in stylish boutique walls in SF's LGBTQ+ heart. *thehotelcastro.com*

Parsonage $$$
Soak up vintage elegance at a Victorian mansion. Two-night minimum. *theparsonage.com*

Where to Eat

Whichever cuisine you're hungry for, you'll find it by the bay. Go north: **Chinatown** is hallowed ground for fans of dim sum and legendary mai tais, while neighboring **North Beach** has a strong Italian accent (pizza and espresso galore). Want seconds? Try sushi in **Japantown**, Mexican in the **Mission** and plant-based food in the increasingly upscale **Haight & Hayes Valley** areas.

SAN FRANCISCO'S FAMOUS FISH STEW

From Dungeness crab fever to passionate debates about the best oyster happy hour, San Franciscans know their seafood. One of the most satisfying ways to taste the bay's bounty is *cioppino*, perfected in San Francisco and ladled up in restaurants across the city. Italian migrants devised this Liguria-inspired recipe in the early 20th century and it rapidly became a favorite among homesick fisherman. A bowl of *cioppino* is a shoal of fish in rich tomato broth: crab, shrimp and whatever the boats haul in. Part of the joy of slurping *cioppino* is in discovering the delights within: dip a wedge of sourdough or garlic bread in the steamy mix to reveal succulent calamari, prise open a clam, and try not to splash yourself as you drop a slippery morsel of snapper back into the soup (hey, that's what the bibs are for). **Scoma's** is a standout and **Sotto Mare** (*sottomaresf.com*) a close runner-up.

BEST PLACES TO EAT & DRINK

La Taqueria $
Humble temple to Mission burritos. They're well stuffed, and you will be too. *lataqueriasf.net*; 11am-8:45pm Wed-Sat, to 7:45pm Sun

Z & Y $$
Standout Chinatown restaurant with extra chili kick. *zandyrestaurant.com*; 11:30am-3pm & 4:30-9pm Wed-Sun

Benu $$$
California ingredients meet Asian flair and a voluminous global wine list; fine dining not to miss. *benusf.com*; 5:30-10:30pm Tue-Sat, reservations only

Scoma's $$$
Slurp *cioppino* studded with crab legs and order a house cocktail. *scomas.com*; noon-9pm Sun-Thu, to 10pm Fri & Sat

Golden Gate Bridge

Crossing the Golden Gate Bridge

Even locals never tire of seeing the Golden Gate Bridge. Rising from San Francisco Bay, often shrouded in fog, this art-deco colossus connects SF's northern Presidio with the Marin Headlands (p180).

Dress for high winds and walk across. First, get a potted history of its hair-raising construction at the Golden Gate Bridge Welcome Center then stride across the burnished bridge, craning your neck at the 746ft-high towers. The color is 'International Orange,' if you're wondering – chosen for safety reasons, its ability to accentuate the sunset is simply a bonus. At the end, either turn back or take a longer hike in the **Golden Gate National Recreation Area**.

LEGENDARY LGBTQ+ SCENES

In 1978 Harvey Milk became California's first openly gay elected official. This appointment put a rainbow-striped stamp on Milk's neighborhood, the **Castro** (just west of the Mission), but San Francisco was already a major hub for LGBTQ+ culture. The US military discharged thousands of gay servicemen during WWII and many settled in SoMa, the Tenderloin and the Castro.

The Castro's streets are paved with Pride flags; soak up some love at **Midnight Sun** (midnightsunsf.com; 2pm-midnight Mon-Wed, to 2am Thu & Fri, 12:30pm-2am Sat, 1pm-midnight Sun) or hang out at **Moby Dick** (noon-2am). Over in SoMa, the **Leather & LGBTQ Cultural District** has been a center of queer life since the 1960s. Every September, the neighborhood's **Folsom Street Fair** unleashes a celebration of kink and queer joy. Meanwhile the reinvigorated **Transgender Cultural District** (transgenderdistrictsf.com) in the Tenderloin is the site of an early fight for queer rights, the 1966 Compton's Cafeteria riots. Today these neighborhoods remain trailblazers for LGTBQ+ activism.

Along the Way We Met...

SAHIL M BANSAL Everybody knows about Pier 39 and the sea lions. But there have been bison in San Francisco for well over 100 years. I also like to take out-of-towners to see Claude the albino alligator at the California Academy of Sciences. The academy also has the oldest fish known in any aquarium, an Australian lungfish called Methuselah – she's over 90 years old.

Sahil is part of storytelling event Odd Salon (oddsalon.com) and the California Academy of Sciences (calacademy.org).

SAHIL'S TIP: *Don't miss the views of downtown from Ina Coolbrith Park in North Beach (there's a hidden staircase).*

Mission Murals

Hundreds of multicolor murals splash the walls of this lively neighborhood. Admire public art and stop for coffee, burritos and boutiques – the heart of SF's Latinx community is a joy to explore.

HOW TO

Getting here: From downtown take BART to 24th St Mission (Balmy Alley) or 16th St Mission (Clarion Alley), depending on where you want to start. From North Beach/Fort Mason, jump aboard bus 49.

Getting around: Wandering is free, but local insights on 90-minute tours with **Precita Eyes** (precitaeyes.org; $25) are priceless.

Start in **Balmy Alley** (balmyalley.org), where artists channeled outrage about human rights abuses into street art. Look for homages to Frida Kahlo and Diego Rivera; these Mexican artists have influenced local creators ever since their visit to San Francisco in the 1930s. Ten minutes' walk west, **La Corneta Taqueria** (lacorneta.com; 10am-9pm) is the place for burritos, emblems of the Mexican food scene. Break up your walk north along Valencia St with life-changing cortado at **Ritual Coffee Roasters** (ritualcoffee.com; 6:30am-7pm Mon-Thu, to 8pm Fri-Sun), shelf-rummaging at **Dog Eared Books** (dogearedbooks.com; 10am-10pm) and taxidermy art at **Paxton Gate** (paxtongate.com; 11am-7pm Wed-Mon).

A block west along 18th St is the impressive Maestrapeace mural adorning the Women's Building, a community center home to women's organizations since 1979. More than 100 volunteers helped artists create this five-story-high homage to Aztec goddesses and feminist revolutionaries.

Continue north to **Clarion Alley** (clarionalleymuralproject.org), a canvas for more than 900 artworks since 1992. The public art gives you instant insights into local sentiments, from gentrification to global politics.

DOLORES PARK

With views of downtown from its grassy slopes, Dolores Park is a beloved hangout for families, artists, tech dropouts and everyone in between, and LGBTQ+ locals flock to 'gay beach' (the park's southwest). Dolores Park was a camp for families made homeless by the 1906 earthquake, and has represented community resilience ever since.

Balmy Alley

Exploring Golden Gate Park

This park is alive with nature and culture. It isn't the place to see the bridge...but you will see bison, splendid museums and rolling parkland.

HOW TO

Getting here: From downtown (Market St) catch bus 5 to reach Golden Gate Park's northern edge. You can also enter the park from the south by catching bus 7 or the N line streetcar.

When to go: The Japanese Garden is glorious during cherry blossom season (March/April).

Bike rental: Rent wheels from **Parkwide Bike** and **Surrey** *(parkwide.com; 2hr rental city/electric bike from $26/52).*

Revel in Art & Nature at World-Class Museums

Enter the park along the northern flank (Fulton St) to start at its powerhouse museums. The **Fine Arts de Young Museum** *(famssf.org/visit/de-young; adult/child $20/free; 9:30am-5.15pm Tue-Sun)* is the crowning attraction: resembling something between Noah's ark and an ancient Egyptian temple, it blends in perfectly with the surrounding greenery. Three floors of beautifully curated works span intricate textile art through to contemporary photography. Enter the womb-like *Skyspace* installation by James Turrell and stare up at the sky through an oculus: the boundaries between art and nature seem to blur.

Walk across the plaza to the **California Academy of Sciences** *(calacademy.org; adult/child from $49/45; 9:30am-5pm, from 11am Sun)* to fire up your inner naturalist. With an aquarium, rainforest and planetarium, this immersive natural history museum plunges you into every realm in the solar system. Our highlights: delving into the deep reefs of the ocean's twilight zone and admiring butterflies in the Osher Rainforest dome.

Smell Roses & the Ocean Breeze

Time to get outside and explore. Walk or cycle to the **Japanese Tea Garden** *(gggp.org/japanese-tea-garden; adult/child $18.75/6.75; 9am-6pm),* which exudes tranquility with its pagodas, Buddha statue (1790), bridge, zen garden and glimmering koi fish. Landscape architect Makoto Hagiwara created it for an 1894 expo but the garden has been preserved and expanded; Hagiwara, tragically, was exiled along

PAINTING THE LADIES

A 10-minute cycle ride east of Golden Gate Park's eastern edge are San Francisco's most colorful dames (outside of the Castro): the Painted Ladies. The term can mean any Victorian house decorated in three or more colors, but the row of blue, green and reddish homes lining Steiner St are icons. Colorist movement pioneer George 'Butch' Kardum is credited with giving these houses their luster. Many of San Francisco's late-19th-century houses were awash in US Navy gray but when Kardum painted his own house rainbow-bright, his neighbors followed suit and the city's emblematic houses were born.

Left: Golden Gate Park;
Below: Japanese Tea Garden

with 120,000 other Japanese Americans during WWII.

Go north of JFK Promenade, which slices through the park, to reach the Rose Garden, a spot popular with picnickers and people on second dates, then head west past Blue Heron Lake to the Bison Paddock. Shaggy mammals have lived in Golden Gate Park since 1891 – many with celebrity names like Sarah Bernhardt and Bill McKinley – and more than 500 calves have come braying into the world thanks to breeding programs in past years. Exit the west side of the park to Ocean Beach, a 3.5-mile sandy stretch with uninterrupted Pacific views.

San Francisco

Things start to look pretty different once you leave San Francisco behind you. As the highway narrows and the buzz of the city fades into forest, you'll be forced to slow your pace, both physically and mentally. Take your time to check out Pacific Ocean views from craggy bluffs or sample freshly baked bread at a village bakery. You've been driving for a while now and you're in a great place to relax.

Margot Bigg

Mendocino

177 MILES — 5.5-HOUR DRIVE

THIS LEG:

- San Francisco
- Marin Headlands
- Sausalito
- Tomales
- Bodega Bay
- Sonoma Coast State Park
- Jenner
- Fort Ross State Historic Park
- Salt Point State Park
- Kruse Rhododendron State Natural Reserve
- Sea Ranch
- Gualala
- Elk
- Van Damme State Park
- Mendocino

PCH near Muir Beach (p183)
NURIA KREUSER/SHUTTERSTOCK

Driving Notes

This section has a bit of everything, from long remote stretches surrounded by farmland and forests to winding roads that can get precariously close to towering sea cliffs. Every so often, you'll come across a village that feels nearly abandoned, until you begin to notice cute art galleries and gourmet bakeries, subtle reminders that San Francisco isn't too far away.

Breaking Your Journey
This stretch is a long one, and you may want to split it into a two-day trip. Bodega Bay is a good midway point, with decent places to eat and stay. If you make a detour to the Napa and Sonoma Valleys, it's smart to spend the night in the area, especially if you plan to do much wine tasting.

Margot's Tips

BEST MEAL Rainbow sandwich at Cafe Aquatica (p181) in Jenner.

FAVORITE VIEW The Golden Gate Bridge from Conzelman Road in the Marin Headlands (p180).

ESSENTIAL STOP Sea Ranch Chapel (p191).

ROAD-TRIP TIP If you have a good pair of binoculars, bring them! They'll come in handy if you pull off at any viewpoints.

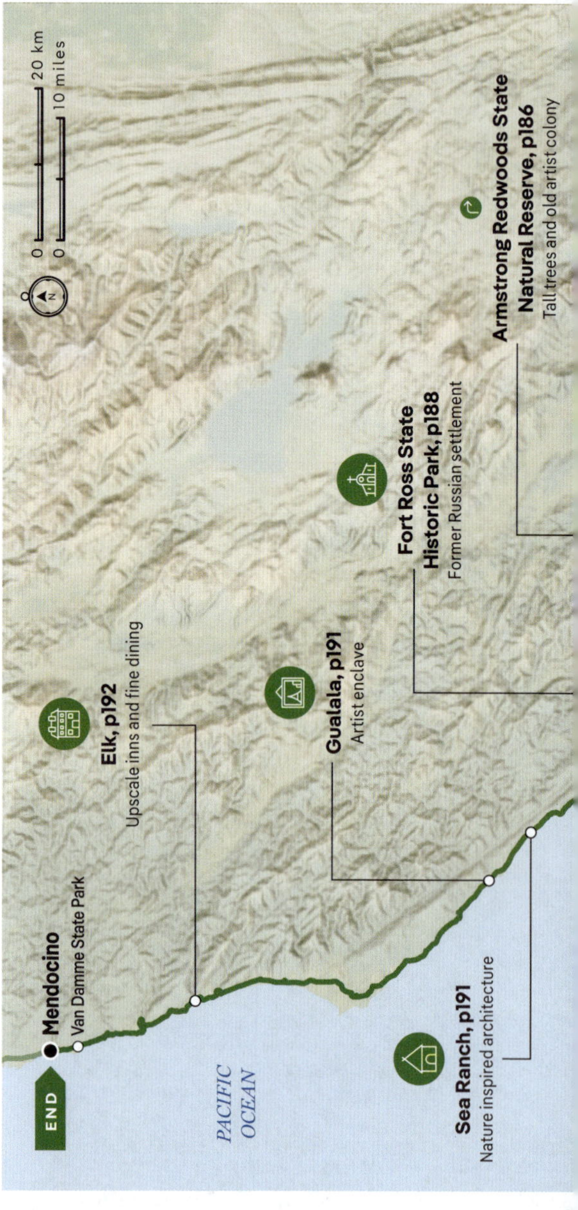

Armstrong Redwoods State Natural Reserve, p186
Tall trees and old artist colony

Fort Ross State Historic Park, p188
Former Russian settlement

Gualala, p191
Artist enclave

Elk, p192
Upscale inns and fine dining

Sea Ranch, p191
Nature inspired architecture

END Mendocino
Van Damme State Park

PACIFIC OCEAN

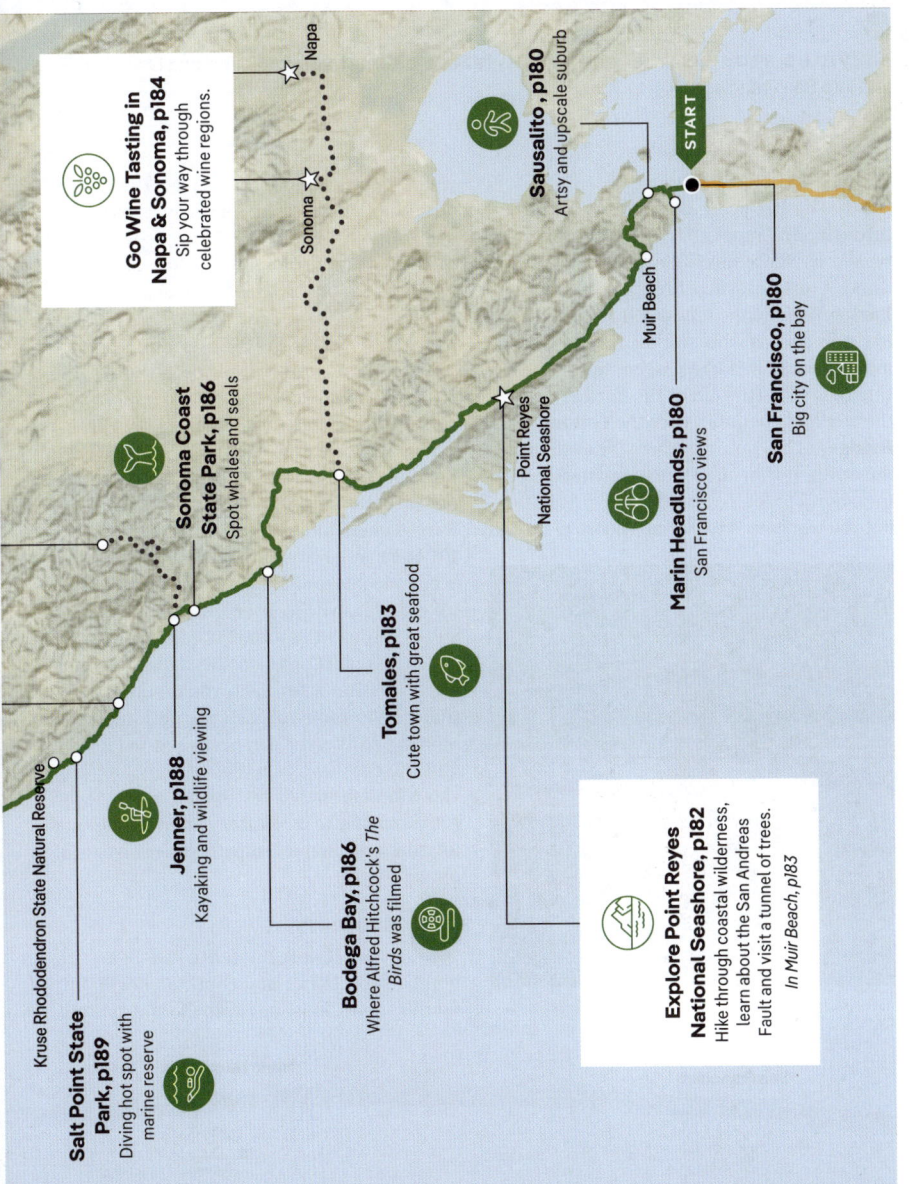

PREVIOUS STOP Continue north from Devil's Slide, passing through Pacifica and Daly City and into San Francisco.

San Francisco

The Pacific Coast Highway goes right through San Francisco (p168), where it's also known as Shoreline Highway. The road continues north, passing through **Golden Gate Park** (p174) and the Presidio, but it looks more like a freeway in this section, so don't expect much scenery if you're passing through. Hwy 1 merges with Hwy 101 at the northern end of the city and continues over the **Golden Gate Bridge** (p172). Note that there is no toll to take the bridge north, but if you're driving the PCH from north to south, you will be charged a toll – but you won't need to stop at a booth to do it. If you're using your own car, you'll get an invoice within a few weeks of your drive; rental-car companies have different billing processes. For more information about tolls, see *goldengate.org/bridge/tolls-payment*.

Marin Headlands

On the northern side of the bridge, the Marin Headlands is the place to go for postcard-worthy pictures of the Golden Gate Bridge against the backdrop of the San Francisco skyline. For the best views, take exit 442 onto Alexander Ave and head west on Bunker Rd to the Barry-Baker Tunnel, which crosses under Hwy 101. You may have to wait, as the tunnel can only accommodate traffic going in one direction at a time, and it switches every five minutes.

Pass through the tunnel to McCullough Rd, which becomes Conzelman Rd at the first traffic circle. Within a few feet, you'll start seeing pull-off viewpoint areas with parking, each offering a different perspective of the bridge and the city beyond it. For some of the best views (and for public restrooms), continue for roughly a mile to the **Battery Spencer** parking lot, where a 0.2-mile footpath leads down to an observation area.

Sausalito

From Conzelman Rd, it's easy to hop back on Hwy 1 and continue north, but families with kids may want to make a pit-

Golden Gate Bridge

San Francisco — 6 miles — Marin Headlands

View of Golden Gate Bridge from Marin Headlands

stop at the **Bay Area Discovery Museum** (*bayareadiscoverymuseum.org*), an indoor-outdoor children's museum with play-based exhibits geared toward the eight-and-under set, before heading north along East Rd to downtown Sausalito. If you can't find street parking, there's a large paid parking lot next to the **Sausalito Terminal Pier** (the terminus for ferries from San Francisco). If you're feeling peckish, head to the **Spinnaker** at the edge of the pier, which offers great food and even better views. Otherwise, consider a stroll down Sausalito's main thoroughfare, the **Bridgeway**, which is dotted with art galleries and expensive boutiques.

continues on p183

BEST PLACES TO EAT

Spinnaker, Sausalito $$$
This swanky spot serves sandwiches, salads and heavier meat and seafood dishes in a bright space with floor-to-ceiling windows that highlight incredible bay views. *spinnakersasausalito.us*; 11am-9pm Sun-Thu, to 10pm Fri & Sat

Marshall Store, Marshall $$
A great place to stop for fresh-from-the-bay oysters, sandwiches and ceviche. *themarshallstore.com*; 11am-3pm Mon-Fri, to 4pm Sat & Sun

Route One Bakery & Kitchen, Tomales $
This bakery is loved for its flaky croissants and its tasty sourdough bread. *routeonekitchen.com*; 7:30-3pm Thu-Sun, to 2pm Mon

Cafe Aquatica, Jenner $
Order a yummy salad or sandwich to have on a river-facing patio at this compact cafe in Jenner. *cafeaquatica.com*; 8am-4pm

---

A great place for a photo stop

7 miles

Sausalito

Explore Point Reyes National Seashore

This protected seashore guards roughly 110 miles of coastal marshes, beaches, forests and grasslands.

HOW TO

Nearest stop: Muir Beach

Getting here: From Muir Beach, head north on Hwy 1 until you pass the town of Olema. Then take a left on Bear Valley Rd, which will lead you to the park headquarters and the Bear Valley Visitor Center.

More info: nps.gov/pore

A federally protected area since 1962, Point Reyes National Seashore offers pristine beaches, historic sites and around 150 miles of trails. The hiking opportunities alone make it worth a visit, with trails suitable for all ages and skill levels. A good place to start your visit is at the **Bear Valley Visitor Center**, where you'll find natural history exhibits, a gift shop and a ranger-staffed information desk. Across the street is a large picnic area with benches and a few trails, including the **Earthquake Trail**, a 0.6-mile paved trail featuring interpretive panels about the San Andreas Fault, which cuts through the national seashore.

From the visitor center, it's just over 11 miles to the **Cypress Tree Tunnel**, a beautiful road flanked with cypresses that form a tunnel with their canopy (note that the road is closed to traffic, so you'll have to park on the edge of Sir Francis Drake Blvd and explore on foot). Another 10 miles south down the same boulevard will lead you to the **Point Reyes Lighthouse**, where there's a visitor center with exhibits on whales and on the lighthouse itself.

Right: Point Reyes Lighthouse

Muir Beach

Hwy 101 and Hwy 1 split again just north of Sausalito, where Hwy 1 regains its Shoreline Highway monicker. The road winds southwest through the suburbs of Tamalpais Valley and crosses through woodlands before reaching Muir Beach, a sandy cove that's popular among dog owners, as dogs are welcome to frolic on the beach without a leash, as long as they are supervised and under voice control. The northern end of the beach is clothing optional. A 450ft-long pedestrian walkway links the parking lot to the beach and to area trails, including the **California Coastal Trail** (p155).

About 1½ miles north of the beach parking lot, the **Muir Beach Overlook** offers magnificent views of the Pacific Ocean. It's especially worth a stop between December and January or March and April, when you can spot gray whales migrating between Baja California and Alaska. From Muir Beach, it's a 20-mile drive north to the **Point Reyes National Seashore**.

Tomales

From Point Reyes, Hwy 1 continues along the eastern shore of Tomales Bay, passing through small unincorporated communities such as Marshall, where seafood restaurants such as the **Marshall Store** (p181) serve oysters freshly harvested from Tomales Bay. The road continues through quiet stretches dominated by vacation cottages and the occasional shop or post office before turning inland toward Tomales, a compact historic town that dates to the mid-1800s. Tomales is a good place for a pit stop. If you're in the mood for a snack, you can pick up tasty pastries at **Route One Bakery & Kitchen** (p181). There are also a few lower-priced hotels in the area, including **Tomales Hotel** (p187), a revamped boutique property in the heart of town. For a bit of beach time, head west for about 4 miles to spacious and sandy **Dillon Beach**, stopping mid-route to snap a picture at **Elephant Rock**, a cluster of boulders on a grassy field that (sort of) resemble a herd of elephants when viewed from certain angles.

DETOUR: The Napa & Sonoma Valleys

If you're at all into wine, it's well worth making a detour inland toward the **Napa and Sonoma Valleys** (p184), two of California's most celebrated viticultural regions. The city of Sonoma in the heart of the Sonoma Valley is around a 30-mile drive away, while the Napa Valley city of Napa is closer to 42 miles from the coast.

continues on p186

PACIFIC GRAY WHALES

While the Pacific Coast Highway is at its busiest during the summer, you'll be in for a treat if you come in winter or spring, when the annual gray whale migration takes place. From November until January, whales head south to the lagoons off the coast of Mexico's Baja Peninsula, before heading north to Alaska around April or May, where they remain through the summer. Pacific gray whales average about 50ft in length and can weigh anywhere from 70,000lb to 90,000lb (females tend to be larger).

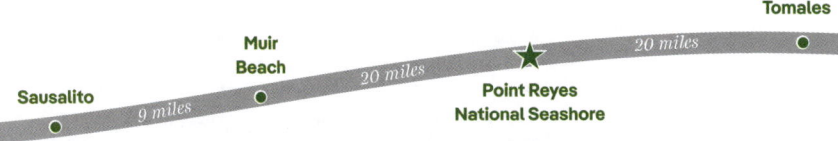

Sausalito — 9 miles — Muir Beach — 20 miles — Point Reyes National Seashore — 20 miles — Tomales

Go Wine Tasting in Napa & Sonoma

Oenophiles take note: the famous wineries of the Napa and Sonoma Valleys are mere miles away. Take a few hours – or a few days – out of your journey for a wine-tasting excursion.

Nearest stop: Tomales

Getting here: To get to the Sonoma Valley, head east on Tomales Petaluma Rd on the south side of Tomales. The region's main city, Sonoma, is about 30 miles away. To get to Napa from Sonoma, take the Sonoma Hwy (Hwy 12) east for another 14 miles.

When to go: Visit between August and October if you want to be in town for the harvest season or come in the winter for fewer crowds and better deals on accommodations.

The Napa Valley

When it comes to California's wine scene, the Napa Valley is the longtime star of the show. It became the first American Viticultural Area (AVA) in California – and on the West Coast – back in 1981. However, the region's rise to fame came five years earlier at the Paris Wine Tasting of 1976, also known as the 'Judgement of Paris,' when wines produced by Napa wineries such as **Stag's Leap Wine Cellars** (stagsleapwinecellars. com) and **Chateau Montelena** (montelena.com) received consistently higher marks than their French counterparts.

While the valley is best known for its big, bold Cabernet Sauvignon, the region also produces a lot of Chardonnay, Merlot and Zinfandel. Wineries worth checking out include **Quintessa** (quintessa.com), a biodynamic property with estate views from its minimalistic tasting room, and **Castello di Amorosa** (castellodiamorosa. com), which looks more like an Angevin castle than a Californian winery. For a particularly fun way to go winery hopping, book a seat on the **Wine Train** (winetrain.com), a vintage steam engine that connects downtown Napa with **Charles Krug** (charleskrug.com) and **V. Sattui Winery** (vsattui.com).

The Sonoma Valley

Although the Sonoma Valley is sometimes left in the shadow of Napa's fame and glory, this neighboring region to the east is actually a better option for many people, and not just because it's a tad closer to the

KNOW BEFORE YOU GO

Many wineries require reservations, so if you have your heart set on a specific spot, check their policies in advance. Most wineries charge for tastings, which can range from around $25 to upwards of $200 in fancier spots. Fees are generally waived with a purchase of two or more bottles. Wineries will usually provide dump buckets, which you can use as a spittoon or to toss out extra wine, both of which are socially acceptable (and smart, if you're the one driving).

Left: Castello di Amorosa; Below: Chateau Montelena

Pacific Coast Highway. Wines here tend to be priced slightly lower, which often has more to do with brand recognition than actual quality, and the tasting experience is often more laid-back and informal in the Sonoma Valley. Like Napa, Sonoma produces a fair bit of Cabernet, but it's Pinot Noir where the region really shines. One of the best spots to try it is at **Gary Farrell Vineyards** *(garyfarrellwinery.com)* in Healdsburg. If you're more of a Zinfandel drinker, visit **Seghesio Family Vineyards** *(seghesio.com)*, which has been around since 1895.

Bodega Bay

A 15-mile drive north of Tomales, Bodega Bay is a fishing village that's morphed into an upmarket getaway destination, complete with upscale inns and a sprawling golf course, the **Links at Bodega Harbour** *(bodegaharbour golf.com).* The town was made famous by Alfred Hitchcock's 1963 film *The Birds,* much of which was shot at the town's **Potter Schoolhouse,** a school turned community center and inn that's now a private residence. Other locations you might recognize from the film include the c 1860 **St Teresa of Avila Church** and the **Tides Wharf & Restaurant** *(innatthetides.com/tides-wharf -restaurant; $$),* which remains a popular seafood stop to this day.

Try Sonoma County's famous wine at **Sonoma Coast Vineyards** *(sonomacoastvineyards.com),* which has a compact tasting room that sits right on the Pacific Coast Highway. From the tasting room, it's just over a mile up the PCH to the **Ren Brown Collection** *(renbrow.com),* which specializes in Japanese artwork and furnishings and has its own Japanese-style garden. If you visit Bodega Bay on a Friday, don't miss the chance to learn about the aquatic world (and see sea creatures!) at the UC Davis Coastal and Marine Sciences Institute's **Bodega Marine Laboratory** *(marinescience.ucdavis.edu/bml)* on a free, hour-long tour.

Sonoma Coast State Park

Sonoma Coast State Park

Just north of Bodega Bay, **Sonoma Coast State Park** *(parks.ca.gov/sonomacoast)* is one of the largest state beaches in California, encompassing roughly 5000 acres and over 10 miles of seashore between Bodega Head and the Russian River. It's particularly popular in the winter, when its many vantage points make for prime whale-watching, while a 5-mile network of trails and four campgrounds draw in visitors from late spring to early fall. The park is also home to one of the largest sea rookeries in the state, and if you come in the spring, you may see harbor-seal pups hanging out near the mouth of the Russian River. If you spot any young seals, keep your distance: mothers are fierce and can attack if they perceive you as a threat.

DETOUR: Armstrong Redwoods State Natural Reserve

The Pacific Coast Highway crosses the Russian River, where it connects to Hwy 116. For an interesting detour that will take you about 17 miles off the route, bear right on Hwy 116 and drive for roughly 4 miles to **Duncans Mills**, a tiny village with a smattering of antique stores and specialty shops offering everything from tea to locally produced wine.

From Duncans Mills, it's another 10 miles to the **Armstrong Redwoods State Natural Reserve** *(parks.ca.gov/?page_id=450)*, which protects over 800 acres of coastal redwood forest. A good place to start is at the visitor center, which has interpretive displays and trail maps, before continuing for half a mile to the **Colonel Armstrong Tree**, which is estimated to be roughly 1400 years old, making it the oldest tree in the grove. Less than 2 miles north of the visitor center sits **Pond Farm Pottery** *(pondfarm.org ; tours $25)*, a former artist colony that ran from the 1940s until becoming part of the recreation area in 1985. Docent-led tours take place on the third Saturday of the month, March to October (booking in advance is recommended).

BEST PLACES TO SLEEP

Tomales Hotel, Tomales $$
This historic small-town property offers cozy rooms and convenient self-check-in. *tomaleshotel.com*

Sea Ranch Lodge, Sea Ranch $$$
Housed in one of the oldest buildings in the design-centric coastal community of Sea Ranch, this boutique property pairs incredible views with natural design. *thesearanchlodge.com*

Harbor House Inn, Elk $$$
The biggest surprise at this upscale inn is that it has its own two-Michelin-star restaurant. *theharborhouseinn.com*

Elk Cove Inn & Spa, Elk $$$
The breakfast is almost as good as the ocean views at this welcoming little inn. *elkcoveinn.com*

Armstrong Redwoods State Natural Reserve

Jenner

Opposite Sonoma Coast State Park, on the northern shores of the Russian River, sits Jenner, sometimes styled as 'Jenner-by-the-Sea,' a tiny resort community with only a handful of businesses. There's a gas station with a minimart, a wine bar–gift shop hybrid and the **Sonoma County Tourism Visitor Center**, which is well stocked with brochures about area attractions (and has a free public restroom). It's next to an excellent cafe – **Cafe Aquatica** (p181) – that serves espresso drinks and tasty sandwiches on a large outdoor patio with views out over the Russian River. Jenner is also the meeting point for **WaterTreks Eco-Tours** *(watertreks.com)*, which offers guided kayaking tours in the Russian River Estuary, including full-moon tours where you can sometimes see bioluminescent plankton, depending on conditions.

Two miles north of town, **Jenner Headlands Preserve** *(wildlandsconservancy.org/preserves/jennerheadlands)* protects 5630 acres of prairie and forest that provide a habitat for a number of rare and endangered species, including red tree voles, spotted owls and peregrine falcons, as well as bobcats, mountain lions, salamanders, newts and butterflies. There's also a network of six trails that range in length from half a mile to 18 miles.

 Fort Ross State Historic Park

A 10-mile drive up the coast from Jenner Headlands Preserve sits **Fort Ross Historic Park** *(parks.ca.gov/fortross)*, which preserves a two-century-old Russian settlement overlooking the ocean. Fort Ross was established

Along the Way We Met...

SUKI WATERS Building a team of local outdoor safety and interpretive staff to help others enjoy the estuary wildlife nursery I grew up with has turned into a life helping others to connect with the natural world that sustains us. Our tourism activities help fund field research for science students from seventh grade through college, and activities for Scouts and many types of youth groups.

Suki is a sustainability and recreational safety expert and educator and a member of the Kashia Pomo Tribe. Suki owns and operates WaterTreks EcoTours in Jenner.

SUKI'S TIP: *Coastal weather is variable. We share the best days and times to explore in our 10-day micro-climate forecast on our website (watertreks.com).*

Sonoma Coast State Park

10 miles

Keep an eye out for seal pups

Jenner

Chapel, Fort Ross State Historic Park

in 1812 by a group of Alaskan Alutiq and Russian explorers where Metini, a Kashya Pomo village, had already existed for centuries. For the Kashya Pomo people, Metini's location was ideal for fishing and harvesting sea salt; for Russian traders, easy access to seal and sea-otter hunting was the primary draw. In the years that followed, the settlers built structures from redwood timber, including stockades, residences and the first Russian Orthodox chapel south of Alaska.

While a few of these structures have been rebuilt, including the chapel, the only original building standing today is **Rotchev House**, which dates to the 1812 arrival of the Russians. There's also a visitor center with interpretive displays spanning topics ranging from Kashya culture to Russian-American traders.

Salt Point State Park

Continuing up the PCH for another 7 miles will take you to **Salt Point State Park** *(parks.ca.gov/saltpoint)*, a 6000-acre park with over 30 miles of hiking and equestrian trails and more than 6 miles of beaches. Just off the shoreline next to the park's visitor center, **Gerstle Cove State Marine Reserve** *(wildlife.ca.gov/conservation/marine/mpas/salt-point-gerstle-cove)* is one of the state's first designated underwater areas. While the reserve is popular among skin and scuba divers, cold

Fort Ross State Historic Park

12 miles

7 miles

Salt Point State Park

Kruse Rhododendron State Natural Reserve

> ### ACCESSIBLE TRAILS ON THE SONOMA COAST
>
> Hiking and visiting beaches are among the most popular things to do on the Sonoma County coast, and there are a few spots that are accessible to people who use mobility devices. The visitor center at the Armstrong Redwoods State Natural Reserve (p186) is accessible, and there are three accessible compacted soil trails in the park that range from a quarter-mile to three-quarters of a mile in length. Sonoma Coast State Park (p186) is also wheelchair-friendly, with accessible campsites, picnic areas and trails, including the 1.9-mile Bodega Head Nature Trail, a great place to take in ocean views.

waters throughout the year mean that you'll probably not want to take the plunge without a high-quality wetsuit.

 ### Kruse Rhododendron State Natural Reserve

Adjacent to the Salt Point, the **Kruse Rhododendron State Natural Reserve** *(parks.ca.gov/?page_id=448)* preserves a mix of second-growth redwood trees, Douglas fir and tanoak, but the real draw is, as the name suggests, the park's abundance of pink rhododendrons, which are usually in bloom between mid-April and mid-June. The thickest section of bushes is found

Salt Point State Park — 3 miles — **Kruse Rhododendron State Natural Reserve**

 Stop here in late spring for a hike through the blooms

by walking around the **Rhododendron Loop Trail** for around 10 minutes.

Sea Ranch

A few miles up the PCH from Salt Point, Sea Ranch is a planned community that was founded in the 1960s. The architecture and landscaping are Sea Ranch's most notable features, with strict regulations that require structures to use locally sourced redwood and Douglas fir for the framing and siding or shingles, following a style that's been dubbed the 'Third Bay Tradition.' A similar aesthetic extends to the grounds, and non native plants and perimeter fences are prohibited. While Sea Ranch has a small number of year-round residents, many of its condominiums and cottages are now used as vacation rentals. There are also 17 rooms for rent at the **Sea Ranch Lodge** (p187), a boutique property fashioned in the quintessential Sea Ranch style.

The most famous building in the community is the **Sea Ranch Chapel** *(thesearanchchapel.org)*, a non-denominational chapel with a fanciful, semi-conical roof that resembles an ornate gnome hat. Inside, there are a few pews where anyone can come and reflect or meditate while watching light trickle in through multihued stained-glass windows. A small trail network extends behind the chapel, but keep an eye out for no-trespassing signs (one of the trails at the southern end of the property is off-limits to visitors).

Gualala

Across the Gualala River from Sea Ranch, the town of Gualala has architecture that feels decidedly ordinary compared to its neighbors down the road. Still, it offers a few good places to stop for a meal, including **Trinks Cafe** *(trinkscafe.com; $)*, which serves pastries, sandwiches and coffee drinks from morning until late afternoon. **Gualala Seafood Shack** *(gualalaseafoodshack.com; $)* is popular for its seafood-dominated menu complete with clam chowder and an oyster bar.

The town's arts scene is enormous for a community of its size. The main institution – **Gualala Arts Center** *(gualalaarts.org; 46501 Old Stage Rd)* – is located half a mile inland from the PCH. The center has two art galleries displaying works by local artists, a clay studio and a performing arts space. More art by Gualala Arts Center members, along with a smattering of jewelry and gift items, is available at the **Dolphin Gallery** on Hwy 1. It's next door to the **Discovery Gallery** *(@discoverygalleryartcollective),* which showcases the works of the 38 members of the Discovery Artist Collective.

Sea Ranch Chapel

The stained-glass windows at the Sea Ranch Chapel are dazzling

Gualala to Elk

Roughly 10 miles north along the PCH will take you to **Schooner Gulch State Beach** *(parks.ca.gov/?page_id=446)*, popular for fishing, surfing and sunset picnics. You'll notice two trailheads at the parking area. The southern one leads to Schooner Gulch Beach, while the trail to the north leads down to **Bowling Ball Beach**, which gets its name from the round mini-boulders that you can see spread across the beach during low tides. While they resemble asymmetrical bowling balls, these mineral formations are actually called concretions.

About an 8-mile drive north of the Schooner Gulch State Beach parking area is the **Point Arena Lighthouse** *(pointarenalighthouse.com)*, which was first constructed here in 1870. The lighthouse features an **Indoor Museum** that gets you up close to a lens dating to 1908. There's also an **Outdoor Museum** that spans 23 acres and features hiking trails, art installations and gardens filled with native plants. If you want to stay a while, you can book an ocean-facing room or **vacation cottage** *($$)* on the same grounds.

Elk

Another 19 miles up the PCH will take you to Elk, a tiny – and undeniably pretty – community with a few upscale lodging options and gorgeous sea-stack views (especially at sunset on rare clear days). One of the most popular spots to stay is the **Harbor House Inn** (p187), but a night here will put you back a pretty penny, especially if you also try the tasting menu at the inn's 20-seat Michelin-star restaurant. **Elk Cove Inn & Spa** (p187) is an equally fine (and typically slightly less expensive) option, with gorgeous views and a sumptuous breakfast.

Elk sits just above **Greenwood State Beach** *(parks.ca.gov/?page_id=447)*, which is worth visiting for its views alone. Before heading down to the shore (accessible via a steep trail from town), it's worth stopping at the **Greenwood Visitor Center** *(Fri-Sun)*. Here you'll find museum displays that give a glimpse into what life was like in Elk during its heyday as a logging town at the turn of the 20th century, when it was still called Greenwood. For souvenirs, head to **Matson Mercantile** *(matsonmercantile.com)*, a few hundred feet from the visitor center, which sells artwork, greeting cards and jewelry crafted by local makers.

Van Damme State Park

Continue north from Elk towards Mendocino, on what is a particularly fog-prone and winding stretch of the highway. You'll mostly pass hotels and vacation homes for the next 14

Point Arena Lighthouse

Gualala

Elk

33 miles

Try Michelin-starred dining in this upscale town

Pygmy Forest Trail

WESTERN SNOWY PLOVER

If you're walking on the beaches of California between March and September, keep an eye out for signage (and possibly fencing) warning of Western snowy plover nesting areas. These tiny threatened shorebirds are known to use driftwood and other ocean debris to make nests in the sand, where they lay itty-bitty eggs that can be harder to see than the camouflageable birds themselves. Snowy plovers also frighten easily, and are known to abandon their nests if they are scared by dogs or even kites flying overhead. Keep your distance.

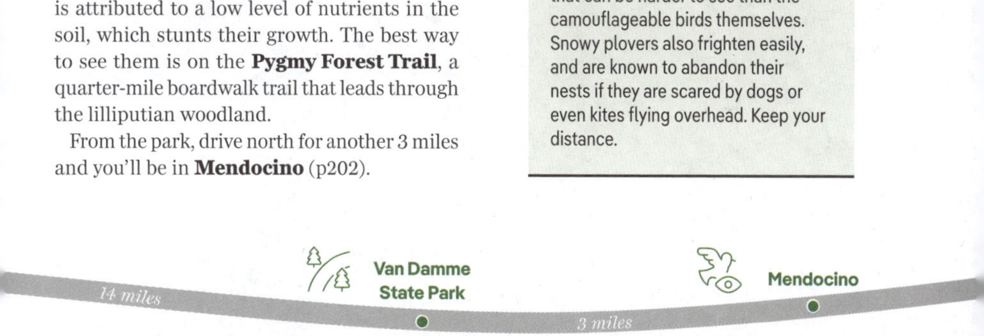

miles until you reach **Van Damme State Park** *(parks.ca.gov/?page_id=433)*, a lush park that's home to a mix of bluffs, beaches, riparian zones and forests. The park's most unusual attraction is its **Pygmy Forest**, where you can see mature, cone-bearing cypress and pine trees that measure between half a foot and 8ft tall, despite being a century old. The trees' small stature is attributed to a low level of nutrients in the soil, which stunts their growth. The best way to see them is on the **Pygmy Forest Trail**, a quarter-mile boardwalk trail that leads through the lilliputian woodland.

From the park, drive north for another 3 miles and you'll be in **Mendocino** (p202).

 Van Damme State Park

 Mendocino

14 miles — 3 miles

PHOTO ESSAY

The Napa Valley

ALTHOUGH WINE IS produced across California, the most famous viticultural region in the state (and the country) is the Napa Valley (p184). A short detour inland from the Pacific Coast Highway, this bucolic region is best known for its bold Cabernet Sauvignon and crisp Chardonnay.

While the Napa Valley's name is synonymous with great wine, its global popularity is fairly new in the grand scheme of things. It became the first American Viticultural Area (AVA) on the West Coast in 1981, only a few years after the pivotal Paris Wine Tasting of 1976, when a slew of Napa wines outperformed French competitors. Today, it's a place of pilgrimage for oenophiles, enticing travelers from across the globe to its expansive vineyards and its grand tasting rooms.

From left:
A visit during fall offers a unique view of the changing colors of Napa's vineyards.
St Helena is home to several wine caves, some of which date back over a hundred years.
Rich soils, rolling hills and varied microclimates make the Napa Valley the picturesque winescape it is.

KIT LEONG/SHUTTERSTOCK

DELLA HUFF/ALAMY

From top:
As far from the light pollution of major cities as it's possible to get in this part of California, Napa offers stunning night skies.

Up, up, and away! Hot air ballooning offers serene unspoiled views of the Napa Valley, especially at sunrise. If heights aren't your thing, hop aboard the Wine Train instead (p184).

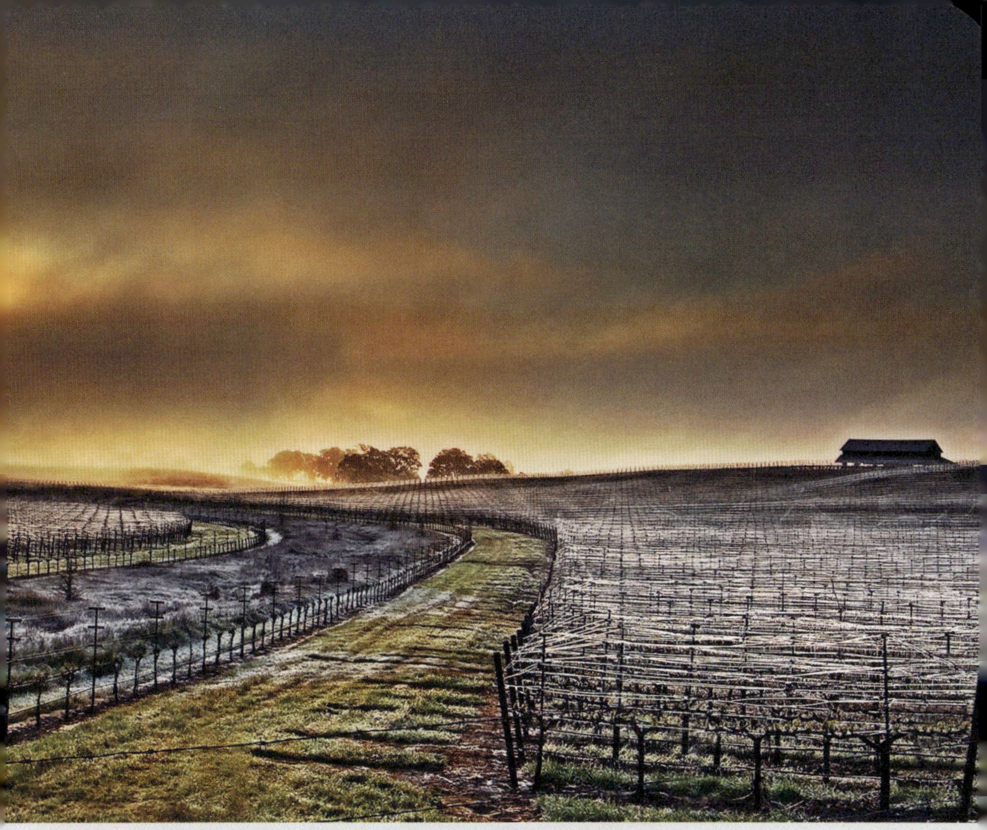

TOP: JEFF TANGEN/ALAMY; RIGHT: DENNIS FRATES/ALAMY

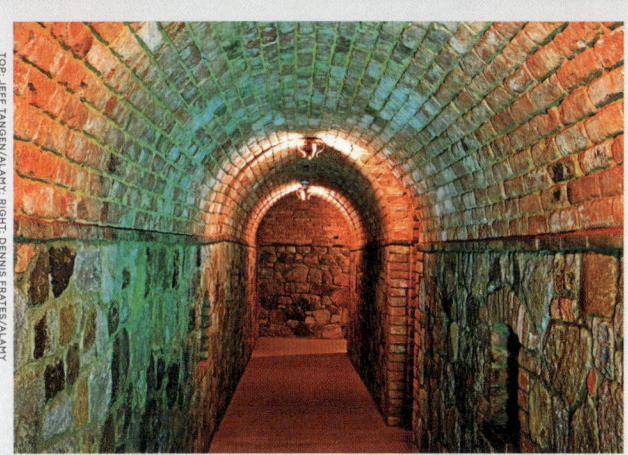

From top:

There is no wrong time to visit Napa – the eerie stillness of the wintry vineyards offers a beauty of its own.

The medieval Tuscan-style castle and winery, Castello di Amorosa (p184), features outdoor terraces, hidden rooms, and wine caves.

Mendocino

One of the biggest shifts in landscape on the PCH happens somewhere between Mendocino and Eureka. After winding along coastal cliffs and past vast expanses of sand and sea, you turn inland, where windswept cypresses give way to mighty hemlocks and Douglas firs. Before you know it, you're driving precariously close to massive redwoods with trunks so gargantuan that you can't help but wonder if you've crossed into a parallel universe inhabited by giants.

Margot Bigg

Eureka

158 MILES
4-HOUR DRIVE

THIS LEG:

- Mendocino
- Mendocino Coast Botanical Gardens
- Downtown Fort Bragg
- Drive Thru Tree Park
- Standish-Hickey State Recreation Area
- Confusion Hill
- Richardson Grove State Park
- Garberville
- Fortuna
- Ferndale
- Humboldt Bay National Wildlife Refuge
- Eureka

PCH near Mendocino (p202)
JOSEPH SOHM/SHUTTERSTOCK

Driving Notes

Expect to see two very different sides of Northern California on this section of your drive. For the first third of the way, you'll be navigating twisty-turny roads that are often blanketed in cotton-like fog. Then you'll turn inland, weaving through a zigzagging forest for 30-odd miles, before being spit out near Leggett, where Hwy 1 ends and redwood adventure begins.

Breaking Your Journey

Garberville is a good place to pick up supplies, get gas or even stop for the night, particularly if you want to do a side trip to the Lost Coast. There's a good choice of restaurants and hotels, too. Fortuna's another option, but it's so close to Eureka that you might as well keep going.

Margot's Tips

BEST MEAL Panang curry at Asian Fusion Thai and Laos Cuisine (p203) in Fort Bragg.

SILLIEST ATTRACTION Confusion Hill

ESSENTIAL STOP The Eternal Treehouse. I have fond memories of visiting as a child, when it was still a gift shop.

ROAD-TRIP TIP The part of this stretch between Mendocino and Rockport can get blanketed in fog, which makes driving on its winding roads extra treacherous. Drive slowly.

Cruise the Avenue of the Giants, p210
Get off the highway and onto a whimsical road flanked by gargantuan redwoods, some with curious backstories.

Humboldt Bay National Wildlife Refuge, p212
Birders' paradise with raptors and waterfowl

Fortuna, p212
Stopover city with organic brewery

Ferndale, p212
Victorian village with cemetery

Avenue of the Giants Ending Point

Avenue of the Giants

END Eureka

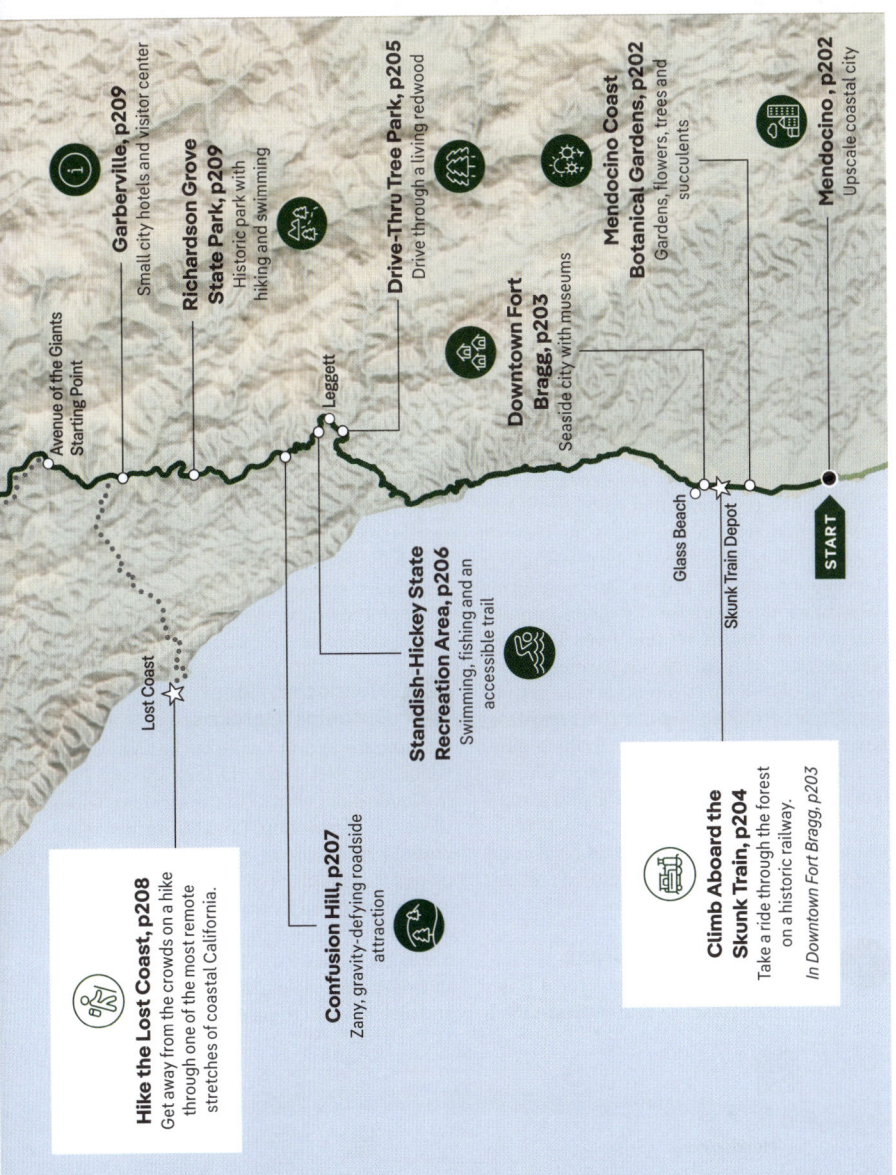

PREVIOUS STOP From Van Damme State Park, continue north for 3 miles to Little Lake Rd. Take a left and you'll be in the heart of downtown Mendocino.

Mendocino

Spread out over a few blocks near a Pacific-facing bluff, compact Mendocino has long been known as a popular but expensive spot for weekending San Franciscans. One of the town's biggest draws is its walkable Historic District full of Victorian houses such as the **Headlands Inn Bed & Breakfast** (p209) that have been turned into charming inns.

If you're into history, a good way to get your bearings is at the **Kelley House Museum** (kelleyhousemuseum.org; Thu-Mon), an 1861 home-turned-museum filled with period furnishings and art. The museum runs Historic District walking tours a few times a week during the summer months (and on Saturday during the winter), along with the occasional haunted tour or tour focused on the 1980s TV series *Murder, She Wrote*, which was partially filmed in the hamlet. Even if you don't take a town tour, it's worth checking out the **Temple of Kwan Tai** (kwantaitemple.org), which dates to 1870, making it one of the oldest Chinese temples in the state. It's open for public tours every weekend in the early afternoon. If you're feeling hungry, you can get a great meal at the **Fog Eater Cafe**, a couple of hundred feet east of the temple.

Mendocino to Fort Bragg

Heading north up Hwy 1 for 3 miles will take you to **Russian Gulch State Park** (parks.ca.gov/russiangulch), a small but mighty park with hiking trails, a beach, a waterfall and an oceanfront sinkhole known as **Devil's Punch Bowl** that looks particularly dramatic during high tide, when churning waves crash against its sides.

From the park, it's about a 2-mile drive north along Point Cabrillo Dr, which runs parallel to Hwy 1, to **Point Cabrillo Light Station** (pointcabrillo.org) parking lot. From here, it's about a half-mile walk to the **Light Station Museum** (travelers with handicap parking placards can drive to and park at the museum). The small museum, which is open every day of the year, tells the story of the lighthouse, which has been in use since 1909. Special lens tours take place on the first weekend of the month from March to October.

Mendocino Coast Botanical Gardens

Continue for around 5 miles up the highway and you'll enter Fort Bragg, the largest coastal city in Mendocino County. On the southern end of town, the **Mendocino Coast Botanical Gardens** (gardenbythesea.org) features 47 acres of bloom-filled gardens with a 4-mile network of compacted gravel footpaths, most of which are around 4ft wide (mobility scooters are available to rent for a small fee). Must-see spaces include rhododendron gardens, a native plant grove and a garden devoted to succulents.

Mendocino

7.5 miles

See one of the oldest Chinese temples in California

Mendocino Coast Botanical Gardens

Downtown Fort Bragg

Drive north up Hwy 1 and you'll soon be in the heart of walkable downtown Fort Bragg. Street parking is widely available, and there's a large public parking lot behind the **Skunk Train** (p204) depot on Laurel St, a block west of Hwy 1. Just south of the depot, the **Guest House Museum** (*fortbragghistory.org*) is a must for architecture and design fans. It was built in 1892 to act as both a residence for the founder of the Union Lumber Company and as a way to showcase what the company could do. The home was made almost entirely from heart redwood and features ornately carved molding, paneling

continues on p205

BEST PLACES TO EAT

Fog Eater Café, Mendocino $$
California cuisine meets the flavors of the southern US at this pretty cafe with an attached wine shop. *fogeatercafe.com; 4-9pm Wed-Sat, 10am-2pm Sun*

Asian Fusion Thai and Laos Cuisine, Fort Bragg $$
Rich, mildly spiced curries and stir-fries steal the show at this downtown spot. *asianfusionsv.com; 11:30am-8:30pm, to 9pm Fri & Sat*

Woodrose Cafe, Garberville $$
At first glance, this local favorite looks like a typical diner, but they specialize in natural and organic food, with a huge menu of scrambles and omelets for breakfast, and sandwiches and burgers at lunchtime. *thewoodrosecafe.com; 8am-3pm Mon-Fri, to 2pm Sat & Sun*

Mendocino Coast Botanical Gardens

2.5 miles

Fort Bragg

Climb Aboard the Skunk Train

Since 1885, the Skunk Train has been making regular journeys through the ancient redwoods of Mendocino County, first as a timber train and later as a tourist attraction.

Nearest stop: Fort Bragg
Getting here: The Skunk Train Depot is in the heart of downtown Fort Bragg, just off Hwy 1 or from East Commercial St in the inland town of Willits.
Cost: Tickets start at $49.95 plus fees for the Pudding Creek Express.
More info: *skunktrain.com*

The Skunk Train offers a number of journeys lasting from 90 minutes to two to three hours. The **Pudding Creek Express** is the most affordable and travels from Fort Bragg, through the Pudding Creek Estuary to Glen Blair Junction, where passengers can disembark for about 45 minutes and explore the forest, or spend even longer in the woods before catching a return train back to Fort Bragg (return tickets are available for the whole day and reservations aren't required). For a fancier experience, you can book a seat in the swanky Presidential Car, which includes priority boarding, snacks and cocktails. For a longer adventure, head to Willits, 35 miles east of Fort Bragg via Hwy 20, to take a ride on the **Wolf Tree Turn** route, a 16-mile (round-trip) journey that plies to the summit of the line at 1740 feet before descending into the Noyo River Canyon. For an adults-only alternative, the **Highball Express** follows the same route and has an onboard bar and a 21-and-over-only policy. Dogs of all ages are welcome for a small fee.

The Skunk Train

continued from p203
and staircases. Colorful stained-glass windows in the grand entry hall add to the wow factor.

Continue south for another 400ft to the **International Sea Glass Museum** (*international seaglassmuseum.com*), tucked in the back end of a compact shopping plaza. This small museum and shop display a rainbow of sea glass, much of which was collected from three 'glass beaches' in and around Fort Bragg. A small room in the back showcases uranium glass glowing under ultraviolet lights. In the same building, **Asian Fusion Thai & Laos Cuisine** (p203) offers a huge and tasty selection of Southeast Asian curries and noodle dishes.

Glass Beach

A 10- to 15-minute walk northwest of downtown takes you to the city's northernmost Glass Beach, which served as an oceanfront garbage dump between 1906 and 1967. Over the years, pieces of glass were transformed by the power of the ocean into tiny rounded pieces of sea glass in hues of wine-bottle green, medicine-bottle amber and tail-light red. While photos of the beach often make it look downright kaleidoscopic, the reality isn't quite as vibrant thanks to years of 'collectors' scooping up loot from the shoreline. These days, collecting sea glass is prohibited, so make sure to take nothing but pictures.

Fort Bragg to Leggett

Continuing up Hwy 1 for about 7 miles will take you to one of the largest beaches in the region: **Ten Mile Beach**, which is actually only about 6 miles long. It's a great place for seriously long walks on the beach and beachcombing, but expect windy conditions. From here, the Pacific Coast Highway continues along sheer coastal cliffs for around 25 winding miles. While your GPS may tell you it will only take 45 minutes or so to drive the stretch, give yourself much longer and expect plenty of fog and long delays for roadwork. Just north of **Rockport**, the highway turns inland, weaving through a hilly forest (watch out for deer) with even sharper turns for the next 15 miles before joining with Hwy 101 in **Leggett**. This is where Hwy 1 ends for good, and Hwy 101 takes over for the rest of the way.

Drive-Thru Tree Park

If you turn right on Hwy 271, just before Hwys 1 and 101 merge, and drive for about a mile, you'll end up at the **Drive-Thru Tree Park** (*drivethrutree.com*), home to the southernmost of a series of 'drive-through trees' spread across the redwood forests of Northern California. As

SANDRA BROCKMAN/SHUTTERSTOCK

Ten Mile Beach

44 miles

Fort Bragg

Drive-Thru Tree Park

Take a ride on the Skunk Train

Chandelier Tree

MIGHTY REDWOODS

Coast redwoods *(Sequoia sempervirens)* are the tallest trees on Earth, and are known to reach heights of over 250ft. While you can't generally see to the top of a redwood if you look at one from below, you can see just how big their trunks are, often measuring upwards of 15ft in diameter.

While the term 'redwood' typically refers to coast redwoods in everyday vernacular, the coast variety are actually one of three types of redwoods found on Earth. The other two are giant sequoias, which are also found in California, and dawn redwoods, which are native to China.

the name suggests, the star attraction here is the **Chandelier Tree**, a 325ft-tall redwood with a 41ft diameter that's believed to be roughly 2400 years old. Its trunk was cut open in 1937 and the poor old tree has been a popular roadside attraction ever since. For $15, you can drive through the tree yourself, but be careful: the opening wasn't cut with huge, modern American cars in mind, and it can be a tight fit for some larger SUVs and trucks. Consider folding your side mirrors in if you want to keep them.

Standish-Hickey State Recreation Area

About a 2-mile drive north of the Chandelier Tree, on the south fork of the Eel River,

Drive-Thru Tree Park — 2 miles — Drive through an ancient redwood tree — **Standish-Hickey State Recreation Area**

Standish-Hickey State Recreation Area (parks.ca.gov/?page_id=423) is a great place to get up close to old-growth and second-growth redwoods without having to dedicate time to a long hike. There are around 10 miles of trails in the park, the easiest of which is the 1.7-mile **Taber Nature Trail**, a wheelchair-accessible loop with great tree views. If you visit on a hot summer day, you can cool off in swimming holes along the Eel River, while fall and winter are popular for salmon and steelhead fishing (licenses are required; see *wildlife.ca.gov*).

Confusion Hill

Continue north for 5 miles and you'll find yourself at the turnout for Confusion Hill *(confusionhill.com)*, among the zaniest roadside attractions in this stretch of the drive. The star of this attraction, which has been operating since 1949, is the **Gravity House**, a seemingly crooked shack accessible via a steep and narrow path where the sensation of gravity feels turned on its side thanks to optical illusions (or, perhaps, a vortex?). You can even sit in a chair that's impossible to get up from without using your hands. For a less confusing experience, there's also a **Mountain Train Ride** that takes visitors on a half-hour ride through the redwoods. While you ride, keep an eye out for the elusive 'chipalope,' a half-chipmunk, half-antelope cryptid that the folks running Confusion Hill will have you believe lives in these woods.

continues on p209

Along the Way We Met...

ADRIENNE LONG Mushroom foraging in this area is pretty amazing because we have a huge diversity of mushrooms. There are over 2000 different species that can be found throughout the year, and at times, you can find up to 50 edibles, which is great if you're into culinary and medicinal mushrooms. It's kind of magical to start learning about how everything in the forest works together, and how trees and plants are reliant on symbiotic fungi.

Adrienne is a mushroom forager and foraging guide. She leads tours in the Fort Bragg and Mendocino areas (mendomushroomforager@gmail.com).

ADRIENNE'S TIP: *Bring clothes for all weather, no matter what time of year you visit. And always be prepared for adventure!*

Always consult an expert if you choose to forage for mushrooms. In severe cases, mushroom poisoning can be fatal.

Confusion Hill

5.5 miles

Watch out for 'chipalopes'

Hike the Lost Coast

This remote stretch of mountainous coastline rewards intrepid travelers with incredible hiking opportunities and plenty of solitude.

HOW TO

Nearest stop: Garberville

Getting here: To get to the most popular destination on the Lost Coast, Shelter Cove, take Redwood Dr from Garberville to the neighboring town of Redway and then head west on Briceland Rd.

Top tip: Some parts of the Lost Coast Trail are impassable at high tide. Check tide tables before heading out.

Shelter Cove is the gateway to the Lost Coast, and if you're coming from Garberville, this is where you'll first end up. It's a good place to base yourself if you plan to spend some time at the coast, with a few inns and campgrounds, plus coffee shops, restaurants and a pizza parlor. The town is also home to the restored **Cape Mendocino Lighthouse** (*capemendocinolighthouse.org*), which was moved from its original location on Cape Mendocino to Shelter Cove's Mal Coombs Park in 2000.

The Lost Coast Trail

Many visitors come to the Lost Coast specifically to hike the 24.6-mile northern section of the Lost Coast Trail, one of the only long-distance coastal hiking trails in the country. The northern section runs from Shelter Cove's aptly named Black Sands Beach to Mattole Beach in the **King Range National Conservation Area**.

If you plan to spend the night along the trail, you'll need to obtain a permit, either online *(recreation.gov)* or at the King Range Visitor Center, located midway between Garberville and Shelter Cove. Permits are not required for day hikes.

Above: Cape Mendocino Lighthouse; Right: Black Sands Beach, Shelter Cove

Richardson Grove State Park

A 25-mile drive north along the highway, **Richardson Grove State Park** *(parks.ca.gov/richardsongrove)* is one of the first of the north coast's many redwood state parks. Nicknamed 'The Grove,' the land now known as the park was used by Sinkyone people for generations until the arrival of non-Indigenous settlers in the late 1860s, who homesteaded much of the park. In the 1920s, a businessman leased some of the land from its owners and built cabins and visitor facilities. The state of California took it over in 1922, thanks to the efforts of the Save the Redwoods League, which was concerned about the environmental impact of mass tourism in the area, and it's been a public park ever since. These days, it's a popular spot to camp among redwoods, with three large campgrounds – most with accessible sites – plus seasonal swimming holes that are open to day visitors. For great views, take the Toumey Trail from just north of the visitor center to **Panorama Point**, about a 2-mile hike away.

Garberville

Seven miles north of Richardson Grove, Garberville is a good place to stop to stretch your legs, get reasonably priced gas or pick up a snack. You can pick up brochures and get information about events in the area at the **Southern Humboldt Chamber of Commerce & Visitors Center** *(garberville.org)*, tucked at the back of a shopping plaza on the main road through town. For a filling meal, head to the **Woodrose Cafe** (p203), a popular spot for breakfast and lunch. Garberville is also a good place to break up your journey for the night, particularly if you're driving the PCH at a reduced pace. The **Benbow Historic Inn** is a comfortable and fairly priced choice.

DETOUR: The Lost Coast

By the time you've passed Garberville, you've made it about a third of the way up a largely inland segment of the PCH that runs roughly from Leggett to Eureka. If you're craving a bit of oceanfront solitude, consider a detour to the Lost Coast, a remote segment of the coastline that's about a 25-mile drive from Garberville.

continues on p212

BEST PLACES TO SLEEP

Headlands Inn Bed & Breakfast, Mendocino $$
This cozy inn offers lovely rooms with pretty views, an English garden and gorgeous breakfasts served right in your room. *headlandsinn.com*

Benbow Historic Inn, Garberville $$
On the banks of the South Fork of the Eel River just outside of Garberville, this historic property has elegant rooms featuring period-inspired decor. Some have gas fireplaces. *benbowinn.com*

Gingerbread Mansion Inn, Ferndale $$
As the name suggests, this ornate Victorian inn with 11 rooms resembles a giant gingerbread house. *thegingerbreadmansion.com*

Cruise the Avenue of the Giants

Unless you're in a serious hurry, it's well worth foregoing Hwy 101 between Garberville and Pepperwood and instead taking the Avenue of the Giants. This 31.6-mile scenic route runs parallel to Hwy 101 and the South Fork Eel River, passing through massive groves of ancient redwoods along the way.

HOW TO

Nearest stop: Garberville (from the south) or Fortuna (from the north).

Getting here: If you're coming from the south, take exit 645 at Phillipsville. From the north, take exit 661 toward Weott.

When to go: The drive is lovely no matter when you visit, but summers can get crowded, especially in the afternoon.

Cost: There's no cost to drive the route, and most of the stops along the road are free.

Along with towering trees, some well over two millennia old, there are plenty of stops along the route, from roadside gift shops to minimarts. If you're coming from the south, the first place you might want to pull over is at **Boiling Grove**, just past the town of Miranda. This was the first grove purchased by the Save the Redwoods League in 1920. From here, it's another 2.3 miles to the **Shrine Drive-Thru Tree** (closed winter). The trunk measures around 21ft in diameter, with an opening large enough to accommodate most small and mid-size vehicles.

Four miles north of the Drive-Thru Tree takes you to the town of Burlington, the gateway to the **Humboldt Redwoods State Park** (humboldtredwoods.org), which encompasses a 53,000-acre expanse west of the Avenue of the Giants. The visitor center is right on the Avenue of the Giants and is full of great resources, from interpretive displays to a theater screening a short film about the park. Staff are on hand to answer questions and provide tips. For a quick hike, head across the street to the **Gould Grove Nature Loop**, a 0.6-mile trail that leads through massive redwoods.

Nine miles north of the visitor center sits the **Eternal Tree**

THE SAVE THE REDWOODS LEAGUE

The reason so much of Northern California's coast redwood forests stand to this day is thanks to the efforts of the **Save the Redwoods League** (*savetheredwoods.org*), a nonprofit organization that was founded in 1918 to help prevent the forest from utter decimation. Over the last century, the league has protected more than 220,000 acres of redwoods and helped the formation of 66 redwood parks, including the Humboldt Redwoods State Park. Their efforts include land purchase, outreach and education.

Left: Shrine Drive-Thru Tree; Below: Immortal Tree

House, a free-to-visit room hollowed out from an old redwood stump. It served as a gift shop for decades, but is now just an empty room (today, the shop is in an adjacent structure). Another 1.6 miles north of the treehouse, discover the **Immortal Tree**, named as such because it's rumored to have survived floods, fires and the threat of loggers (an axe sticks out of the side of the trunk, about 15ft above the ground).

From here, it's about 3 miles to the junction with Hwy 101.

DETOUR: Avenue of the Giants

Although staying on the PCH is the fastest way to continue your drive north, you're better off taking the scenic route, especially if you want to see some magnificent redwood trees. Eight miles north of Garberville (via exit 645), the Avenue of the Giants (p210) is a 31.6-mile road that runs (mostly) parallel to Hwy 101, passing through groves of massive trees and alongside picnic areas and redwood-themed roadside attractions.

Fortuna

The Avenue of the Giants meets up with the Pacific Coast Highway again just after the town of Pepperwood. From here, it's another 20 miles north along the highway to the city of Fortuna. Like Garberville, this small city is a good place to fill your tank (or charge your electric vehicle) or grab a bite. For a hearty meal or a cold pint of all-natural beer, stop at **Eel River Brewing Co.** *(eelriverbrewing.com; $$),* the first certified organic brewery in the country.

Ferndale

A 7.5-mile drive west of Fortuna, tiny Ferndale has fewer amenities but way more charm. This beautifully preserved Victorian town is lined with colorful old buildings, many of which have been transformed into artsy gift shops. If you're looking for a place to stay the night, consider the **Gingerbread Mansion Inn** (p209), an opulent home-turned-hotel, complete with latticed balconies and a turret. Don't miss the **Ferndale Historic Cemetery** *(ferndalecemetery.com),* which dates to 1868. The expertly carved tombstones in this sprawling graveyard stretch across a beautifully manicured hillside, complete with a flurry of rhododendron bushes.

Humboldt Bay National Wildlife Refuge

About 10 miles up Hwy 101 from the Fortuna and Ferndale area, the **Humboldt Bay National Wildlife Refuge** *(fws.gov/refuge/humboldt-bay)* is a wonderful place for a short hike, and most of the trails here are only around half a mile. It's also a fantastic spot for year-round bird-watching, but peak season for raptors and waterbirds runs from November through April. To the north of the refuge sits **Eureka** (p214), the county seat of Humboldt County and the largest city on California's North Coast.

CANNABIS IN HUMBOLDT COUNTY

Although recreational cannabis has been legal in California since 2016, Humboldt County has been known for its marijuana cultivation since the late 1960s. For decades, young people from across the West Coast would come to the area for seasonal jobs trimming cannabis flowers, creating a summer surge of temporary residents. Today, the scene has moved aboveground, and most Humboldt towns have dispensaries that will sell weed to anyone over 21 with ID. You can even visit a pot farm yourself by taking a tour with **Humboldt Cannabis Tours** *(humcannabis.com).*

Humboldt Bay National Wildlife Refuge

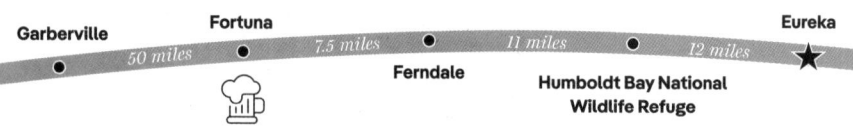

CITY GUIDE:
Eureka

Although Eureka is the largest city on the North Coast, it's far from a metropolis. This compact coastal community has a similar appeal to many of the smaller seafront villages along the coast, with cute shops and restaurants and a heavy dose of Victorian architecture.

HOW TO

Getting there: The PCH runs right through Eureka and into its historic old town.

Getting around: The old town is flat and walkable, and there's plenty of street parking that's metered during the week and free on Sundays.

Sleeping: There are loads of places to stay in Eureka, from budget chain motels such as the **Super 8 by Wyndham Eureka** (wyndhamhotels.com/super-8; $) to historic mansion inns such as the **Pinc Lady Mansion** (pincladymansion.com; $$). Your best bet is to find a spot in or near the Old Town, where most of the city's key attractions and best restaurants are located.

More info: VisitEureka.com

While there are plenty of great places to base yourself throughout the redwood region, Eureka offers far more in terms of amenities, with plenty of places to eat and stay the night, plus all sorts of events, including the **Kinetic Grand Championship** (kineticgrandchampionship.com), a human-powered sculpture race held every spring.

Eureka's architecture is another big draw, and ornate Victorian mansions such as the **Carson Mansion** (ingomar.org), now a private members' club, certainly add a heavy dose of old-timey appeal. And once you've had enough urban fun, redwood forests and tranquil dunes are mere miles away.

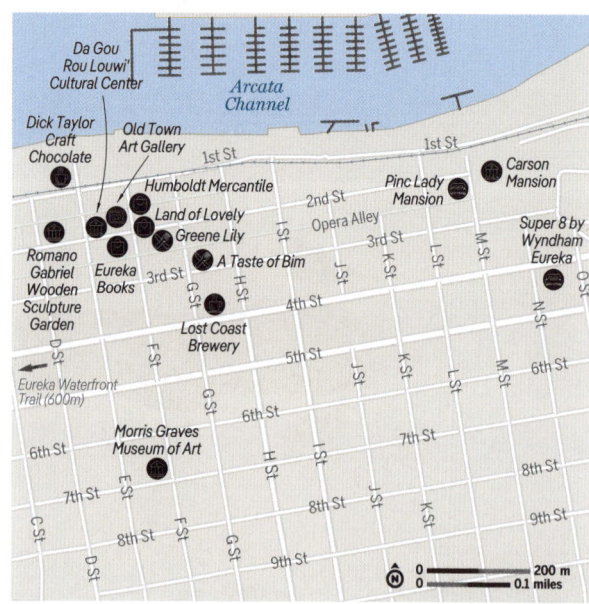

EUREKA'S ART SCENE

Despite its small size, Eureka has a thriving art scene, with loads of galleries, museums and events. Many of the best galleries are right in Old Town, including the **Old Town Art Gallery** (oldtownartgallery eureka.com), a cooperative art gallery that's been showcasing sculpture, photography, paintings and jewelry by local artists for more than half a century. A few blocks away, the **Romano Gabriel Wooden Sculpture Garden** features a selection of wooden creations by Italian-Eurekan artist Romano Gabriel, who died in 1977.

South of Old Town, the **Morris Graves Museum of Art** (humboldtartscouncil.org) is worth the short trek. Along with a large collection of works by American artist Morris Graves, the museum showcases works by other artists from the area, including Romano Gabriel.

If you happen to be in Eureka on the first Saturday evening of the month, it's worth checking out **Arts Alive!**, a celebration of the arts that takes place from 6pm to 9pm. Galleries stay open late, while musicians and other performers come down to the streets to showcase their talent.

Eureka Books

The Da Gou Rou Louwi' Cultural Center

Just west of the Plaza de California, Eureka's main square, the **Da Gou Rou Louwi' Cultural Center** (wiyot.us) tells the story of the Wiyot Tribe, who've lived in the Humboldt Bay region for many thousands of years. The ground floor features a gift shop selling souvenirs and tribally made crafts, while a loft area upstairs hosts changing exhibits focused on Wiyot culture and artistic traditions. Docent-led tours are available by appointment, but drop-in visitors are welcome to explore on their own.

Old Town Shopping

Eureka's Old Town is a great place to shop, with loads of boutiques selling art, gifts and edible treats. **Eureka Books** (eurekabookshop.com) is a great place to pick up new and used books by local and international authors, while **Land of Lovely** (landoflovely.com) is the place to go for women's apparel and colorful gifts. For a sweet snack, head to **Dick Taylor Craft Chocolate** (dicktaylorchocolate.com), which specializes in small-batch chocolates with a nautical theme, or visit **Humboldt Mercantile** (thehumboldtmercantile.com), where you can make your own gift basket full of gourmet goodies from local purveyors.

BEST PLACES TO EAT & DRINK

A Taste of Bim $$	Greene Lily $$	Lost Coast Brewery $$
Tasty Caribbean cuisine, from curries to jerk chicken. atasteofbimeureka.com; 11:30am-8pm Mon-Sat, 1-8pm Sun	Brunch spot with vintage vibes. thegreenelily.com; 9am-2pm	Brewery with a large selection of pub fare. lostcoast.com; 11:30am-9pm Sun-Thu, to 11pm Fri & Sat

INSIGHT

Legends of the Coast

Hwy 1 holds more than postcard views. Between the cliffs and swell, the road gathers stories of creation and catastrophe, of phantoms in lighthouse towers, Bigfoot in the redwoods, dark watchers on the bluffs and sea serpents in the bay.

WORDS BY **CHRISTABEL LOBO**
Christabel is a writer and illustrator based between Abu Dhabi and wherever her next flight lands

MOST ROAD TRIPS down Hwy 1 begin the same way: cliffs and curves, endless swaths of breathtaking roadway, Instagram-worthy sunsets. But as you follow the coast north, the scenery starts to carry whispers. Stories cling to these headlands and harbors – of spirits, giants, phantoms and sea monsters.

The road itself becomes the storyteller, each mile marker a new chapter in California's ongoing mythology. It's easy to believe in things that don't quite make sense – and maybe that's the point.

Today, those stories still linger. In forest clearings and lighthouse towers. In roadside museums and diners. Half-remembered tales of yore that make the drive between Los Angeles and Oregon feel less like sightseeing and more like myth-hunting.

Coastal Cosmologies

Long before the road, before the rumble of tires on asphalt, the Pacific was the first storyteller. For the Indigenous peoples of this coastline, the ocean has always been more than scenery. It's spirit. It's ancestor. It's lifeblood.

In Chumash oral traditions, a rainbow bridge once stretched from Santa Cruz Island (p81) to the mainland, linking people to the creator. Anyone who fell into the sea was transformed into a dolphin. Whales, waves and surf served as messengers, and *tomols* – plank canoes crafted from redwood – cut through the swells to connect island and shore, uniting the physical with the sacred.

Further north, Ohlone and Esselen narratives speak of land emerging from water after a great flood, leaving only a single peak where eagle, hummingbird and coyote took refuge. When the

Bigfoot statue, Garberville (p209)

waters receded, they descended to a newly dry earth to begin the work of populating the land. Walk the shore at Point Lobos (p134) or Big Sur (p126) and those stories start to feel possible. Rocks jut out like they've been placed there with intent. Tide pools reveal shapes you're not sure are seaweed or something else.

The line between land and myth blurs. Mist moves like breath. Waves crash like memory. And if you listen long enough, the coast tells you what it remembers.

Shadows on the Cliffs

Along the ridges of the Santa Lucia Mountains – where Big Sur's cliffs make their final plunge into the Pacific – hikers have long whispered about the 'dark watchers.' Seen most often at twilight, these human-shaped silhouettes stand utterly still, gazing out to sea or into the canyons.

The Chumash are said to have spoken of these figures in their stories, which were later folded into Spanish colonial lore. John Steinbeck mentioned them in his 1938 short story *Flight* and poet Robinson Jeffers wove them into verse. Reports today remain eerily consistent: a hiker glances up from a trail, spots a distant figure, and before they can call out, it vanishes.

Skeptics blame tricks of light, fog or fatigued eyes. But on a late-afternoon hike in Julia Pfeiffer Burns State Park (p129), or gazing from Pfeiffer Ridge, when the wind stills and the shadows stretch, it's easy to believe some watchers never leave their post.

Giants in the Trees

North of Mendocino, Hwy 1 winds inland to its end at Leggett, where Hwy 101 takes over and threads into redwood country. Here the tallest trees on Earth can reach over 350 feet – some older than 2000 years and higher than the Statue of Liberty. Driving the Avenue of the Giants (p210), the canopy knits so tightly overhead that it turns midday into twilight.

That uncanny stillness is part of why Northern California has become ground zero for Bigfoot lore. In 1958, Humboldt County made headlines when local journalists reported on massive, human-like footprints found near Bluff Creek. The name 'Bigfoot' stuck, and in 1967 the Patterson–Gimlin film captured a broad-shouldered figure vanishing into the trees, cementing the region's place in cryptid lore.

Today, Bigfoot is a cottage industry. In Willow Creek (p129) – the self-proclaimed Bigfoot Capital of the World – you can visit the China Flat Museum's cryptid room, browse plaster casts of alleged prints or snap a selfie with towering redwood Sasquatches outside shops. On forest trails in Six Rivers National Forest, the rustle of leaves or a crack of wood underfoot can make you understand why people keep looking.

Haunted by the Sea

California's coastal lighthouses have guided ships through fog and fury for more than a century – and collected their share of ghost stories along the way. Point Sur Lighthouse in Big Sur runs ghost tours in October where docents tell of phantom footsteps and locked doors swinging open. Battery Point Lighthouse in Crescent City (p230) – reachable only at low tide – has tales of cold spots, creaking floors and unseen hands brushing past.

Monterey Bay fishermen still tell of Bobo – a mournful-faced, long-necked creature said to surface over the deep submarine canyon. In 1938, the *Monterey Peninsula Herald* reported that an entire sardine boat crew watched Bobo doze at the surface before it awoke with a snort, fixed them with coal-black eyes, and vanished into the depths.

Add the mournful call of foghorns, the flicker of bioluminescence on black water or the sudden rise of a rogue wave, and it's easy to see how legend takes root here.

The Pacific Coast Highway is more than a scenic drive where myths are carried on salt air and histories etched in stone. Whether you're chasing the perfect photo or the possibility of something unseen, the journey reminds you that some stories are worth the detour.

Eureka

I have a soft spot for this final stretch of the road, partially because of how remote it feels. Even during the peak of summer, when the parking lots at visitor centers and trailheads fill up with cars bearing license plates from across the US and Canada, it's still pretty easy to jump off the route and find yourself a quiet spot to stop and take in the majesty of towering redwoods or the vast Pacific Ocean.

Margot Bigg

PCH near Klamath (p228)
SPRING IMAGES/ALAMY

Crescent City

111 MILES · 2-HOUR DRIVE

THIS LEG:

- Eureka
- Humboldt Coastal Nature Center
- Arcata
- Trinidad
- Sue-meg State Park
- Redwood National and State Parks
- Klamath
- Trees of Mystery
- Del Norte Coast Redwoods State Park
- Crescent City
- Jedediah Smith Redwoods State Park
- The Oregon Coast

Driving Notes

This final segment is fairly short, and the highway is straight and wide throughout much of the stretch, making it easy to get through quite quickly. Still, big things can come in small packages, and you'll find plenty of things to make you want to pull over and get out of your car in this sub-100-mile drive.

Breaking Your Journey

Arcata is a great alternative to Eureka, with a few hotels and some great restaurants. Trinidad is even lovelier if you're looking for peace and views, but expect to pay a premium. If you're continuing your journey into Oregon, consider a night in Crescent City, which has some of the lowest-cost accommodations on California's North Coast.

Margot's Tips

BEST MEAL Wicked Thai Peanut Stirfry at Wildflower Café & Bakery (p223).

FAVORITE VIEW Sunset from atop Trinidad Head (p225).

ESSENTIAL STOP Sue-meg State Park.

ROAD-TRIP TIP Save a few bucks by skipping the drive-through trees further south and visiting the one in Klamath instead.

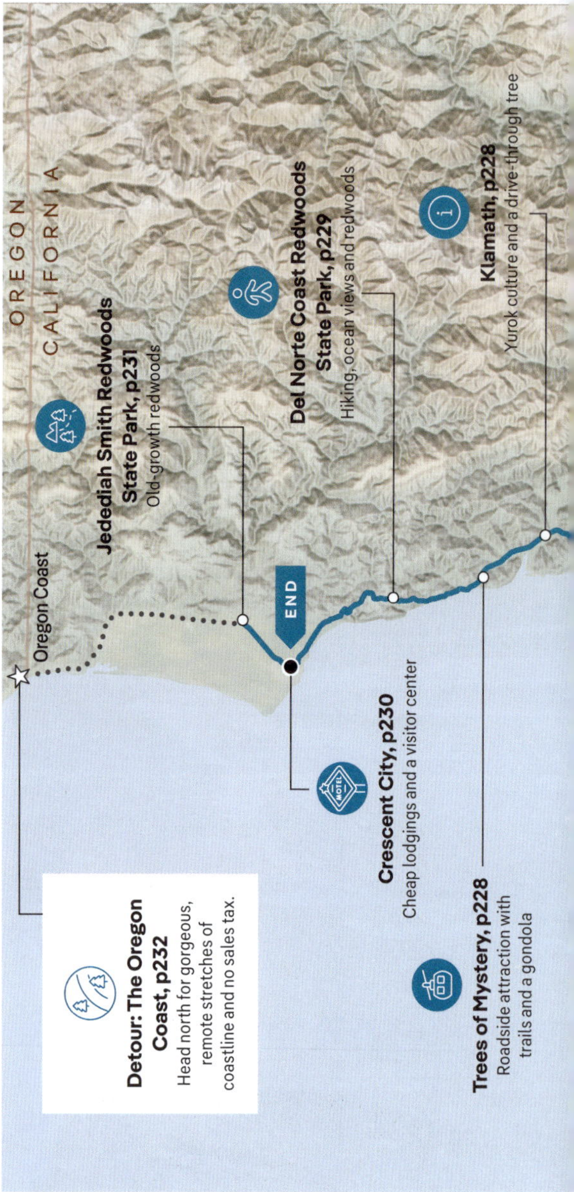
OREGON
CALIFORNIA
Oregon Coast
END
Jedediah Smith Redwoods State Park, p231
Old-growth redwoods
Del Norte Coast Redwoods State Park, p229
Hiking, ocean views and redwoods
Klamath, p228
Yurok culture and a drive-through tree
Detour: The Oregon Coast, p232
Head north for gorgeous, remote stretches of coastline and no sales tax.
Crescent City, p230
Cheap lodgings and a visitor center
Trees of Mystery, p228
Roadside attraction with trails and a gondola

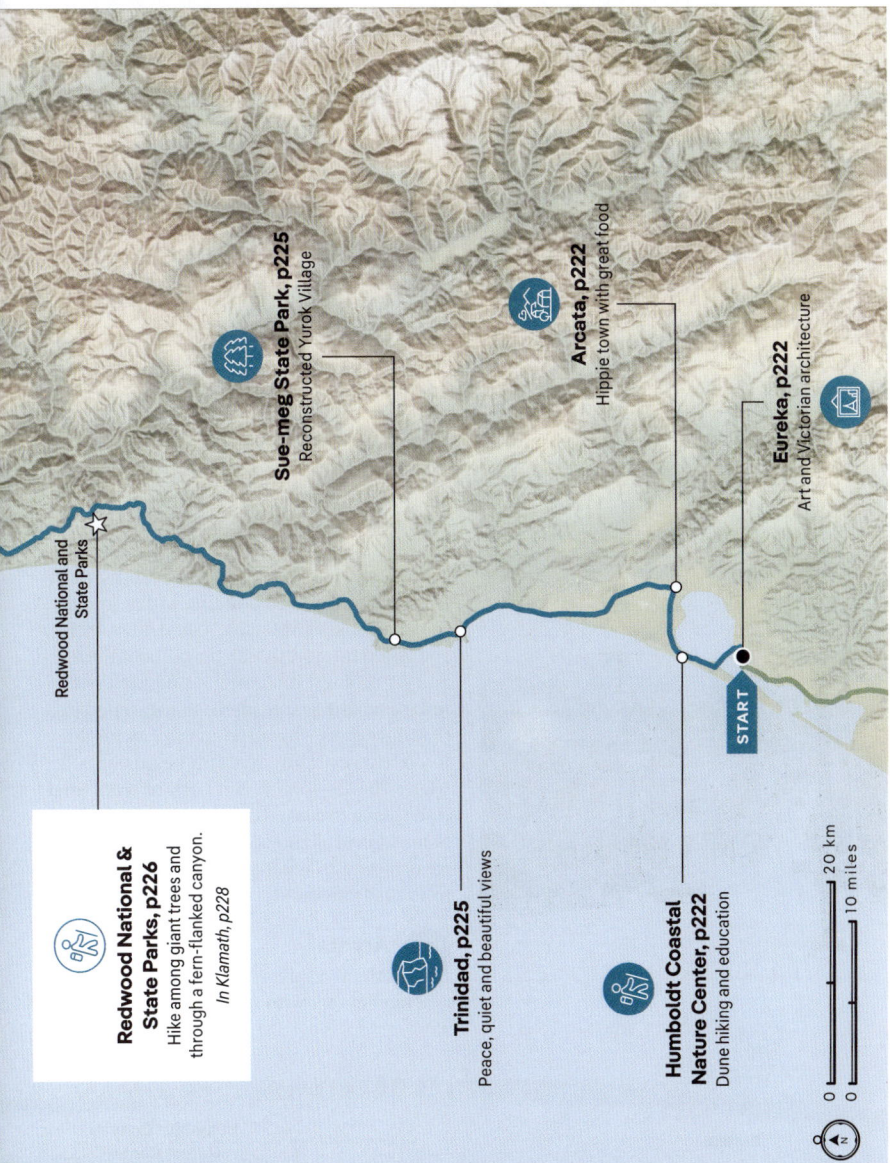

PREVIOUS STOP The highway continues north through the Humboldt Bay National Wildlife Refuge and into Eureka.

Eureka

Eureka (p214) is the cultural and economic hub of Humboldt County and the largest city on the North Coast. It's anchored by a charming old town full of Victorian buildings and independent shops and restaurants. The Pacific Coast Highway (locally known as the Redwood Highway) runs right through the historic center of town, where it splits into two one-way streets that run parallel to each other, rejoining into one highway on Eureka's northeastern outskirts.

As of summer 2025, cyclists (and ambitious walkers) can travel from Eureka up to neighboring **Arcata** without having to worry about cars, thanks to the **Humboldt Bay Trail**, which connects the two cities via a paved multi-use path that runs along the riverfront. The trail is made up of multiple smaller trails that, in turn, are part of the 307-mile-long **Great Redwood Trail**.

Humboldt Coastal Nature Center

Across the Humboldt Bay from Eureka, the **Humboldt Coastal Nature Center** (*friendsofthedunes.org*) is an excellent starting point for visiting the bay's north spit. The one-room center is housed in the Stamps Dune House, a greige-hued building with a rounded roof that makes it resemble a sand dune. Inside, you'll find interpretive displays about the area and its ecology, including a poignant sculpture of a baby seal made from cigarette butts that illustrates why littering is an awful thing to do. However, the real fun begins outside, where there's a small network of trails that leads down to coastal dunes, crossing through a small forest along the way. If you plan to hike, wear mosquito repellent, available to borrow from the front desk.

Arcata

About 8 miles north of Eureka, Arcata is a smaller city with its own unique vibe. It's

Arcata

FROM LEFT: CONOR P FITZGERALD/SHUTTERSTOCK, BOLANE/SHUTTERSTOCK

Beach near Eureka

home to Cal Poly Humboldt (formerly known as Humboldt State University) and has long been famous as a hippie enclave, with natural food stores, bohemian boutiques and a strong cannabis scene that predates the legalization of marijuana in California by many decades.

At the heart of the city, Arcata Plaza is a good place to get a feel for the city, especially if you come on a Saturday, when a year-round farmers market showcases fresh produce from across the region. On the northern end of the plaza, the **Hotel Arcata** (p224) offers simple rooms at one of the most convenient spots in town. Just south of the plaza, **Havana Restaurant and Bar** is among the best addresses in town

BEST PLACES TO EAT

Havana Restaurant and Bar, Arcata $$$
A fancy alternative to Arcata's more casual cafes, this Cuban spot serves heavy stews and sandwiches and Caribbean cocktails. *havanainarcata.com; 5-10pm*

Wildflower Café and Bakery, Arcata $
This long-established breakfast and lunch spot serves up huge portions of vegetarian and vegan baked goods, scrambles, burgers and sandwiches. *wildflowercafebakery.com; 9am-4pm Wed-Mon, plus 5:30-9:30pm Fri & Sat*

Beachcomber Café, Trinidad $$
An all-day menu of brunch classics and filling sandwiches keeps this local hot spot busy most of the time. Many of the ingredients, from the chevre to the focaccia used for the sandwiches, come from local suppliers. *beachcombercafetrinidad.com; 7:30am-2pm*

Go tide-pooling at Luffenholtz Beach Park

Arcata

Luffenholtz Beach Park

BEST PLACES TO SLEEP

Hotel Arcata, Arcata $$
It doesn't get more convenient than this historic hotel overlooking Arcata Plaza, where a popular farmers market takes place every Saturday, no matter the season. *hotelarcata.com*

Lookout at Trinidad Bay, Trinidad $$$
This ultra-intimate property offers four bright rooms with Trinidad Bay views and includes gourmet breakfasts to sweeten the deal. *lookouttrinidadbay.com*

Lighthouse Inn, Crescent City $
This family-run, no-frills hotel is far from fancy, but the rooms are spacious, and some have fireplaces. Free breakfast adds to the value appeal. *lighthouse101.com*

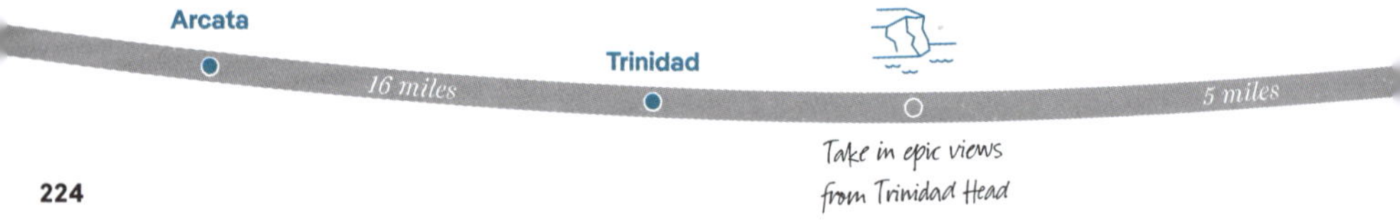

for a fancy dinner date or a cocktail. About a half-mile walk north of the plaza, **Wildflower Cafe and Bakery** (p223) is an excellent spot for breakfast or lunch. About a mile east of the city center, the **Arcata Community Forest** *(cityofarcata.org/197)* is a great place for a hike among the redwoods and has a small network of trails with minimal elevation gain.

Arcata to Trinidad

Hwy 101 continues north out of Arcata, passing through the little city of McKinleyville about 15 miles before reaching Trinidad. There

Arcata — 16 miles — Trinidad — 5 miles

Take in epic views from Trinidad Head

are a few great beaches just beyond McKinleyville, starting with **Clam Beach County Park** (*humboldtgov.org/facilities/facility/details/clam-beach-4*), a good spot for flying kites and one of the few beach parks in the state that allow beachfront camping. **Little River State Beach** (*parks.ca.gov/?page_id=419*) is the next beach up and features a mix of flat beach and dune formations, accessible from the North Beach Trailhead. It's less than half a mile north to **Moonstone Beach County Park** (*humboldtgov.org/facilities/facility/details/moonstone-beach-14*), a popular (and dog-friendly) spot that's a favorite among surfers and boulderers. From Moonstone Beach, the mile-long Scenic Dr (yes, that's the road's official name) leads to **Luffenholtz Beach Park** (*trinidadcoastallandtrust.org*), a popular tide-pooling spot that's accessible via a steep trail.

Trinidad

Just north of Luffenholtz Beach Park, Trinidad is a tiny coastal hamlet with some of the prettiest ocean views in Humboldt County from its beaches and headlands. The town itself is spread out over just a few blocks, but it packs quite the punch, with numerous restaurants, boutiques and galleries, plus a handful of bed-and-breakfasts, including the cozy **Lookout at Trinidad Bay**. For filling, nutritious bowls and sandwiches and great coffee drinks, head to **Beachcomber Cafe** (p223), a popular community hangout. To sample red, white and even orange wine made right in Humboldt, drop by the **Moonstone Crossing Winery** (*moonstonecrossing.com*) tasting room. Kids love the **Telonicher Marine Lab** (*humboldt.edu/marine-lab; closed weekends & holidays*), a marine station with aquatic displays and touch tanks.

Just west of town, **Trinidad Head** is the place to go for views, especially at sunset or during the winter whale-watching season. Birders may want to bring along binoculars as two of the offshore sea stacks, Green Rock and Flatiron Rock, account for roughly a quarter of the California coast's most significant seabird colonies. At the top of the headland, **Trinidad Head Lighthouse** (*blm.gov/visit/trinidad-head-lighthouse*) is open for tours on the first Saturday of the month from 10am to noon.

Sue-meg State Park

Directly north of Trinidad, about 7 miles from the heart of town, **Sue-meg State Park** (*parks.ca.gov/?page_id=417*) packs a lot into one park, with a visitor center, hiking trails, beaches and multiple campgrounds spread across 640 acres. The park's star attraction is a reconstructed Yurok village, named **Sumêg** (which means 'forever' in the Yurok language). It was reconstructed by a Yurok crew in 1990 and features three family homes, three changing houses, a sweat house, a dance pit and a redwood canoe, all crafted from redwood lumber.

Just south of the village is a native plant garden where you can see plants used by Yurok people for medicine, food, ceremonies and basketry. For a short and scenic hike, follow the 2-mile-long **Rim Trail**, and take in spectacular views of forests and the Pacific Ocean.

continues on p228

Sue-meg State Park — See a reconstructed Yurok village — *17 miles* — Go kayaking at the Humboldt Lagoons — **Redwood National and State Parks**

Redwood National & State Parks

Some of the best hikes in the redwoods are found in the southern section of the Redwood National and State Parks. Highlights include the Fern Canyon Trail, the Lady Bird Johnson Grove Trail and the Tall Trees Grove.

HOW TO

Nearest stop: Sue-meg State Park

Getting here: From Sue-meg State Park, continue north along Hwy 101, which cuts right through the park. For the Lady Bird Johnson Grove Trail or the Tall Trees Grove, take a right on Bald Hills Rd (not recommended for RVs or buses). For the Fern Canyon Trail, go left on Davison Rd.

Book ahead: Reservations are required if you want to drive to Fern Canyon from May 15 to September 15, and year-round if you wish to hike the Tall Trees Grove.

More info: *nps.gov/redw/index.htm*

Lady Bird Johnson Grove Trail

About 3 miles up Bald Hills Rd, the Lady Bird Johnson Trail is one of the most popular hikes in this part of the forest, especially with families and those who don't want to do too much walking. This 1.5-mile path loops through a pristine old-growth forest of towering redwoods that are much bigger and grander than many of the second-growth woodlands in the area. Just come early if you want to see it for yourself; because of the trail's popularity, the parking lot remains full for much of the day.

Tall Trees Grove

Hikers who want to see some of the most glorious redwoods in the forest, and who are up for a 4.5-mile hike with 1600ft in elevation gain, should seriously consider a visit to the Tall Trees Grove, which was made famous by a 1963 article in *National Geographic* that showcased the grove's famous Libby Tree, which was the tallest known tree on Earth until 1988, when it lost its top. This article drew attention to the need to protect redwoods and was a catalyst for the creation of Redwood National Park. Visitor numbers are limited to 50 groups per day and permits are required. You can reserve your permit online between 180 and 24 hours in advance *(nps.gov/redw/planyourvisit/talltreespermits.htm)*.

ELK SPOTTING

If you want to see elk in the wild, you've come to the right place. A good place to look for these majestic beasts is Elk Prairie, on the Newton Drury Scenic Pkwy, just before you reach the Prairie Creek Visitor Center. Elk Meadow, on Davison Rd, just off Hwy 101, is another promising spot. Just remember that while elk can be cute, they are very dangerous. Keep your distance to avoid winning a Darwin Award.

From left: Lady Bird Johnson Grove Trail; Fern Canyon Trail

Fern Canyon Trail

For a different type of foliage, take a hike on the mile-long Fern Canyon Trail, which takes you into a canyon with emeraldine ferns blanketing its steep walls. This lush hike is fairly flat, but does require trudging through a small creek, so expect to get your toes wet, especially if you visit outside of the June to September high season, when the parks service sets up temporary foot bridges to keep hikers from soaking their socks.

Sue-meg State Park to Klamath

Just north of Sue-meg, **Humboldt Lagoons State Park** *(parks.ca.gov/?page_id =416)* is a wonderland for wildlife-watchers, attracting large numbers of migrant birds and Roosevelt elk, especially after the rainy season. It's also a popular spot for kayaking (Freshwater Lagoon is particularly good, as it gets the least amount of north wind). The highway continues north after the Humboldt Lagoons, passing through the town of Orick before cutting through the southern section of the **Redwood National & State Parks** (p226), which encompasses **Prairie Creek Redwood State Park** and some of the most spectacular trails in the region. If you end up stopping at the parks, your best bet is to travel north along the more scenic (but slower) **Newton B. Drury Scenic Pkwy**, which eventually joins up with Hwy 101 near the northeastern-most tip of the park. The road starts to weave inland after a few miles, running parallel to Waukell Creek and into the Yurok Indian Reservation before crossing the Klamath River (California's second-largest river) and into the community of Klamath.

Klamath

Just north of the Klamath River, the **Klamath Tour Thru Tree** is worth a visit if you haven't already had the chance to drive through the Chandelier Tree (p206) or the Shrine Drive-Thru Tree (p210) farther south. The tree is not always staffed, so bring a $5 bill to leave in the dropbox if you come after hours.

Less than a mile up the road, the **Yurok Country Visitor Center** *(visityurokcountry. com)* feels almost like a mini-museum, with interpretive displays and interactive exhibits that tell the story of the land, the tribe and the Yurok language. It's also a good place to pick up souvenirs, including jewelry crafted by Native American artists from the area. The visitor center is also the departure point for **canoe and jetboat tours** *(visityurokcountry .com/adventure)*. Canoe tours give visitors the chance to paddle down the Klamath River in one of the world's only traditional dugout redwood canoes, while jet-boat tours visit Blue Creek and include guided narration about Yurok culture and area history. Depending on when you visit, you might spot ospreys, seals or even bears.

Trees of Mystery

As you continue driving toward the northern end of Klamath, look to your right and you'll see a three-story statue of Paul Bunyan – a legendary giant lumberjack of North American folklore – and his trusty sidekick, a blue ox by the name of Babe. Pull into the parking lot and you'll be at **Trees of Mystery** *(treesofmystery.net)*, Klamath's quintessential redwoods mega-attraction. While plenty of people simply stop for a selfie or two with Paul and Babe, there's a lot more to do here, including a gargantuan gift shop full of plush toys displayed ever so strategically at the eye level of the average seven-year-old. Spread across a series of galleries at the back end of the gift shop is a surprisingly comprehensive museum featuring baskets, clothing, art and other artifacts from Indigenous groups from the West Coast and beyond.

Behind the museum and gift shop is where the outdoor fun begins, with a trail network that winds through forests of massive redwoods

Redwood National and State Parks

20 miles

Klamath

Stop by the Yurok Visitor Center to learn about the tribe

Damnation Creek Trail (p230)

and other supersized conifers. Aerial suspension bridges give you a different perspective on the big trees, and there's a gondola ride that provides even better views on clear days. Don't miss the small outdoor collection of wooden sculptures made using loggers' tools (namely, a chainsaw and a jackknife).

 ### Del Norte Coast Redwoods State Park

Just north of the Trees of Mystery, the Pacific Coast Highway enters **Del Norte Coast Redwoods State Park** *(parks.ca.gov/?page_id =414)*, the southernmost of two contiguous redwood state parks established in the area in

> ### TIDE-POOL SAFETY
>
> While checking out tide pools can be a lot of fun, it doesn't come without risks, both for people and sea creatures. These tips can help avoid problems.
>
> Before you set out, make sure to check tide tables, as the ocean can come in quickly.
>
> Never turn your back to the ocean, even if you aren't in the water.
>
> Be careful where you step: what might look like rocks could actually be barnacles or other living beings.
>
> Don't touch anything. Take pictures, not creatures (it's also illegal to take starfish from within 1000ft of the tide line).

Trees of Mystery

5.5 miles

1 mile

Del Norte Coast Redwoods State Park

 You won't be able to miss it: just look for the huge statues

> **BANANA SLUGS**
>
> If you take a hike in a redwood forest after the rain has fallen, you're likely to see some of Northern California's best-known residents: banana slugs. Named because of their resemblance to bananas, these mollusks are crucial to the forest ecosystem, helping out with everything from eating detritus to spreading seeds. Because of their prevalence, banana slugs have become an unofficial Humboldt County mascot, and you'll see plenty of toys and souvenirs bearing their image. There's even a bagel bakery in Arcata, **Los Bagels** *(losbagels.com; $)*, with roll-shaped bagels named after the famous slugs.

the late 1920s. If you're game for a steep hike, follow the **Damnation Creek Trail** through forests of ferns and trees toward the coast, or hike part of the **Coastal Trail**, which runs through the park.

Crescent City

Soon after crossing Del Norte Coast Redwood State Park, you'll be in Crescent City, the largest city on this last little stretch of the route. It's a popular place to stay the night, with loads of budget chain and franchise hotels. The **Lighthouse Inn** (p224) is a popular, budget-friendly option. Most people use the city more as a place to rest between redwood adventures, but if you're interested in marine life, stop by the **Northcoast Marine Mammal Center** *(northcoastmmc.org)* to learn about their work rescuing and rehabilitating sea creatures and visit their gift shop.

Along the Way We Saw...

WILD FLOWERS Although I've driven the northernmost stretch of the Pacific Coast Highway more times than I can count, I wasn't expecting to see quite as much vibrant color as I did on my most recent trip, thanks to a flurry of wildflower blooms that blanketed many of the meadows (and even roadside patches of grass) that I saw along the way. Throughout the course of my journey, I spotted stalky lupines with indigo blooms, bright-yellow buttercups and a delicate cream-colored flower that I'd later learn had the foreboding name of Fremont's deathcamas. What I spotted the most of, unsurprisingly, were bright-orange California poppies, the state's official flower.

Margot Bigg

Del Norte Coast Redwoods State Park — 15 miles — **Crescent City** — 5 miles — **Jedediah Smith Redwoods State Park** — 16 miles — *Continue north to the Oregon Border*

Jedediah Smith Redwoods State Park

Crescent City is the jumping-off point for visiting **Jedediah Smith Redwoods State Park** *(parks.ca.gov/?page_id=413)*, a 10,000-acre expanse of old-growth coast redwoods that starts just 5 miles east of the city. The park has a visitor center at its headquarters inside the **Newton B. Drury Center** *(cnr K & 2nd Sts, Crescent City)*, where you can pick up brochures and get hiking recommendations from rangers. If you don't end up visiting Crescent City, you can still get all the information you need at the **Hiouchi Visitor Center** *(Hwy 199)* in the heart of the park.

 DETOUR: Crescent City to the Oregon Border

After visiting Crescent City and Jedediah Smith Redwoods State Park, you have the option to turn around and drive the PCH in the opposite direction or carry on towards the Oregon Coast, where the Pacific Coast Highway continues. You can also just drive up to the border if you want to complete the entire road clear up to the northernmost part of the California coast.

The stretch between Crescent City and Oregon is almost exactly 20 miles, passing through the town of Fort Dick, home to the wetlands and beaches of **Tolowa Dunes State Park** *(parks.ca.gov/?page_id=430)*, a great place for birding and whale-watching. Soon after, you'll see a large sign welcoming you to Oregon. Just note that if you go up to the border and turn back around, you'll be stopped for a mandatory produce inspection, where you'll be asked if you're carrying any fruits that could introduce pests from Oregon to California.

Wildflowers at Crescent City coast

Detour: The Oregon Coast

If you have the time, it's worth continuing your drive up into Oregon to visit as much of the state's beautiful – and usually uncrowded – coast as you can.

Nearest stop: Crescent City

Getting here: From Crescent City, drive north for 20 miles and you'll be in Oregon. The first city, Brookings, is about a 5-mile drive north of the border.

When to go: Summer offers the best weather and driest conditions.

Good to know: Oregon doesn't have sales tax, which makes it a great place to pick up supplies and gifts.

More info: *visittheoregoncoast.com*

While the Pacific Coast Highway is often used to describe the Californian segment of Hwys 1 and 101, Hwy 101 continues all the way up through the Pacific Northwest, from Oregon's remote southern coast clear up to the Olympic Peninsula in Washington State.

South Coast

When you cross the border, you'll immediately be on the South Coast, a remote stretch known for its scenery. Highlights include the **Samuel H Boardman State Scenic Corridor** and **Humbug Mountain**, which rewards incredible Pacific Ocean views to travelers willing to hike for 5.5 miles to its 1765ft summit. Further north, cliffside **Shore Acres State Park** requires much less exertion to visit (just drive right up) and has some mighty fine views itself, especially during stormy times of the year, when crashing waves get precariously close to the park's viewing platform.

Central Coast

Oregon's Central Coast is a bit more populated, with a mix of sweeping beaches, forested parks and fishing communities. Highlights along the route include the **Oregon Dunes National Recreation Area**, which protects the largest expanse of coastal dunes in North America (and was the inspiration for Frank Herbert's sci-fi novel, *Dune*). It's not far from the **Darlingtonia State Natural Site**, a small park with a walkway that leads through a bog of carnivorous plants.

THE SAMUEL H BOARDMAN STATE SCENIC CORRIDOR

Even with just a couple of hours on the Oregon Coast, you'll have enough time to drive what many will argue is its prettiest section: the **Samuel H Boardman State Scenic Corridor**. It starts just north of Brooklyn and continues for around 12 miles, weaving alongside towering cliffs with views out over arch-shaped sea stacks. If you come during low tide, stop at **Secret Beach**, about a third of a mile south of milepost 345. A 0.75-mile trail descends to this tiny cove that's beloved for its secluded feel.

Left: Shore Acres State Park; Below: Gray whale at Depoe Bay

North Coast

This is the busiest part of the Oregon Coast, partially because it's easy to get to from Portland. Don't miss **Depoe Bay**, one of the few places where you can see whales in the summer, and **Lincoln City**, which is both the kite-flying and the glassblowing capital of the coast. Further north, you can visit the **Tillamook Creamery** to sample its nationally famous cheese or drive to **Astoria**, the northernmost city in Oregon. This Victorian city is where 1980s cult classic *The Goonies* was filmed.

Condor, California coast
SUSANA MIRANDA/SHUTTERSTOCK

INSIGHT

The Return of the Condor

European-American settlement in North America nearly wiped out the continent's largest land bird, the California condor. Thanks to the Yurok Condor Restoration Program, these sacred birds have returned to Yurok Ancestral Territory for the first time since 1892.

WORDS BY MARGOT BIGG
Margot is a travel writer from the Pacific Northwest whose interests include nature and conservation.

FOR THOUSANDS OF years, humans and California condors (*Gymnogyps californianus*) lived in harmony. Many Indigenous peoples, including the Yurok, whose ancestral lands extend through much of what is now called Northern California, considered the birds sacred and made sure not to harm them. Traditional practices, including the use of prescribed fire known as cultural burning, helped nourish the biodiversity of prairies, key foraging grounds for the birds.

Like all scavenger species, California condors play a vital role in maintaining healthy ecosystems and preventing the spread of disease. These gargantuan birds, which can weigh up to

25lb and have a wingspan of 9.5ft, are obligate carnivores and feed on large, slow-to-decompose animals. While many smaller scavengers are unable to rip through the tough skin of whales and other big mammals, condors' strong beaks and jaws make it easier for them to open carcasses and break remains into smaller, more manageable pieces for other creatures to eat.

When Euro-American settlers began moving to the west in the 1800s, California condors had a wide range that extended from the reaches of Baja California in present-day Mexico up the coast of what is now known as British Columbia. By the end of the century, conservationists had already begun documenting a decline in populations across the western US. Factors such as habitat destruction, hunting and poaching all played a part in this decline, as did environmental contaminants – including spent lead from bullets and the use of DDT, a now-banned insecticide that causes eggshell thinning. By 1967, only 60 individuals existed in the wild, and the birds were officially declared an endangered species by the US federal government. By early 1982, fewer than two dozen of the birds existed in the wild. In Yurok country, the disappearance of condors came much earlier, with the last documented sighting in 1892.

Flying Home

The decline of California condors spurred wildlife officials to round up the remaining birds and put them into breeding programs in a last-ditch attempt to save the species from disappearing. Their efforts succeeded, and the California Condor Recovery Program (CCRP), a multi-entity program spearheaded by the US Fish & Wildlife Service, began re-establishing wild flocks in Southern and Central California in the 1990s. By the turn of the 21st century, flocks were present in many parts of the state, as well as in Utah and Arizona, but they remained absent from Yurok country.

In 2003, a panel of Yurok elders who had been tasked with determining priorities for natural and cultural restoration decided to focus efforts on bringing California condors – known as *prey-go-neesh* in Yurok – back to the tribe's ancestral territory. This laid the foundation for the Yurok Condor Restoration Program (YCRP), which started in 2008.

'*Prey-go-neesh* are deeply culturally important to the Yurok and surrounding peoples, featuring heavily in our world renewal ceremonies,' says Tiana Williams-Claussen, director of the Yurok Tribe Wildlife Department, which administers the program. 'Yurok people have, since time immemorial, taken an active and relationship-based approach to conservation and ecological restoration,' she explains. 'While we are called to steward the spiritual and physical wellbeing of our world, we are one species amongst many that contribute to the health of the ecosystem.'

Over the years that followed, YCRP scientists assessed coastal northern California for contaminants such as DDT and lead, as well as for the presence of ecological conditions that would support condor reintroduction, including suitable habitat and the availability of food sources. This period was also used to build awareness about condors while encouraging hunters to transition from lead-based to copper-based ammunition through the tribe's Hunters as Stewards program. In 2022, after nearly two decades of preparation, four condors were released on lands that were historically shared by several tribes in the area. Today, there are 25 condors in the area.

Cultural Restoration

While the reintroduction of condors is helping restore ecological diversity to Northern California, the vultures' return is also significant to the cultural identity of the Yurok community. 'Bringing condors home to Yurok country in a very real way means restoration of the Yurok people, as well,' says Williams-Claussen. 'This next generation is the first in over a century who will grow up living in a community with condors. I now see condors show up in our poems, artwork and community stories,' she continues. 'A critical component of who we are has been restored to us.'

Toolkit

First Time
238

Money
239

On the Road
240

Cycling
244

Where to Stay
245

Access, Attitudes & Safety
246

Responsible Travel
248

The Spotter's Guide
250

PCH at Santa Monica (p66)
GEMNANNER8/SHUTTERSTOCK

First Time

 For information on arriving, see the San Diego City Guide (p34), Los Angeles City Guide (p62) and San Francisco City Guide (p168).

LANGUAGE

Up until roughly 200 years ago, the region that is now called California had around 80 to 90 languages across 20 families. Today, English is the most commonly spoken language in the state, and most US Americans are monolingual. While some attractions offer brochures and secondary sign-posting in Spanish, a general command of English (or a good translation app) is crucial.

Visas & Visa Waivers

Most visitors to the US need to either obtain a visa before traveling or apply for a visa waiver through the Electronic System for Travel Authorization (ESTA). Travelers from roughly 40 countries – including the UK, EU member states, Singapore, Japan and Australia – are eligible to use ESTA. Canadian and Bermudan passport holders do not need an ESTA for stays of up to 90 days.

Medical Insurance

Health care is extremely expensive in the United States, and many US citizens with employer-subsidized health care still have to pay a large chunk of their earnings to have health insurance. It's crucial to obtain health insurance before traveling to the US, as even minor emergencies – or short ambulance rides – can result in bills in the tens of thousands of dollars.

Phones & Data

It's a good idea to purchase an eSIM with a US plan and data before you set out. Most US plans include unlimited incoming and outgoing texting, and SMS is more popular than WhatsApp or other messaging apps. Data coverage is spotty in sections of the PCH, but wi-fi is free at most hotels and some restaurants.

Smoking

Cannabis and tobacco products are legal in California for adults aged 21 and over, but don't expect clouds of smoke at every turn. Smoking in bars, restaurants and other workplaces is banned in California, and cigarette smoking is frowned upon in many circles, in some cases more so than marijuana. Note that driving under the influence of marijuana carries the same legal repercussions as drunk driving.

PHOTO ID

You'll need valid photo ID in the US not only for entering the country, but also for checking into hotel rooms, purchasing alcohol and entering some clubs and venues.

TIME ZONE

California is on Pacific Standard Time (PST/GMT -8) in the winter and Pacific Daylight Time (PDT/GMT -7) from March until November.

ELECTRICITY 120V/60HZ

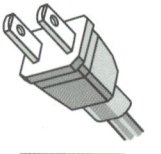

Type A: 120V/60Hz   **Type B:** 120V/60Hz

Money

Budget
How much to budget for a Pacific Coast Highway road trip depends entirely on how you like to travel, and accommodation prices vary quite a bit (summer hotel costs along the 90-mile-long Big Sur coastline are particularly exorbitant). If you plan to stay in budget or mid-range hotels, you'll still need around $375 to $500 per day for two people during the summer high season; if you camp and cook your own meals, $200 will be enough.

Money-Saving Tips
Visit in the low season Come between October and March to score significantly cheaper accommodations with the added benefit of fewer crowds.
Skip the restaurants You can save a good chunk of cash by picking up sandwich fixings at grocery stores or staying at vacation rentals where you can cook proper meals.
Check for discounts Many attractions offer discounts for children and visitors 60 and over, and some offer reduced group rates for families.

TIPPING AND SALES TAX
What you see isn't always what you pay in California. There's a 7.25% statewide sales tax tacked onto most bills (non-prepared food at grocery stores is exempt). Some areas have additional district taxes that range from 0.1 to 2%, additional taxes on hotel rooms, or both. Tipping is expected at restaurants; 20% of the pre-tax bill is customary. Always tip hotel cleaners at least $5 per day.

Cards & Contactless Payments
Credit cards, debit cards and contactless phone payments are widely accepted in California, though some small shops will occasionally charge a credit-card processing fee or require a minimum purchase to use a card (usually around $5). Visa and Mastercard are always accepted at spots that take cards, but not all businesses accept American Express. ATMs are widely available, and it's a good idea to have a little bit of cash handy to tip hotel cleaning staff.

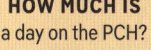

HOW MUCH IS a day on the PCH?

Coffee and snacks	$20
Museum entry	$15
Hotel room	from $150
Lunch with taxes and tips	$40
Dinner with taxes and tips	$60
Parking	from $10
Gas per day	$40
Car rental per day	$50
Total (per day for two adults)	**$375**

Free Attractions
There's no shortage of free attractions on the Pacific Coast Highway, from beaches to hiking trails to roadside attractions. California state parks typically charge a day-use vehicle fee that's assessed per car, not per person (most such parks allow cyclists and pedestrians to visit free of charge). Architecture fans will find that many of the prettiest historic buildings along the route are best experienced from the outside at no cost.

CLOCKWISE FROM TOP LEFT: MARKUS MAINKA/SHUTTERSTOCK, MADELE/SHUTTERSTOCK, KOSOFF/SHUTTERSTOCK

On The Road

Driver's Licenses

While some US states require overseas or Canadian visitors to carry international driver's licenses, people from all over the world can use their licenses in California without worry. However, if your license is issued in a language other than English, you may want to obtain an international license with a translation anyway, just to play it safe. This is an especially good idea if your home country uses a non-Roman script, such as Cyrillic or Abjad.

Speed Limits & Signage

Speed limits in California are posted on white signs with black numbering and are always in miles, not kilometers. Going below the speed limit is OK, within reason, and it can be a good idea during periods of heavy fog or rain. In some areas, particularly on winding roads with hairpin turns, you may see yellow signs with black numbers – these are suggested speeds, and while they aren't legally enforceable, it's a good idea to follow them for safety's sake.

Electric Vehicles

Electric vehicles are increasingly commonplace in the US, especially in California, where gas prices are some of the highest in the country. Many gas stations have charging stations, as do some higher-end hotels and even big-box stores, but fewer options exist in remote parts of the route, and some stations require you to bring your own charging cable. For a mapped-out list of EV charging stations, visit *chargehub.com* or download the ChargeHub app.

GOOD TO KNOW

Drive on the right

.08

Legal blood alcohol limit 0.08%

65

Speed limit 65 mph (on wide, straight stretches)

HOW TO

PUMP YOUR OWN GAS

Self-serve is the standard at California gas stations, a daunting proposition if you're used to attendants. You'll usually need to swipe or tap your credit card before inserting the pump into your vehicle and lift up the lever to dispense fuel. Most fuel stations have attached minimarts. If you only have cash, you will have to go inside and pay an attendant.

FOUR-WAY STOPS

If you're not from North America, you may not be familiar with seeing four-way stops at intersections, in which all cars are required to come to a complete stop and take turns proceeding. The order is typically based on order of arrival, but in cases where two people arrive at the same time, the driver to the right gets the right of way.

Santa Monica (p66)

TOLLS

Tolls are rare on the PCH, except when heading south over the Golden Gate Bridge. Tolls are levied on vehicles crossing many bridges and freeway express lanes in busier parts of the state through an automated system known as FasTrak (fastrak.org). If you don't have a FasTrak account, a bill will be sent to your home (or rental-car company) and will incur administrative fees.

Traffic-Light Laws

In California, you are allowed to turn right on a red light, as long as you come to a complete stop first and check for oncoming traffic. The only exception to this is when there's a sign clearly stating 'no turn on red' or when there's a red arrow light rather than a circular traffic light. Traffic lights in California turn from green to yellow (amber) to red. If a light changes to yellow and you can't safely come to a complete stop, it's OK to continue, but you should be in the intersection before it turns red or you may get a ticket.

GPS & Maps

Many rental cars have built-in navigation systems with GPS, which can be a boon if you find yourself in one of the many stretches of the PCH without cell service. Rental companies often offer the option to add on a portable navigation system, but you can also just use your phone (especially if your car comes with a phone mount or if you have a co-passenger to navigate). Both Google Maps and Apple Maps allow you to download offline maps that rely on GPS alone, meaning that they work even when you don't have an internet connection.

HOW TO

RENT A CAR

Renting a car in the US is fairly straightforward: you just need a driver's license and a major credit card. Cars with automatic transmissions are standard, but manual vehicles are usually available.

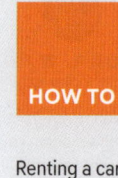

One-Way Rentals
Most car-rental companies will allow you to pick up at one city and drop it off in a different location, but this option is typically more expensive than if you drop your car in the same city where you pick it up. Still, it's a good option if you want to do the route in just one direction. If you're planning to drive from San Diego to the northern tip of California and don't want to turn around and drive all the way back again, consider carrying on to Medford, Oregon – about 110 miles northeast of Crescent City – where the closest major airport with direct flights to San Diego, Los Angeles and San Francisco is located.

PCH near Point Mugu (p78)

Money Matters
Debit cards aren't typically accepted, even if they have a Visa or Mastercard endorsement, as the rental company will want to place a hold on your card (usually of around $300, but the fees can vary considerably). Cars go out with a full tank of gas, and if you don't return yours with a full tank, you can expect to pay an exorbitant per-gallon refueling fee.

Younger Drivers
If you're under 25 years of age, things can get a bit more complicated, as many rental companies only rent to drivers aged 25 and older due to liabilities associated with younger drivers. However, some companies, such as Enterprise, will rent to drivers 21 and over for an additional fee. People under 21 aren't allowed to rent cars in California (or in most US states, save for Michigan and New Jersey).

HOW TO BOOK A RENTAL CAR

While you can try showing up and seeing what's available, it's best to book in advance, both to guarantee availability and to score the best deals. Listed prices are for one person and do not include fees for additional drivers or insurance. Expect a hard sales pitch for supplemental insurance when you arrive at the rental desk.

PROBLEM-BUSTER

What happens if I get pulled over by the police? If an officer stops you, they will tell you why they are pulling you over and ask for your driver's license, registration and proof of insurance for verification. They may issue you a citation or give you a verbal warning. If you receive a citation, you'll have the option of paying online or contesting the charges, either in writing or by appearing in court.

What happens if I get in an accident? If you get in a minor accident, remain calm and pull over to the side of the road. If another vehicle is involved, you'll need to exchange insurance and driver's license details with the other driver. It's also a good idea to take photos of both vehicles to share with your insurance company. If anyone is seriously injured, call 911.

What happens if my car breaks down? If your car breaks down, it's best to call your rental company and ask what to do. If you are driving a personal vehicle, it's a good idea to sign up for a roadside assistance program such as AAA before your trip.

What happens if I run out of fuel? If you run out of gas, you could be in for a long walk to the nearest gas station, where you can buy a plastic gas container, fill it up at the pump and take it back to your car. Or you can call roadside assistance, but it might take longer and end up costing you a premium.

Tow truck, Oregon Coast (p232)

CYCLING TOOLKIT

Cycling

BRING YOUR OWN BIKE

Bringing your own bike is often easier than renting, especially if you're doing the route one way. You can check your bike on most domestic flights in the US (as special sporting equipment) and on most Amtrak trains.

Road Rules for Cyclists

When cycling the PCH, make sure to ride in the same direction as traffic (ie on the right), staying in bike lanes where the exist or as far to the shoulder as possible when there's no alternative. Cyclists are expected to obey traffic laws, and must come to a full stop at stop signs (though there have been ongoing attempts to change this law). Helmets are not required for adults over 18, but they are a good idea.

Preparing for the Journey

While cycling the Pacific Coast Highway can certainly be rewarding, it requires a lot of preparation, especially if you live in a flatter area and aren't used to cycling up and down hills. Make sure to pack bottled water (and a filter straw), basic bike repair tools and plenty of layers. The Adventure Cycling Association *(adventurecycling.org)* is an excellent resource to help you get road-ready.

OVERNIGHT OPTIONS

Many hotels and inns along the PCH will let you bring your bike into your room, but it's a good idea to call in advance to make sure you won't have to lock your bicycle up outside for the night. Many California state parks have dedicated 'hike or bike' campsites that are specifically for hikers and cyclists, typically available on a first-come, first-served basis. A great resource for cyclists looking for a place to crash for the night is *warmshowers.org*.

Cyclists, San Francisco (p168)

Where to Stay

Hotels

Hotels are widely available all along the Pacific Coast Highway, with most budget-friendlier options found in the outskirts of larger cities. Some sections of the route, particularly those within weekending distance of San Francisco – such as Big Sur and the Mendocino Coast – tend towards high end, with price tags to match. A simple continental breakfast is often included at hotels and chain hotels, while higher-end inns sometimes provide guests with a gourmet cooked meal to start the day.

Campsites

Camping can be a fun and cost-effective way to explore the Pacific Coast, especially if you have an RV. Camping is widely available in California state parks and on federally managed land, and while some campsites are available on a first-come, first-served basis, most of the best spots need to be reserved in advance. Camping outside of campgrounds on Bureau of Land Management (BLM), known as dispersed camping, is also an option; more details are available at *blm.gov/visit*.

Vacation Rentals

Vacation rentals are an excellent option if you want some of the comforts of a hotel, but also want to be able to prepare your own meals. They're also a good choice if you want to stay in a smaller community that doesn't have many (or any) hotels. Just note that quality can vary quite a bit, so you should spend a bit of time looking through reviews from previous guests before you book.

PCH near Big Sur (p126)

HOW MUCH FOR A NIGHT IN A...

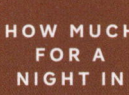

Campsite (tent site) from $20

Motel room from $120 (high season)

Vacation rental with kitchen from $130

HOW TO: BOOK A CAMPSITE OR RV SITE

If you plan to camp, you can reserve state park sites at *reservecalifornia.com* or campsites and cabins in national forests at *recreation.gov*. Both open for reservations six months in advance. For private campsites, RV sites and cabins, *koa.com* and *hipcamp.com* are solid resources, while *goodsam.com* is a good resource for finding RV parks.

Access, Attitudes & Safety

SOLO ROAD TRIP SAFETY TIPS

Consider sharing your location. Apps such as Life360 and Google Maps are popular options.

Pace yourself. Enjoy the journey and take breaks every couple of hours.

Download podcasts. It's easy to get sleepy when you don't have anyone to chat to. Podcasts are the next best thing.

Back up important info. Keep a written record of hotel addresses, just in case something happens to your phone.

Senior Travel

Road-tripping is a popular post-retirement activity in the US, and plenty of seniors buy RVs after retiring and set out on the open road. Many major attractions offer senior discounts (sometimes for people as young as 60 or 65), and some supermarkets even offer senior discount days. Some hotels offer special rates to members of the AARP *(aarp.org)*, formerly called the American Association of Retired Persons. Membership is open to anyone 50 or over.

Civil Rights in California

California has strong civil rights laws in place that are designed to ensure equitable treatment to all people, irrespective of race, cultural background, gender expression, sexual orientation or age. This extends to the right to use the restroom facilities consistent with your gender identity, without question. For more information or to make a report, contact the California Civil Rights Department *(calcivilrights.ca.gov)*.

Women Travelers

Plenty of women travel the Pacific Coast Highway every year, and many make the journey solo. Most women have a seamless experience, and there aren't any widely held taboos in California about women traveling alone. Precautions worth taking include not telling random people that you're traveling alone, never saying your hotel room number aloud and always remembering to bolt the interior lock in your hotel room. Most importantly, always trust your instincts.

Accessibility Resources

AccessibleGo *(accessiblego.com)* Online platform with a community forum, plus accessible hotel, car and equipment bookings.

Society for the Accessible Tourism & Hospitality *(sath.org)* Nonprofit membership organization offering accessible travel tips and destination guides.

TravelAbility *(travelability.net/destination/california)* Accessibility resources in California.

TSA Cares *(tsa.gov/travel/tsa-cares)* Airport and security information for travelers with disabilities and access needs.

San Diego Zoo (p38)

TRAVELING WITH BABIES

Road-tripping with babies takes some extra planning, but it's certainly doable. Most women's restrooms, and an increasing number of men's restrooms and all-gender/family restrooms, have baby-changing tables, and disposable diapers and baby food are widely available. The right to breastfeed in public is legally enshrined in California law, though some people prefer to cover up with a blanket.

Family Travel

The Pacific Coast Highway makes for a great family road trip, with kid-friendly attractions ranging from the **Bay Area Discovery Museum** (p181) to the **San Diego Zoo** (p38). Children are welcome in most restaurants, and chain restaurants typically have kids menus that usually feature smaller portions and blander, simpler foods. Many hotels allow children to stay free, and some provide cots or pull-out beds for kids. Children under eight years of age are legally required to be in a car or booster seat, with additional requirements for those weighing less than 40lb. Car-seat rentals are typically available through rental agencies, with advance notice.

CRIME

While violent crime exists in California, you're unlikely to fall victim to it during your trip. Your biggest concern will likely be for the safety of your vehicle. While actual vehicle theft is rare (and increasingly difficult), break-ins do happen, and the risk is higher in Los Angeles County and in San Francisco. To reduce your risk of a smash-and-grab, keep valuables, bags and shiny objects out of view, especially after dark.

Accessible Travel

Travelers with disabilities are protected in the US under the Americans with Disabilities Act (ADA), and public spaces in California typically have wheelchair ramps and accessible toilets (historic buildings are an exception). Wheelchair-accessible trails are found across the state, too, including the **Elephant Seal Boardwalk & Trail** (p127) in San Simeon and the **Bodega Head Nature Trail** (p190) in Sonoma State Park. Larger hotels typically have wheelchair-accessible rooms with wide doors and roll-in showers, and many have facilities for blind or deaf visitors, such as braille signage and visual fire-alarm systems and doorbells.

Responsible Travel

Climate Change & Travel
It's impossible to ignore the impact we have when traveling; Lonely Planet urges all travellers to engage with their travel carbon footprint, which will mainly come from air travel. While there often isn't an alternative, travelers can look to minimise the number of flights they take, opt for newer aircrafts and use cleaner ground transport, such as trains. One proposed solution – purchasing carbon offsets – unfortunately does not cancel out the impact of individual flights. While most destinations will depend on air travel for the foreseeable future, for now, pursuing ground-based travel where possible is the best course of action.

The **ICAO's carbon emissions calculator** allows visitors to analyse the CO2 generated by point-to-point journeys

The **UN Carbon Offset Calculator** shows how flying impacts a household's emissions

WILDFIRES
Wildfires occur regularly in California, sometimes in populated areas. Officials have many measures in place to reduce fire risks and prevent spread, and campfires and certain types of outdoor cooking devices are often banned from spring until fall, when risks are at their highest. While fire itself is an obvious danger, wildfire smoke has many risks of its own and can lead to respiratory issues in vulnerable populations. N95 masks are a good idea during periods of poor air quality.

Bottle & Can Recycling
Expect to pay a $0.10 deposit on most bottled and canned beverages in California. This deposit, charged at points of sale, is designed to encourage people to return empty containers rather than throwing them in the trash. You can get your cash back by bringing empty bottles to recycling kiosks found at most major supermarkets.

VEGGIE TABLES
Animal agriculture is among the largest causes of climate change. One way to offset the impact of your road trip is by opting for plant-based meals along the way, even if just some of the time. The Happy Cow app *(happycow.net)* is a great resource for finding options without meat or dairy. Opting for restaurants that emphasize locally sourced ingredients is another great way to reduce your impact.

Los Angeles wildfire

FROM TOP: JASONDOIY/SHUTTERSTOCK, MAURO PEZZOTTA/SHUTTERSTOCK

Snowy plovers, Moss Landing State Beach (p148)

Protecting Beaches

Large numbers of visitors can often hurt coastal ecosystems. Keep your impact to a minimum by being careful where you walk and keeping your dogs on leashes except in designated areas. Be mindful of Western snowy plover nesting areas (p193) and be very careful when walking near tide pools, as it's easy to accidentally step on barnacles or other living things. Never remove sea creatures (including snails or sea urchins) from marine protected areas – this is considered poaching. If you see anyone removing sea life or littering, contact the California Department of Fish and Wildlife's CALTIP (Californians Turn In Poachers and Polluters) hotline at 1-888-334-2258 or text CALTIP to 847411.

Indigenous Americans

California's human history certainly didn't start with the arrival of the Spanish in 1769, and archaeological evidence points to at least 12,000 years of human settlement in the area. Today, the state is home to around 110 federally recognized tribes. To learn more about Indigenous people in California, skip museums (which are often guilty of presenting Native American cultures as a monolith) and instead make a point of stopping at tribally owned and operated cultural centers, such as the **Yurok Country Visitor Center** (p228) in Klamath and the **Da Gou Rou Louwi' Cultural Center** (p215) in Eureka.

Drinking Water

Most tap water in California is potable, unless signposted otherwise. Avoid plastic waste by carrying a refillable bottle or bottles with you and filling them up at your hotel or rest areas.

HOW TO

SUPPORT LOCAL COMMUNITIES

Shop at Farmers Markets
One of the easiest ways to keep your tourism dollars in local communities is by eschewing corporate supermarkets, most of which are stocked with subpar produce from megafarms, and heading to farmers markets for provisions. Not only will you be buying directly from small farmers, but you'll also get much fresher produce.

Buy Locally Made Souvenirs
Many gift shops are stocked with chintzy souvenir shot glasses and stuffed animals. These are often made in big factories with questionable labor practices, and buying them doesn't do much for the local economy. Instead, seek out locally made handicrafts.

Choose Family-Run Inns over Chain Hotels
You'll find lots of little inns up and down the Pacific Coast, many of which are both owned and operated by local families. If it's within your budget to stay in locally owned properties, it's worth giving them a shot. These inns often come with all the bells and whistles of a small hotel but have a more intimate, home-like feel.

Hire Guides
The best way to understand a destination is by spending time with a person who lives there. Whether you want to go kayaking or mushroom foraging, consider hiring a guide to share their insider knowledge with you.

The Spotter's Guide

From towering redwoods to tiny butterflies, nature is omnipresent along the Pacific Coast Highway. Here are some species to look out for.

❶ **Joshua Tree** *(Yucca brevifolia)* A spiny monocot tree found in Southern California, especially in the Mojave Desert. ❷ **Monarch Butterfly** *(Danaus Plexippus)* Migratory butterflies that feed on milkweed and are frequently spotted on the California coast, particularly in Pismo Beach and in the Monterey area. ❸ **Humpback Whale** *(Megaptera novaeangliae)* Baleen whales that are known for breaching (jumping above the ocean's surface), often spotted off the coasts of Southern California and Monterey. ❹ **Coast Redwood** *(Sequoia sempervirens)* The tallest trees on Earth and some of the longest-living; mostly seen in Northern California, with smaller groves in Santa Cruz County. ❺ **California Poppy** *(Eschscholzia californica)* Ubiquitous flowering perennial with orange, yellow and red blossoms; the official state flower of California (p230).

6 Tule Elk *(Cervus canadensis nannodes)* A rare, smallish subspecies of elk that's only found in California, particularly in Central and Northern California. **7 Sea Otter** *(Enhydra lutris)* Marine members of the weasel family found across the California coast, with large numbers in the Monterey Bay (p134). **8 American Black Bear** *(Ursus americanus)* California's state animal is the California grizzly bear, but you won't see any during your visit. They're extinct. You may see black bears in forested areas. They're not generally dangerous if left alone. **9 Cougar** *(Puma concolor)* Also known as mountain lions, these big cats are found everywhere from forests to deserts, but prefer to avoid humans. **10 California Quail** *(Callipepla californica)* California's state bird with pretty hat-like plumage.

Index

Journey legs 000
Map pages **000**

17-Mile Drive 144
4WDing 112

accessible travel 190, 246-7
accommodations 245, *see also* camping, *individual locations*
activities, *see individual activities*
amusement parks
　Disneyland 58-9, 60-1
　Knott's Berry Farm 59
　LEGOLAND 49, 50
Anaheim 56
Andrew Molera State Park 134
animals, *see* wildlife
Aptos Village 148
aquariums
　Aquarium of the Pacific 57
　Bodega Marine Laboratory 186
　Telonicher Marine Lab 225
Arcata 222-4
architecture 116-17, *see also* missions
　Crystal Cove State Park 54
　Eureka 214
　Los Angeles 70
　oddities 26, 122
　San Diego 38
　Santa Barbara 95
art galleries & museums
　Broad, The 70
　Hawthorne Gallery 131
　Laguna Art Museum 54
　Los Angeles County Museum of Art 69
　Museum of Contemporary Art 70
　Museum of Contemporary Art Santa Barbara 98
　Old Town Art Gallery 215
　San Luis Obispo Museum of Art 124
　Santa Barbara Museum of Art 97
Astoria 233
Avenue of the Giants 210-11
Avila Beach 112-13

B

Balboa Peninsula 55
banana slugs 230
beaches 8-11, 249
　Andrew Molera Beach 134
　Bowling Ball Beach 192
　Capistrano Beach 51-2
　Capitola Beach 149-50
　Carmel Beach 144
　Carmel River State Beach 144
　Carmel Sunset Beach 144
　Coronado 40
　Dillon Beach 183
　El Capitán State Beach 108
　Emma Wood State Beach 82
　Fletcher Cove 46
　Glass Beach 205
　Gray Whale Cove State Beach 153
　Greenwood State Beach 192
　Humboldt Bay 225
　Huntington State Beach 56
　Laguna Beach 54
　Leucadia 49
　Malibu 77
　Manhattan Beach 66
　Moss Landing State Beach 148
　Muir Beach 183
　Natural Bridges State Beach 161
　New Brighton State Beach 148-9
　Oxnard 79
　Pfeiffer Beach 132
　Rincon Park County Beach 82
　San Mateo County 151
　San Onofre State Beach 51
　Schooner Gulch State Beach 192
　Seacliff State Beach 148
　Ten Mile Beach 205
　Willow Creek Beach 129
bicycling, *see* cycling
Big Sur 129-35, 136-9
Big Sur River Inn 133
biking, *see* cycling
bird-watching
　Elkhorn Slough 148

Humboldt Bay National Wildlife Refuge 212
Malibu 77
Bixby Bridge 134
boating
　Newport Beach 55
　Ventura Harbor 79-80
Bodega Bay 186
budget 239, 245
Buellton 110-11
butterflies 104-5, 106, 107-8

Camarillo 79
Cambria 126
camping
　Carpinteria State Beach 83
　Clam Beach County Park 225
　Goleta 107-8
　Leo Carrillo State Park 77-8
　Loma Vista 132
　Pfeiffer Big Sur State Park 132
　Point Mugu State Park 78-9
　Richardson Grove State Park 209
campsites 245
cannabis 212
canoeing, *see* kayaking & canoeing
Capitola Village 149-50
Cardiff 46-7
car rental 242
car travel 240-1, 243
Carlsbad 49
Carmel-by-the-Sea 144
Carmel-by-the-Sea to San Francisco 140-55, **142-3**, *see also* San Luis Obispo to Carmel-by-the-Sea, San Francisco to Mendocino
　accommodations 142, 149
　food 145
　highlights 142
　route 142-3
Carpinteria 83
caves
　Gaviota Wind Caves 109
　Sunny Jim's Sea Cave 39

252

cell phones 238
Channel Islands National Park 80, 81
children, travel with 247
cinemas
    El Capitan Theatre 68
    Fremont Theater 122
    TCL Chinese Theatre 68
climate change 162-5
condors 234-5
conservation 211, 249
Coronado 40-1
costs 239, 245
courses 57
crafts
    Harmony Glassworks 123
    Pond Farm Pottery 187
credit cards 239
Crescent City 230
crime 247
Crystal Cove Historic District 54
cultural centers
    Da Gou Rou Louwi' Cultural Center 215
    Greek Theatre 67
    Gualala Arts Center 191
    Hollywood Bowl 68
    SLO Film Center 122
    Walt Disney Concert Hall 70
culture 216-17, see also indigenous people & culture
cycling 244
    Coronado 41
    Emma Wood State Beach 82
    Fort Ord Dunes State Park 145
    Half Moon Bay 154
    Humboldt Bay 222
    Huntington Beach 56
    Pismo Beach 115
    San Clemente 51
    San Diego to Los Angeles 55
    Wilder Ranch State Park 151

Dana Point 52, 54
Deetjen's Big Sur Inn 130
Del Mar 46
disabilities, travelers with 190, 246-7
Disneyland 58-9, 60-1
drinking, see individual locations
drinks, see tap water, wine
driver's licenses 240
driving 240-1, 243

DTLA 70-1
Duncans Mills 186-7
dunes
    Guadalupe-Nipomo Dunes Complex 112
    Oceano Dunes 112
    Oregon Dunes National Recreation Area 232

electric vehicles 240
electricity 238
elephant seals 127, 151
Elk 192
elk (animals) 227
Encinitas 48
Esalen Institute 129
Eureka 212, 214-15, 222, **214**
    accommodations 214
    drinking 215
    food 215
    transportation 214
Eureka to Crescent City 218-33, **220-1**, see also Mendocino to Eureka
    accommodations 220, 224
    food 223
    highlights 220
    route 220-1
events, see festivals & events

family travel 247
farms
    Avila Valley Barn 112
    Lavender Fields Forever 111
    Lompoc Flower Fields 109
    Luffa Farm 112
    Ostrichland USA 110
    Toro Canyon 86
    Vega Vineyard & Farm 110
festivals & events
    Big Sur Folk Festival 138
    Buellton Fall Festival 110
    Chicano-Con 38
    Half Moon Bay Art & Pumpkin Festival 154
    Kinetic Grand Championship 214
    Pismo Beach Clam Festival 114
    San Luis Obispo International Film Festival 122
Ferndale 212

films 111, 160, 186
food 16-19, 37, see also individual locations
Fort Bragg 203, 205
Fort Ord Dunes State Park 145
Fortuna 212

Garberville 209
gardens, see parks & gardens
Garrapata State Park 134
Gaviota State Park 108-9
gay travelers 172
Golden Gate Bridge 172, 180
Golden Gate Park 174
Goleta 104
golf 46, 186
Griffith Park 67
Guadalupe 112
Gualala 191

Half Moon Bay 151, 154-5, **155**
Harmony 123
Hearst Castle 126
Henry Miller Memorial Library 130
hiking 12-15
    Andrew Molera State Park 134
    Año Nuevo State Park 151
    Arcata Community Forest 224
    Burton Mesa Ecological Reserve 109
    Cambria 126
    Del Norte Coast Redwoods State Park 230
    Devil's Slide 153
    Fort Ord Dunes State Park 145
    Garrapata State Park 134
    Goleta 107
    Half Moon Bay 154
    Humboldt Bay 222
    Humboldt Redwoods State Park 210
    Jedediah Smith Redwoods State Park 231
    Julia Pfeiffer Burns State Park 129-30
    Leo Carrillo State Park 78
    Limekiln State Park 129
    Lost Coast, the 208
    Montecito 87
    Natural Bridges State Park 150-1
    Ojai 85
    Pfeiffer Big Sur State Park 132

hiking *continued*
  Pismo Beach 115
  Point Lobos State Natural Reserve 134-5
  Point Mugu State Park 78-9
  Point Reyes National Seashore 182
  Redwood National & State Parks 226-7
  Russian Gulch State Park 202
  Salt Point State Park 189
  San Luis Obispo 122
  San Simeon 127
  Sonoma Coast 190
  Sonoma Coast State Park 186
  Standish-Hickey State Recreation Area 207
  Sue-meg State Park 225
  Van Damme State Park 193
  West Cliff Drive 161
  Wilder Ranch State Park 151
historic buildings & sites
  Carson Mansion 214
  Chapman Estate 115
  Ferndale Historic Cemetery 212
  Half Moon Bay City Hall 154
  James Johnston House 151
  Larkin House 146
  Lucia Lodge 129
  Old Fisherman's Wharf 146
  Point Sur Naval Facility 134
  Potter Schoolhouse 186
  Rancho La Patera 104
  Rancho San Andrés Castro Adobe Park 148
  Robert Louis Stevenson House 146
  Rotchev House 189
  San Benito House 154
  Sea Ranch Chapel 191
  Stearns Wharf 98, 104
  Temple of Kwan Tai 202
  Top Gun House 51
historic parks
  Fort Ross State Historic Park 188-9
  La Purísima Mission State Historic Park 109
  Pigeon Point Light Station State Historic Park 152
  Point Sur State Historic Park 134

history
  Chicano 38
  culture 116-17, 125, 136-9
  Indigenous people & culture 83, 249
  missions 20-3, 52, 109, 113
Hollywood Blvd 68
Hollywood Walk of Fame 68
horse racing 46
horse riding
  Moss Landing State Beach 148
  Salt Point State Park 189
  Summerland 87
  Wilder Ranch State Park 151
hotels 245
hot springs 112
Huntington Beach 56

I

Indigenous people & culture 83, 249
insurance, medical 238

J

Jenner 188
jetboating 228
Julia Pfeiffer Burns State Park 129-30

K

kayaking & canoeing
  Coronado 41
  Jenner 188
  Klamath 228
  Santa Cruz Island 81

L

La Jolla 39
Laguna Beach 54
landslides 135
Leggett 205
LEGOLAND 49, 50
Leucadia 48-9
LGBTQ+ travelers 172
lighthouses
  Cape Mendocino Lighthouse 208
  Piedras Blancas Light Station 127
  Pigeon Point Light Station 152
  Point Arena Lighthouse 192
  Point Cabrillo Light Station 202
  Point Reyes Lighthouse 182
  Point Sur Lightstation 134
  Trinidad Head Lighthouse 225

Limekiln State Park 129
Lincoln City 233
Loma Vista 132
Lompoc 109
Long Beach 57
Los Angeles 62-71, **64**
  accommodations 65
  drinking 65, 71
  food 65
  itineraries 64
  transportation 62
Los Angeles to Santa Barbara 72-87, **74-5**, *see also* San Diego to Los Angeles, Santa Barbara to San Luis Obispo
  accommodations 74, 80
  food 78
  highlights 74
  route 74-5
Lost Coast, the 208

M

Malibu 76-7
Mendocino 202
Mendocino to Eureka 198-215, **200-1**, *see also* San Francisco to Mendocino, Eureka to Crescent City
  accommodations 200, 209
  food 203
  highlights 200
  route 200-1
Mission San Juan Capistrano 53
missions 20-3, 113
  Carmel Mission Basilica 144
  La Purísima Mission 109
  Mission Basilica San Buenaventura 80
  Mission San Juan Capistrano 53
  Mission San Luis Obispo de Tolosa 124
  Old Mission Santa Barbara 97
mobile phones 238
Monarch Butterfly Grove at Ellwood Mesa 104-5
money 239
monuments, *see* statues & monuments
Montecito 86, 87
Monterey 146-7, **147**
Morro Bay 123
Moss Landing State Beach 148

motels 245
mountain-biking, see cycling
museums, see also art galleries & museums
  Academy Museum of Motion Pictures 69
  Autry Museum of the American West 67
  Bay Area Discovery Museum 181
  California Academy of Sciences 174
  California African American Museum 71
  California Science Center 70
  Cambria Historical Museum 126
  de Young Museum 174
  Getty Center 69
  Guest House Museum 203
  Hollywood Museum 68
  Huntington Beach International Surfing Museum 56
  International Sea Glass Museum 205
  Kelley House Museum 202
  La Brea Tar Pits 69
  Light Station Museum 202
  Lucas Museum of Narrative Art 71
  Molera Ranch House Museum 134
  Morris Graves Museum of Art 215
  Morro Bay Maritime Museum 123
  Museum of Ventura County 80
  Natural History Museum of Los Angeles County 70-1
  Ocean Institute 54
  Pacific House Museum 146
  Petersen Automotive Museum 69
  Queen Mary 57
  Santa Barbara Historical Museum 99
  Santa Barbara Museum of Natural History 97
  Santa Cruz Surfing Museum 161
  South Coast Railroad Museum 104
  Trees of Mystery 228-9
  UCLA Hammer Museum 69
Mussel Shoals 82

Napa Valley 183, 184-5
national & state parks & reserves
  Andrew Molera State Park 134
  Año Nuevo State Park 151
  Armstrong Redwoods State Natural Reserve 186-7
  Channel Islands National Park 80, 81
  Crystal Cove State Park 54
  Del Norte Coast Redwoods State Park 229-30
  Fitzgerald Marine Reserve 153
  Forest of Nisene Marks State Park 148
  Fort Ord Dunes State Park 145
  Garrapata State Park 134
  Gaviota State Park 108-9
  Henry Cowell Redwoods State Park 160
  Humboldt Lagoons State Park 228
  Humboldt Redwoods State Park 210
  Jedediah Smith Redwoods State Park 231
  Julia Pfeiffer Burns State Park 129-30
  Kruse Rhododendron State Natural Reserve 190-1
  Leo Carrillo State Park 77-8
  Limekiln State Park 129
  Monterey State Historic Park 146
  Natural Bridges State Park 150
  Pfeiffer Big Sur State Park 132
  Point Lobos State Natural Reserve 134
  Point Mugu State Park 78-9
  Point Reyes National Seashore 182
  Redwood National & State Parks 226-7
  Richardson Grove State Park 209
  Russian Gulch State Park 202
  Salt Point State Park 189-90
  Shore Acres State Park 232
  Sonoma Coast State Park 186
  Standish-Hickey State Recreation Area 206
  Sue-meg State Park 225
  Tolowa Dunes State Park 231
  Torrey Pines State Natural Reserve 46
  Van Damme State Park 192-3
  Wilder Ranch State Park 151
Nepenthe 131
New Camaldoli Hermitage 128
Newport Beach 55
Nipomo 112

observatories 67
Oceano 112
Oceanside 49
Ojai 82, 84-5, **84**
  accommodations 84
  drinking 85
  food 85
  transportation 84
Oregon 231, 232-3
Oxnard 79

Pacific gray whales 183
Pacifica 153
parks & gardens
  Balboa Park 38
  Darlingtonia State Natural Site 232
  Dinosaur Caves Park 114
  Dolores Park 173
  Golden Gate Park 174, 180
  Griffith Park 67
  Japanese Tea Garden 174-5
  Lotusland 87
  Mendocino Coast Botanical Gardens 202
  Price Historical Park 115
  Romano Gabriel Wooden Sculpture Garden 215
  Toro Canyon Park 86-7
  Ventura Botanical Gardens 82
Pfeiffer Beach 132
Pfeiffer Big Sur State Park 132
piers
  Malibu Pier 76
  Pismo Beach Pier 114
  Sausalito Terminal Pier 181
  Seal Beach Pier 56
  Ventura Pier 80
Pismo Beach 114-15
planning 28-9
Point Reyes National Seashore 182
Point Sur State Historic Park 134
pop culture 69

Ragged Point 126
recycling 248
Redwood National & State Parks 226-7

redwoods 206, 211, 226
responsible travel 248-9
Rincon Point 82
road closures 135
roadside attractions 24-7
- Avenue of the Giants 210-11
- Confusion Hill 207
- Drive-Thru Tree Park 205-6
- Klamath 228
- Mystery Spot 160

rock formations
- Keyhole Rock 132
- Morro Rock 123

Rockport 205
routes 28-9

S

safe travel 246-7
- tide pools 229

Samuel H Boardman State Scenic Corridor 232-3
San Clemente 51
San Diego 34-41, **36**
- accommodations 37
- food 37
- itineraries 36
- transportation 34

San Diego to Los Angeles 42-59, **44-5**, *see also* Los Angeles to Santa Barbara
- accommodations 44, 51
- food 47
- highlights 44
- route 44-5

San Francisco 168-75, 180, **170**
- accommodations 171
- drinking 171
- food 171
- itineraries 170
- transportation 168

San Francisco to Mendocino 176-93, **178-9**, *see also* Carmel-by-the-Sea to San Francisco, Mendocino to Eureka
- accommodations 178, 187
- food 181
- highlights 178
- route 178-9

San Juan Capistrano 52
San Luis Obispo 122-3, 124-5, **124**
- accommodations 124
- drinking 125
- food 125
- transportation 124

San Luis Obispo to Carmel-by-the-Sea 118-35, **120-1**, *see also* Santa Barbara to San Luis Obispo, Carmel-by-the-Sea to San Francisco
- accommodations 120, 131
- food 126
- highlights 120
- route 120-1

Santa Barbara 94-9, 104, **95**
- accommodations 96
- drinking 96
- food 96
- itineraries 95
- transportation 94

Santa Barbara to San Luis Obispo 100-15, **102-3**, *see also* Los Angeles to Santa Barbara, San Luis Obispo to Carmel-by-the-Sea
- accommodations 102, 107
- food 105
- highlights 102
- route 102-103

Santa Cruz 150-1, 156-61, **158**
- accommodations 159
- drinking 159
- food 159
- itineraries 158
- transportation 156

Santa Cruz Island 81
Santa Monica 66
Sausalito 180-1
Sea Ranch 191
Seal Beach 56
senior travelers 240
shopping 249
- Bodega Bay 186
- Camarillo 79
- Cambria 126
- Carmel-by-the-Sea 144
- Carpinteria 83
- Del Mar 46
- Elk 192
- Eureka 215
- Gualala 191
- Half Moon Bay 154-5
- Loma Vista 132
- Montecito 87
- Monterey 146
- Ojai 85
- San Francisco 173
- San Juan Capistrano 52
- San Luis Obispo 125
- Santa Barbara 98
- Seaport Village 38
- Solana Beach 46
- Summerland 87

smoking 238
Solana Beach 46
solo travel 246
Sonoma Valley 183, 184-5
spas
- Avila 112
- Ojai 85
- San Luis Obispo 125

sports
- Angel Stadium 56
- Honda Center 56
- LA teams 69

state parks & reserves, *see* national & state parks & reserves
statues & monuments
- Cardiff Kook Statue 47
- Chromatic Gate 104
- Dana Point 52

street art 108, 173
studio tours 66
Sumêg 225
Summerland 87
SUP 41
surfing
- Cardiff State Beach 47
- Emma Wood State Beach 82
- Half Moon Bay 154
- Huntington Beach 56
- Leo Carrillo State Park 78
- Malibu 77
- Moonstone Beach County Park 225
- Moss Landing State Beach 148
- Pismo Beach 114
- Rincon Point 82
- San Diego to Los Angeles 57
- Santa Cruz 160
- Schooner Gulch State Beach 192
- Silver Strand Beach 79
- Surf Beach 51
- Swami's Beach 48

sustainability 248-9

swimming
  Cardiff State Beach 47
  Emma Wood State Beach 82
  Harbor Cove Beach 80
  Huntington Beach 56
  Leo Carrillo State Park 78
  Malibu 77
  Moonlight State Beach 48
  Richardson Grove State Park 209
  San Onofre State Beach 51
  Seacliff State Beach 148
  Standish-Hickey State Recreation Area 207

tap water 249
tide pools 229
  Cardiff State Beach 47
  Luffenholtz Beach Park 225
time zones 238
tipping 239
tolls 241
Tomales 183
Toro Canyon 86
traffic laws 240-1
trains
  Redwood Forest Train 160
  Skunk Train 204
travel seasons 28-9
trekking, see hiking
Trinidad 225
trolleys 97

Vandenberg Space Force Base 109
Vandenberg Village 109
Venice 66
Ventura 80, 82
Ventura Harbor 79
viewpoints
  Battery Spencer 180
  Heisler Park 54
  Marin Headlands 180
  Muir Beach Overlook 183
  Panorama Point 209
  Sunset Cliffs 41
  Trinidad Head 225
  Willow Creek View Point 129
vineyards, see wine
visas 238

walking, see hiking
walking tours
  Half Moon Bay 154-5, **155**
  Monterey 146-7, **147**
  Santa Barbara 98-9, **99**
water parks 59
wellness 129
West Cliff Drive 161
Western snowy plovers 193
waterfalls
  McWay Falls 129-30
  Pfeiffer Falls 132
whale-watching
  Depoe Bay 233
  Santa Cruz 161
  Ventura Harbor 79-80

wildfires 248
wildflowers 46, 230
wildlife 250-1, see also banana slugs, bird-watching, butterflies, condors, elephant seals, elk, Pacific gray whales, Western snowy plovers, whale-watching
wildlife centers & reserves
  Gerstle Cove State Marine Reserve 189-90
  Humboldt Bay National Wildlife Refuge 212
  Humboldt Coastal Nature Center 222
  Humboldt Lagoons State Park 228
  Jenner Headlands Preserve 188
  Monterey Bay National Marine Sanctuary 134
  Northcoast Marine Mammal Center 230
  Ventana Wildlife Society's Discovery Center 134
windsurfing, see surfing
wine 18
  Lompoc 109
  Napa Valley 184
  Santa Barbara 98
  Sonoma Valley 184-5
  Trinidad 225
women travelers 246

zip-lining 110
zoos
  San Diego Zoo 38
  Santa Barbara Zoo 104

THIS BOOK

Destination Editor
Akanksha Singh

Production Editor
Sofie Andersen

Coordinating Editor
Kate James

Assisting Editor
Helen Koehne

Image Researcher
Megan Cassidy

Cartographer
Vojtech Bartos

Cover Illustration
Guy Shield

Map Illustration
James Gulliver Hancock

Product Development
Anne Mason, James Smart,
Marc Backwell, Katerina Pavkova

Series Development Leadership
Darren O'Connell, Piers Pickard, Chris Zeiher

Thanks
Alison Killilea, Kellie Langdon, Kate Mathews, Charlotte Orr, Saralinda Turner

All rights reserved. No part of this publication may be copied, stored in a retrieval system, or transmitted in any form by any means, electronic, mechanical, recording or otherwise, except brief extracts for the purpose of review, and no part of this publication may be sold or hired, without the written permission of the publisher. Lonely Planet and the Lonely Planet logo are trademarks of Lonely Planet and are registered in the US Patent and Trademark Office and in other countries. Lonely Planet does not allow its name or logo to be appropriated by commercial establishments, such as retailers, restaurants or hotels. Please let us know of any misuses: lonelyplanet.com/legal/intellectual-property.

Mapping data sources:
©Lonely Planet, ©OpenStreetMap, ©Natural Earth, ©GEBCO, ©Esri, ©NASA Earth Observatory, ©USGS-ASTER and the GIS User Community